The New Organic Grower

The
NEW ORGANIC GROWER

A Master's Manual
of Tools and Techniques
for the Home and Market Gardener

BY
ELIOT COLEMAN

Illustrations by Sheri Amsel

CHELSEA GREEN
CHELSEA, VERMONT

Library of Congress Cataloging-in-Publication Data

Coleman, Eliot, 1938–
    The new organic grower: a master's manual of tools and techniques
for the home and market gardener/by Eliot Coleman.
        p. cm.
    Bibliography: p.
    Includes index.
    ISBN 0-930031-22-9 (alk. paper): $19.95
    1. Vegetable gardening. 2. Organic gardening. 3. Truck farming.
4. Organic farming. I. Title.
SB324.3.C65   1989   89-7295
635.0484 – dc20   CIP

To SN and HKN

One of the intangible legacies the Shakers left to the world is their demonstration that it is possible for man to create the environment and the way of life he wants, if he wants it enough. Man can choose.

The Shakers were practical idealists. They did not dream vaguely of conditions they would like to see realized; they went to work to make these conditions an actuality. They wasted no time in raging against competitive society, or in complaining bitterly that they had no power to change it; instead they built a domain of their own, where they could arrange their lives to their liking.
—MARGUERITE FELLOWS MELCHER
The Shaker Venture

CONTENTS

INTRODUCTION

AS AN AVID READER OF BOOKS ON GARDENING AND agriculture, I am convinced that virtually everything intelligent that can be said and written about the subject exists already, almost certainly in English. From Fukuoka to Jekyll, from Thoreau to Berry, from Rodale to Jeavons, all aspects of these earthly crafts that coax life from dirt have been thoroughly detailed for new or seasoned practitioners. And yet when asked to write this introduction to Coleman's book on gardening, I agreed immediately because in this instance the world needs and deserves another book.

A teacher once advised me to read the book that saved me from reading ten others. *Farmers of Forty Centuries* is such a book; so is *Nutrition and Physical Degeneration*. There must be dozens of books that are offshoots of these, some without even knowing it. When seeking specific knowledge of soil and plant, it can be fairly said that most of the literature one reads is derivative and borrowed. With Eliot's book, this is not the case. Eliot is committing himself to print after two decades of intensive work in field and garden, work which has produced spectacular results not only in yield and bounty but in thought and insight. Simply stated, I know of no other person (what shall we call him—field gardener, truck farmer?) who can produce better results on the land with an economy of effort and means. He has transformed gardening from a task, to a craft, and finally to what Stewart Brand would call "local science."

As I write, the decennial echo of Rachel Carson has once again been heard in Congress and the media, this time in the voice of Meryl Streep imploring our leaders that as a mother she no longer wishes to conduct the experiment of factory farming with its attendant poisons on her children in the form of Alar-laced apples. But this is not merely an echo, for every time the awareness of manmade toxins in our food arises, the lines at farm stands and organic food stores get a bit longer. There is, here and abroad, a slow, incremental but ineluctable movement towards food that nourishes both person and place, that is grown with a far richer knowledge and awareness of biology than can be found in the five-gallon cans of chlorinated hydrocarbons provided by Shell or Uniroyal. If the problems of modern agriculture are centralization, simplification, and biological reductionism, then the answers include diversity, complexity, and local knowledge. Such intelligence cannot be obtained in most of our land grant universities, and it is a pity this is so. For while we are justifiably confident that when it comes to anthropology, physics, and biogenetics, our universities uphold the highest standards of inquiry and experimentation, it is in the area of our land and food where they have failed us utterly. Here we must look to the land itself, and in particular to those people who "husband" it to find standards of truth that we can live by and that allow us to live in turn.

It is satisfying and tempting to think that the major problems of our day have major answers, but I doubt it. The problems that we face—eroded lands, vanishing topsoil, genetic loss, toxic food, poisoned wells—were created by the temptation to find simple solutions. The answers reside in intimate knowledge of species, biota, soil, climate, and place, a type of observation that is embodied before it is taught or transmitted. Eliot not only embodies this intimate science of place, but has been throughout his life the untrammeled observer, unphased by theories of any one school of thought, enamored of experience. It is this seasoned knowing that he shares here.

It was Hans Jenny, a soil scientist, who first pointed out that there is often more life below and within the soil than there is above it, including homo sapiens. This inversion of soil as medium to soil as life itself should be enough to convince any agri-scientist to adopt only those means of agriculture that support and nurture this life. But that has not been the case. It will be gardeners, truck farmers, and small land holders who have and can recognize this fact and act on it. Just as those who broke the prairie sod were pioneers, the new pioneers are those who restore native land and soil. As biota leaves the soil, so does life vanish from society and civilization as we know it. The act of learning to garden and farm, so sincere and simple on its face, is in the hands of Eliot an act of restoration that has implications far beyond one lifetime. It is a practice. And like any practice, it can only be learned through repetition, dedication, and good teaching. This is the good teaching.

PAUL HAWKEN

PREFACE

I STRONGLY BELIEVE IN THE VALUES AND REWARDS of the small farm. I wish to encourage them. And so this book is written for those with a small-farm dream. But it also has a wealth of ideas to offer the serious home gardener. The efficient, professional techniques described here are basically scale neutral and can be used to make everyone's vegetable-growing efforts more productive and enjoyable. And who knows? The best home gardeners often move up to become small farmers.

Organic growing is not complicated. Nor is it difficult. It is the most straightforward way of raising plants. Difficulties usually arise from a misunderstanding of how it works. Once the principles are clear, gardeners from backyard to back forty can tune into the existing balances of the natural system and grow the crops they have always dreamed of.

I have been fortunate to learn from a number of excellent teachers over the years. I owe a debt to all of them. As in any learning situation, my teachers were books, people, models, and most important of all, my own curiosity. The lessons I was fortunate to learn from them influenced the form and function of my approach to farming and helped create this book.

The New Organic Grower

Chapter ✤ 1 AGRICULTURAL CRAFTSMANSHIP

WHY AND HOW DO PLANTS GROW? WHY AND HOW do they fail? Why do plants seem to grow successfully for some people and in some places and not others? The answers lie in those factors that affect the growth of plants: they include light, moisture, temperature, soil fertility, mineral balance, biotic life, weeds, pests, seeds, labor, planning, and skill. The grower can influence some of these factors more than others. The more they can be arranged to the crop's liking, however, the more successful the grower's operation will be.

The Biology of Agriculture

Working with living creatures, both plant and animal, is what makes agriculture different from any other production enterprise. Even though a product is produced, in farming the process is anything but industrial. It is biological. We are dealing with a vital, living system rather than an inert manufacturing process. The skills required to manage a biological system are similar to those of the conductor of an orchestra. The musicians are all very good at what they do individually. The role of the conductor is not to play each instrument but rather to nurture the union of the disparate parts. The conductor coordinates each musician's effort with those of all the others and combines them in a harmonious whole.

Agriculture cannot be an industrial process any more than music can be. It must be understood differently from stamping this metal into that shape or mixing these chemicals and reagents to create that compound. The major workers—the soil microorganisms, the fungi, the mineral particles, the sun, the air, the water—are all parts of a system, and it is not just the employment of any one of them but the coordination of the whole that achieves success.

I remember a conversation I had a few years ago with a Kansas farmer in his sixties who farmed some 700 acres. His methods were considered unconventional because he had always farmed without purchasing herbicides or pesticides and bought only small quantities of lime and phosphorus. I asked him on what theory he based his farming. He said there really wasn't any theory that he knew of. It was simply the same now as it had ever been. He mentioned a favorite book of his, a 1930s agricultural textbook that stressed the value of biological techniques such as crop rotation, animal manures, green manures, cover crops, mixed cropping, mixed stocking, legumes, crop residues, and more. He said he used those practices on his farm simply because they worked so well. The book never mentioned any "theory" and probably never knew one. The book referred to these biological techniques as "good farming practices."

My Kansas friend assured me that by basing his crop production on those good farming practices his yields were equal to and often far better than his neighbors'. He saw no yield increase from soluble fertilizer when he had tried it. His crop rotation and mixed-farming system made weeds, pests, and diseases negligible problems. When fertilizer prices rose he felt as secure as ever because his production techniques were so fundamentally independent of purchased materials. And as long as those good farming practices worked and continued to make his farm profitable, he would continue to use them. He concluded by saying that if there were any theory involved, he would call it "successful farming."

I have long followed similar good farming practices—biological techniques—in my system. The secret to success in agriculture is to remove the limiting factors to plant growth. These practices do that by efficiently and economically generating a balanced soil fertility from *within* the farm rather than importing it from without. They power the system through nurturing the natural processes of soil fertility, plant growth, and pest management and enable them to work even better. In the words of Cole Porter, they "accentuate the positive." When chosen carefully and managed perceptively so as to take full advantage of specific aspects of the natural world, these good farming practices are all the farmer needs. As a further bonus they eliminate such negatives as soil erosion, fertilizer run-off, and pesticide pollution at the same time.

Creating a System

I have been compiling and evaluating information on biologically based food production techniques ever since I started farming. At first I collected this material as a commercial vegetable grower because I needed the information to ensure the success of my own operation. In the process I became aware of the enormous untapped potential of this way of farming and became enthralled by the discovery and practice of the simple techniques of an agriculture in harmony with the natural world.

In order to develop a dependable vegetable production model, I concentrated on collecting information in four subject areas:

- How to simplify production techniques

- How to locate the most efficient machinery and tools

- How to reduce expenditures on purchased supplies

- How to market produce in the most remunerative manner

From my experience, these four areas represent the basic information needed for small-scale, economically successful, biologically based food production.

The first category explains just how straightforward and rational a successful vegetable production system can be. Although growing commercial crops is often considered for "experts" only, it most emphatically is not. The world of plants is vital, vigorous, and self-starting. Drop a seed in the ground and it wants to grow. The common wisdom possessed by the successful farmer is that he understands how to help the seed do what it is already determined to do. The more successful the farmer, the better he understands how to enhance the natural processes without overwhelming them. That simply stated idea is the key to successful food production.

Next is the importance of efficient and dependable machinery and tools that match the needs of small-scale production. The small farmer can and does compete and succeed economically and practically when he has access to equipment scaled and priced within his means and designed for his tasks. The fact that such equipment has not been readily available has been a contributing factor in the demise of the small farm and the concurrent belief that it cannot succeed. Too often unwarranted and problematic growth in farm size has been dictated by the need to justify expensive and oversized equipment because nothing else was available.

In order to find, try out, and modify the right equipment, I have looked all over the world. The equipment ideas included here originated in many different countries. The recommended tools do their jobs admirably. New models will no doubt appear in the future and should be even better. But I expect the basic relationship of the tasks to the system to remain fairly constant.

Third, the economic success of any operation must be ensured. In order to keep costs down I emphasize the importance of "low-input production practices." By that I mean practices such as crop rotation, green manures, animal manure management, efficient labor, season extension, and so forth. Production benefits are gained from careful management rather than expensive purchases. Not only will these practices save money in the short run, but they will also increase the stability and independence of the farm in the long run. The more production needs are farm-generated or labor-saving, the more independent and secure the operation becomes. The farm and its economy cannot then be held hostage by the unavailability or high prices of commodities from outside suppliers. The most stable farm economy is one that is built upon the greatest use of farm-generated production aids.

Finally, no matter how successful I might be in the first three areas, it would be of little use to me if I did not have a successful marketing program. Marketing has always been the make-or-break area for small-scale producers. Much depends on highly developed marketing skills that probably would not have led someone to farming in the first place. The recent growth of "farmers' markets" has in many instances helped the marketing of local produce. But there are other solutions. I have noticed on both sides of the Atlantic that farmers who enjoy the greatest economic success have found competitive niches in the larger marketing system. The extent of this market for small-scale growers and ways to reach it are described in the chapter on marketing.

But It Can't Be Done, Can It?

Most sections of the United States were once fed by small local farms. Today that is considered an impossible dream. Even where professional farmers are involved, the idea of the economically viable small farm is criticized as visionary. Many agricultural experts state that it just cannot work. Their opinion is based primarily on economic and production conclusions drawn from large-scale agricultural operations. Unfortunately, little consideration has been given to the advantages inherent in the small end of the spectrum.

If you understand how the economic and practical realities change when low-cost production methods are allied with the right machinery and marketing practices, then the case does not seem hopeless at all. In fact, the negative opinion of the experts is contradicted by the number of successful examples of small-scale food production operations both here and abroad. Those numbers will increase as improved low-cost technologies become more widely available and consumer demand grows for high-quality local produce.

From my experience, one-half to five acres is a highly productive scale of vegetable growing. The management skills needed for an operation this size are enjoyable rather than onerous. It is a comprehensible size for commercial food production—large enough to make a living yet small enough to retain the emphasis on quality; diverse enough so that the work is never dull yet compact enough so it is never out of control.

There is a distance, to be sure, between the isolated example and the consistent success. Consistent success can only result if the system makes practical sense, has been well tested and proven over a number of years, and is followed with diligence and understanding. The experts have been mistaken before and they will certainly be mistaken again. What they have failed to realize in the case of the small farm is that with careful planning, organization, and desire, there is nothing that "can't be done."

Chapter ❧ 2   L A N D

EVERYONE SHARES A KINSHIP WITH THE LAND. No matter where we are in time or distance, the desire for an ideal country spot is very real. Whether the image comes from books, childhood experiences, or the depths of our souls, it has an indelible quality. The dream farm has fields here, an orchard there, a brook, and large trees near the perfect house, with the barns and outbuildings set off just so. The dream is effortless. The difficulty comes in trying to find such a place when you decide to buy one.

I suggest not trying to find that perfect place. Rather than the finished painting, look for the bare canvas. Every ideal farm at one time began as field and woodland. Its transformation was the result of some predecessor's planning, organization, building, and management. This is a satisfying process in itself, and the end result may be far more successful if it springs from the changes the farmer makes himself. This is not a hard and fast rule, merely a suggestion from experience. If you already own or can obtain a productive farm that is well established, then by all means do so. But if that is not possible, then do not hesitate to buy the raw land and create the farm.

A few suggestions follow on things to take into account when looking at a piece of land with an eye toward turning it into a successful small-scale farm.

Soil Type

Almost any soil can be made productive for growing crops. The difference lies in the amount of effort needed to make it so. The less ideal a soil is to begin with the more attention must be paid to modifying its characteristics. Extreme soil types require an inordinate amount of work. Pure clay or pure sand and gravel are obviously less desirable than a rich loam. On the other hand, while the transformation of imperfect soils requires time and energy, the result can be as productive as initially more promising soils. I have grown magnificent produce on a very sandy-gravelly soil that began with a pH of 4.3. It took a few years of manuring and liming, adding phosphorus, potassium, and trace elements, growing green manures, and establishing a rotation, but it became, and has remained, a highly productive piece of ground.

The dream soil for vegetable production is sandy loam. This is a general term describing the proportions of three ingredients: clay, silt, and sand. Clay consists of fine particles that help the soil hold water and provide a potentially rich storehouse of plant nutrients. Sand consists of larger particles, mostly silicates, which keep the soil open for air and water penetration and aid early warming in the spring. Silt falls somewhere between these two. A fourth soil ingredient—humus or organic matter—is the key to productivity. It opens up heavy clay soils for better air and water movement and easier working. Humus also helps hold together and give structure to light sandy soils, creating more stable conditions for the provision of water and nutrients to plants.

My advice is to look for the best soil possible, but not to be put off if it is not perfect. The cultural practices recommended in this book will help put in the organic matter and nutrient supply to make a productive success from a wide range of initial soil types.

Soil Depth

Old adages apply to soils as well as to people. Don't be fooled by a pretty face. What is underneath the surface of the soil will be important in the future, so investigate it from the start. Investigations with a shovel can be augmented by requests to the local Soil Conservation Service office for information on that particular soil or others like it in the area.

Soil depth should be considered in three ways. Some soil problems are more easily modified than others. First consider the depth to bedrock. This can't be changed to any degree. So ask hard questions about it and take cores with a soil sampling auger if you are not satisfied. Rock outcrops in the surrounding topography are warning signs of a shallow soil. Then there is the depth to the water table. Land that otherwise appears acceptable may have a seasonally high water table during wet times of the year. This could make early spring planting difficult or impossible. A too-high water table also limits the depth of usable soil by hindering root penetration. In most cases the condition can be cured through surface or subsurface drainage, but these modifications are expensive.

The third consideration is the depth of the topsoil. There are layers in the soil that make up the soil profile. The uppermost layer, the topsoil, is commonly from 4 to 12 inches deep. If you dig a hole, it is relatively easy to determine where the darker topsoil ends and the lighter subsoil begins. Normally, the deeper the topsoil the better, since topsoil depth is closely related to soil productivity. This is the one of the three soil-depth factors that can be most easily modified over time. Subsoil tillage, manuring, deep-rotary tillage, and the growing of deep-rooted, soil-improving crops will all help to deepen the topsoil, techniques that will be described in a later chapter.

Aspect of the Land   The lay of the land in most of the northern half of the United Sates is a very important factor. Land with a southern aspect has a number of advantages. A southern exposure warms up sooner in the spring. The more perpendicular a slope is to the angle of the sun, the faster it warms up. The grower who plans to compete for the early vegetable market needs this advantage. Land in the northern hemisphere at about 43° latitude (the northern border of Massachusetts, Illinois, or California) that slopes 5° to the south is actually in the same solar climate as level land three hundred miles to the south.

The logical application is to choose land with a southern slope for early crops. A southwestern slope is preferable to a southern or southeastern slope. On a southwestern slope, less direct radiation is employed to evaporate dew or frost in the early morning, and more is available for absorption once the initial daily warming has occurred. However, in this as in other areas, a compromise may have to be made.

A practical approximation of a southern exposure can be created on a flat field by hilling it up in east-west ridges with the southern surface sloped at approximately 40°. This gives the effect of many small south-facing slopes. Calculations

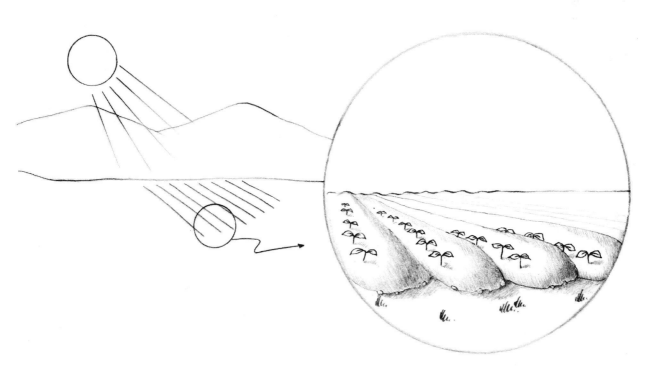

have shown an average 30-percent gain in total heat absorption by the soil from this practice. Early crops planted just up from the base of the *southern slope* of these ridges have a significant head start in the spring over similar crops planted on the flat.

Air Drainage

Plants and gardens need to breathe fresh air. A low area with no air movement is undesirable for a number of reasons. Stagnant air encourages fungus diseases, holds air pollutants around plants, and stays colder on frosty nights. The last is an important consideration, because cold air, which is heavier than warm air, "flows" downslope and collects in hollows and valleys. A farm in such a location is at a great disadvantage. Conversely, one on a hillside or near the top of a slope is better protected from frosts because the cold air of late spring and early fall flows down the hillside and settles in the valley. In many cases this cold-air drainage can result in a longer frost-free growing season of 2 and even 3 weeks at *both* ends of the season.

Of course the land does not want to be so sloped that it is either difficult to farm or is subject to erosion. Actually, a flat area on the edge of a slope enjoys as much air drainage as the top of the slope does and is probably the ideal situation.

Wind Protection and Sunshine

Although some air motion is good, more is not always better. An excessively windy site can cause physical damage to plants, cause windborne soil erosion, and provide less than ideal growing conditions due to the cooling action of the moving air. A windbreak, which can be anything from trees and tall hedges, to low stone or board walls, to strips of wheat or rye, can minimize the damaging effects of strong winds and optimize the benefits of solar warmth. The temperature of the soil is raised in shelter because as more surface warming takes place the accumulated heat is conducted downward into the soil. Windbreaks also help to create more ideal growing conditions by preventing the loss of transpired moisture. Reduction in evaporation means a consequent reduction in heat loss. In many ways a wind shelter does more than just lower wind speeds. It creates a beneficial microclimate far different from that in nearby ground.

Windbreaks of hedges and trees require long-term planning if such shelter does not already exist. Fortunately, effective short-term protection can be had by using temporary shelters. Two parallel lengths of snow fence 4 feet high and 60 feet apart can increase air temperature by 1° to 4°F. The slightly more substantial protection of a snow fence combined with a hedge can mean an average air temperature increase of 5°F in April and 7°F in May. Even a temporary 2-foot hedge of spruce boughs can keep the air temperature of the protected plot 2° to 3°F higher than that of nearby open field.

Unfortunately, too much of a good thing always causes a loss somewhere else. Too much wind shelter can mean inadequate sunshine. A balance must be struck somewhere between adequate wind protection and excessive shade. In order to achieve that ideal in the right place and at the right time, you must pay close attention to the path of the sun. It is not enough to merely say that the sun is higher in the sky in summer than in winter. It also traces a different path in the sky, rising and setting farther to the north in summer and to the south in winter. The ideal May windbreak is planned so as not to shade the January greenhouse.

Sunlight is the motive power for photosynthesis. Every effort must be made to take full advantage of it, especially during the early and late months of the growing season. Sometimes that means cutting down a tree to reduce shade. When faced with this situation, I think long and hard about whether the shade cast is serious enough to warrant removal of the tree. If the decision goes against the tree, I don't hesitate to cut it down, but I always replace it with another one that is more suitable for the location. Sunshine is one of the most dependable free inputs in a food-production system, and the grower should make every effort to maximize its contribution.

Water

Excess water is a flood and too little water is a drought. The farmer must make provision for both. River-bottom land is usually fertile and easy to work, but the grower must have access to higher land for dependable early crops in wet years. If the flood-prone land can be planned for a summer rotation or later crops, it will be less likely to cause a failure. Droughts are the other side of the coin. Water supply for irrigation is a major concern in some areas of the country. On average, provision should be made for applying one inch of water per week during the growing season if it is not supplied by natural rainfall. When looking for a good piece of land for vegetable growing, water is a key factor.

The ideal solution is a year-round spring or stream that can be tapped into and is sufficiently higher than the cultivated fields to allow for gravity feed. The piping for such a system can be laid inexpensively on top of the ground in spring and drained in fall, thus avoiding the expense of burying a long water line. Second best to a gravity system is a dependable pond from which water can be pumped. A well is a good third choice, but it is difficult to be sure of an adequate supply to meet the needs of production at the height of the season. One way or the other, don't forget water.

Geographic Location

This is too broad a subject to cover in detail. North, South, East, or West; hot or cold; wet or dry; urban, suburban, rural, or remote: crops can be grown in any and all of these places. The main consideration regarding location is proximity to market. Obviously, a suburban location close to many customers, stores, and restaurants is appealing, but the cost of the land in such areas is high. Land is less expensive in rural areas, but a greater effort must be made to develop and reach an adequate market. One compromise is to locate your farm in a rural area that attracts summer visitors. That market will not be available year round, but it will appear during your most productive cropping season.

Access   Both you and your customers need to be able to get to and about your land. Access in both instances is often not taken into account. A market location on a busy highway must provide plenty of space for safe parking. If it doesn't, few will stop. A long, unpaved, or seasonally impassable road to the farm will also discourage customers and increase the costs of access and operation. Streams on the property may be picturesque, but if they must be crossed often to get from one field to another, they become a liability. Land for a successful food production operation should be easy to enter, work in, and work around. It should be accessible to large equipment required for deep cultivation and spreading manure. Careful consideration should be given to the flow of activities from seeding through harvest, and provision made so that access to one part of the operation is not hindered by activities in another.

Security   The depredations of both two- and four-legged invaders can prove costly to a small farm. Dirt bikes and other off-road vehicles can destroy a whole spring's work in a thoughtless moment. Fields of raspberries, strawberries, and other fruit are tempting targets for midnight thievery unless they are protected by a fence or are located near inhabited dwellings.

Crows, pigeons, and other winged invaders of newly seeded crops can be stopped a couple of ways: either by beating them or joining them. To beat them the grower might use the floating crop covers described in Chapter 12. These covers protect seedlings from the birds, but joining the birds can also work. An old-timer once gave me the obvious answer to hungry crows: feed them. His method was to place small piles of corn in easily accessible places around the field, figuring that crows with full bellies won't pull up newly sprouted corn. The feeding continues until the corn is past the susceptible stage. I have followed his suggestion for many years and am very fond of this ingenious and benign solution.

Four-footed marauders also need to be considered. In a few short hours deer can graze off a whole field of newly transplanted seedlings. Raccoons are notoriously fond of sweet corn crops. Although there are a number of temporary measures (chemical repellents, organic repellents, radios tuned to all-night talk shows, and scarecrows, to name a few), the most consistently effective barrier is a good fence. The best fence is powered by an electric charger. The new, light-weight electro-plastic fencing units are reasonably priced, simple to erect, easy to move, and can be designed to keep out everything from raccoons to deer. They will provide your most dependable protection.

Pollutants Pollutants are a fact of life in most areas. It makes sense to give some thought to this problem in order to know what can be done before it surfaces. Both lead from exhaust and cadmium from tire wear have been found in excessive amounts on food grown within 200 to 300 feet of heavily traveled highways. A 6- to 8-foot-high evergreen hedge bordering the highway can block out the bulk of this pollution before it reaches the fields beyond. Lead from old paint and plaster can be a serious soil pollutant in areas where buildings once stood. Under certain conditions lead and other heavy metals in the soil can be taken up by plants in amounts that are highly detrimental to consumers, especially young children.

Residues from toxic waste dumps can travel downstream or downwind at far greater distances than is commonly recognized. Crops irrigated with water from an aquifer contaminated by one of these sites will cause toxic residues to accumulate both in and on the crops. Areas downwind of large industrial smokestacks suffer a continual dusting of questionable substances, including gases such as ozone, which are directly harmful to plant growth.

These problems may exist to a greater or lesser degree. They are mentioned here as one more factor to be considered in selecting land on which to farm. As with anything that may affect the success of a farm operation, it is best to know beforehand. Nothing could be more discouraging than to put a lot of work into establishing a small farm and to then find that because of unanticipated circumstances the site will not produce quality food. Forewarned is forearmed.

Acreage How much land should you purchase? Some people buy twice what is needed and sell half of it. Perhaps in addition to fields you'll need wooded land for firewood. You might want to purchase an adjacent area to set aside as wildlife or native plant habitats. Maybe what it comes down to is you just want some extra space.

All these decisions are personal ones. The premise of this book is that you can make a good living on five acres or less of intensive vegetable production. Thus it is those acres that concern us most. If five acres is all the land you can afford, it is more than sufficient for an economically successful farm. If you can afford more, another five acres perhaps, then more options open up. The crop rotation could include small live-stock on pasture to take advantage of the long-term soil fertility benefits of leaving land in deep-rooting grass and legume pastures for a few years before rotating it back into vegetable crops. Another one or two acres might be used for berry crops. Beyond that, you must watch out for the trap of more, more, and more. It is easy to farm a lot of land with a pencil and paper, but a lot harder to actually do it. The best advice is to buy only as much land as you will use and to buy the best land you can afford.

Soil Tests In my experience, the utility of soil tests is controversial. Soil tests appear to be part science and part necromancy. A sample of soil is sent to a laboratory where it is supposedly analyzed, investigated, and divided into its component parts. You then receive a report on its good and bad points. Despite the guise of the laboratory, there is more art than science to a good soil "test." The secret of using the results of a soil test lies in their interpretation. Not everyone agrees on how that should be done. Nor do people agree on how many useful conclusions can be drawn from the data. I recommend in all cases that you make an initial basic soil test on the fields you intend to use for vegetable production. Better yet, have two or three tests made on the same soil sample, each by a different laboratory. Have a state university lab make one of the tests and then send the same sample to one or two private labs. The results are often similar to the old saying, "A man with one watch knows what time it is; a man with two watches is never sure." Still, given the lack of certainty inherent in soil testing, it is better to have two or three opinions from which to draw your conclusions than only one.

The interpretation of soil test results is something that I suggest growers do for themselves. It won't be done mystically or according to one particular theory, but rather by common sense. If the test shows the soil is low in a nutrient, then add it. The method and manner of adding these nutrients is explained in Chapter 10. My recommendation is to add nutrients in their most available but least soluble form. By "most available" I mean that they should be finely ground, and by "least soluble" I mean not immediately water soluble but rather gradually water soluble through the action of soil bacteria and dilute soil acids—through the natural soil processes.

In taking a soil test you want to obtain as homogeneous a picture of the field or plot to be cultivated as possible. Instead of taking one sample from a spot in the middle of a field, a number of random samples should be taken over the whole area and then combined and mixed. The soil sent to be analyzed will be a more accurate representation of what you have. It is best to do this sampling and mixing with tools whose composition will not affect the results of the test. For example, if you are testing for iron, don't sample with a rusty iron trowel. In general, a stainless steel soil probe for the samples and a hard plastic bucket for mixing them are best. Addresses are given in the Chapter Notes for the labs whose tests I have found to be the most reliable.

The Ideal Small Farm

I doubt if you will find the ideal small farm (I never have), but the best of luck to you anyhow. Described below is what I believe the perfect piece of land would look like. Please remember that none of this is carved in stone. The determined farmer can transform even the most unlikely site into a model farm by applying the basic techniques of soil building.

> FOR SALE: 30 acres. 20 acres mixed hardwood forest, 10 acres pasture. DESCRIPTION: Reasonably flat (about 5 percent slope to south or southwest), set on the brow of a hill with good air drainage to the valley below. Protected on the north by higher land and dense forest. Excellent year-round gravity water supply. Soil on the cleared land is clay loam on one half and sandy loam on the other half. 12 inches of topsoil, well drained, very few stones, highly fertile, naturally neutral pH, and presently growing a grass-legume sod.

Chapter 3 SCALE AND CAPITAL

THE ECONOMISTS ARE ALWAYS TELLING US THAT American farms have to get bigger to survive. Small vegetable farms have almost entirely disappeared. But the weakness of small farms has not been one of scale. It has been one of *useless information*. Like a traveler with an outdated map, the small farmer has had to rely on outmoded concepts. Since the standard information sources (the United States Department of Agriculture, the land grant colleges, the agricultural supply industry) have not thought small farming possible, they have neither been compiling nor dispensing information on how to do it. To understand this situation we need to understand our underlying attitudes toward farming in America.

Bigger Is Not Better

The most common attitude holds that bigger is better, and the admonition to "get big or get out" is frequently heard. There is a basic assumption in American agriculture that a farmer with a few acres and mixed production is less successful and less advanced than the farmer who practices industrialized monoculture on a huge scale. In the recent history of American agriculture, such an assumption may have been defendable. American farmers with ambition and entrepreneurial ability took advantage of the resources of capital, transportation, and the agricultural technology that all blossomed in the 20th century to expand their operations, buy more land, and become increasingly specialized. This should not, however, be seen as the only or even the best way to farm. The economic and environmental problems of large-scale agriculture now make headlines every day. It seems the warning should be changed to "get big *and get out.*"

The major obstacle I had to overcome when I started farming was a lack of models. There were almost no commercially successful organic small farmers from whom I could get inspiration and with whom I could share ideas. My prototype of the economically viable five-acre farm didn't even exist. But highly productive small vegetable farms used to exist, so I began with the assumption that if it could be done once it could be done again. The know-how had to be available somewhere. At the start, old books and old-timers were my best sources of information and support. They were a good beginning, but they left me in the past. Nevertheless, I made some headway, but in the process I became aware of the reasons why small farming had died out. The product was excellent, but the process was exhausting. It was neither cost effective nor efficient. But I wasn't ready to give up. I knew there had to be suitable techniques and equipment somewhere that would bring this production process up to date.

The European Model

There are sections of the industrial world where the small farm has been and continues to be a success. Western Europe is such an area. The recent history of European agriculture is quite different from ours. There, the small farmer is an institution. Whether through tradition or stubbornness, the European small farmer has persevered and his equipment and information resources have kept up with him.

Entrepreneurial farming in Europe led to *better* rather than *bigger*. In part because more land was not readily available, increased income lay in improving production on existing acreage rather than expanding. As a consequence, the output of the average European farm is remarkably efficient and diverse, obvious corollaries of intensive agriculture. Europe's small farmers have traditionally produced the bulk of the food eaten in Europe and have made a good living for themselves in the process. There is no reason why regionally based, small-scale food production cannot be successful again in the United States, especially since dwindling supplies of fossil fuels are likely to drive up transportation costs between now and the next century. Unlike grains, fully ripened fruits and vegetables are highly perishable. They are particularly well-suited for local markets.

In the process of finding the tools and technologies I needed, I also learned a great deal about scale and the advantages of staying small. I learned right from the start that one must totally re-evaluate the basis for size in farming. The best way to do that is to wipe the slate clean and start thinking from scratch. All the when, where, what, why, and how questions need to be asked anew. How much production can one person or family handle? What kinds of equipment and techniques can be efficiently employed on the family farm? What helps the farm family do more with less?

The Five-Acre Answer

The answers are illuminating. Five acres is the optimum size because it is about as much land as a couple or small family can manage. By manage, I mean both practically and professionally—practically by using the low-cost equipment and simple techniques that fit the tasks, and professionally by making sure there are enough *people* per acre to stay on top of things. To effectively manage a farm operation I believe there is a person-to-land-area ratio that cannot be exceeded. Producing quality food requires an investment of effort on the part of the grower that naturally limits the amount of land farmed. For diversified vegetable growing, I place that upper limit at somewhere around 2½ acres per person. That ratio is small only in numbers. Two and a half acres is more than sufficient land to grow a year's worth of vegetables for 100 people. Anyone feeding that many folks can honestly consider himself to be running a highly productive farm.

In order to fully understand the potential for practical and economic success on the small farm, it must be understood that scale is not necessarily limiting or static. Size is only one of the components of an economic operation, and growth is more than just a change in size. It is generally accepted that a business must grow and respond to change in order to survive. The same applies to the small farm. But there are countless ways in which a farm can expand: quality, variety, and service are a few examples. I feel strongly that growth and change in the direction of *better* will ensure the economic and agronomic survival of the small farm more assuredly than growth and change in the direction of *bigger*.

It also helps if one can learn to ignore the well-meaning advice of economists, because their understanding of scale is industrial rather than agricultural. Their advice does not apply to biological production. The truth is that what can be accomplished on a small scale in agriculture cannot always be duplicated on a larger scale. The small farmer's aim is to produce a quality product for an appreciative clientele. The production of red, green, or orange-colored cellulose for a mass market is not the same thing.

The most encouraging aspect of small-scale farming is that the capital requirements to start up are reasonable. In this and many other ways small scale in agriculture should be understood as a very *positive* factor.

Equipment

The basic high-quality equipment needed to manage five acres of vegetable production can be purchased new for about $6,000. If used models are available, that cost can obviously be reduced. However, since much of the equipment I recommend has only recently become widely available, that option may not exist. This equipment consists of:

Walking tractor-tiller	$3,500
Wheel hoes	500
One-row seeder	100
Soil-block equipment	800
Hoes and hand tools	400
Carts and wheelbarrows	700
	$6,000

The single most important concept that keeps the capital investment at this very reasonable level (and simplifies the skills needed for operation and maintenance of the equipment) is the size of the equipment. Instead of a four-wheel tractor with costly implements, I recommend a much simpler two-wheel walking tractor/tiller for soil preparation along with hand-powered tools for seeding and cultivating. Reliance on these tools is not a concession to economics. Their outstanding performance and flexibility alone recommend them.

Additional capital investment for equipment other than the above may be required (or at least desired by the farmer) under many growing and marketing conditions. This should not amount to more than another $6,000. In this category I include:

Greenhouse	$3,500
Irrigation	2,000
Undersowing seeder	500
	$6,000

If the whole $12,000 were spent and paid back over 5 years (the depreciation life of the equipment) at 15-percent interest, the total cost per acre per year on 5 productive acres would be about $700. Allowing a generous figure of $1,300 per-acre per-year for annual operating costs (seed, fertilizer, fuel, hired equipment, and repairs) brings the total per acre per year cost to approximately $2,000. If you compare that to the $8,000-plus per-acre income an efficient vegetable operation should realize, you can see that the economics of small-scale vegetable farming are promising. If the local market permits a degree of specialization in the higher-priced crops, the income figure can be raised substantially. The "Food Guild" program suggested in Chapter 18 offers an innovative marketing concept that can help achieve those goals.

The small farmer operates in a unique situation. Definitions of the possible, the economic, the realistic, and the practical are completely changed. More than anything else, a lack of understanding of these definitions and a parallel lack of information on down-scaled biological and mechanical technologies have added to the belief that human-scale, regionally based agriculture "can't be done." It can.

PART-TIME HELP

Chapter
❧ 4

"YOU CANNOT GET GOOD HELP NOWADAYS."
"People don't work hard enough." "People don't care."
"They want too much money." "They aren't dependable."
Labor can be a problem. Many of these comments may be
valid, others not, but all are worth noting. It is wise to make
some serious choices ahead of time before you find yourself
muttering those very sentiments.

Family Labor

My suggestions in this area are consistent with the food-
production premise of this book—small, manageable, and
efficient. The family is the best source of labor for the small-
scale farm. So, the most important recommendation is to set
up an operation that is small, manageable, and efficient
enough to be run mainly by family labor. Why? Because
farming is hard work, and the rewards at the start are measured more in satisfaction and pride than in large salaries.
The farm family will do the work because it is their dream. It
is their canvas, and they are painting it the way they've
always wanted it to look. Hired help who can involve themselves from the start on such an intense level of participation
are not easy to find.

My production system is planned to make the most of
family labor in the following ways:

- I have chosen equipment for ease and efficiency of use and repair.

- I recommend growing a broad range of crops to spread the work more evenly over a long season.

- I take a management-intensive approach for fertilization and pest control.

- I stress forethought and pre-planning to avoid panic.

- I propose imaginative marketing approaches to save time and energy.

- Most important, this system is based upon a philosophy that aims at stability by establishing long-term, self-perpetuating, low-input systems of production as opposed to short-term, high-input systems.

Outside Labor

The best-laid plans don't always run true, and chances are the grower will need outside labor sometimes. When paid helpers are required, I have some suggestions.

If you find good employees, plan to keep them. Pay a fair wage and investigate profit-sharing options, insurance, and other rewards. One good worker familiar with your operation is worth three inexperienced workers. Be imaginative. What does the farm have to offer that will attract the ideal people? The usual pool of labor available for part-time farm work has never been the best. But think further. For many people, farming is exciting. Most everyone has a farming urge hidden behind their urbanized facade. While most are still dreaming about it, your farm is a reality. So offer potential helpers not so much a job but rather a part-time outlet for their dream. It is surprising how many people share it but have not yet decided to pursue it. Offer that reward to those people.

Finding Willing Workers

The potential labor pool extends from the young to the old, from students to retirees. Homemakers whose children are now in school or college are often looking for a new challenge. Working on an organic farm can give them meaningful part-time work and a chance to turn their energy and competence into valuable assets. There are many such people who are reliable, intelligent, hard-working, interested, motivated, and would love the chance to share in someone else's dream. For them the rewards are only partially financial. Since work hours are often limited to evenings or early mornings (harvesting for market, say) the possibility of fitting farm work into standard schedules is increased. Where to look for willing workers? Some of the following are good places to start:

- Retirement communities
- Supermarket bulletin boards (put up help-wanted signs and specify the benefits)
- Local colleges
- Food co-ops
- Ethnic groups
- Garden clubs
- Condominium and apartment dwellers

Be Flexible Be efficient. Maximize skills, minimize deficiencies. Labor should be hired to do what the boss does not do best or what he does not need to do. Ideally, the boss is going to be good at growing and marketing. Fine. Then hire help to pick, wash, crate, and distribute. Whoever is best-suited for a certain area of the operation should spend his or her time doing that as well as it can be done. Overall efficiency will be greater. Hire labor to complement rather than replace family skills.

Be flexible. Work out a solution for the particular labor needs of the moment. If the labor arrangement of the farm does not parallel that of modern agriculture, let it be of no concern. Many unique situations are successful. A farm may be next door to a large vegetarian community that will buy everything at a premium and help out to boot. Students from a nearby college may provide all the part-time labor on a work-study program. The farmer may have a dozen brothers and sisters living nearby who eagerly come and help out whenever they are needed. Ignore any claims that a farm only succeeds because of a special arrangement. Success simply means that a farmer is doing something right. Remember, too, that no matter how good a deal is, it should never be assumed to be permanent. Always have an alternative solution or two on hand.

Getting Quality Work

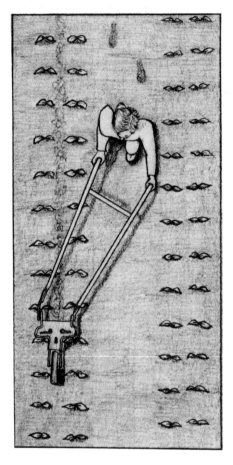

Jobs should be done correctly. The complement to labor is management. That is what the boss must do, and the quality of his management determines to a large degree how well labor performs. Horticulture is a skilled profession, and there is a need to work quickly but precisely. Standards must be set. In Europe, horticulture is respected and understood. The employees are professionals, are proud of their work, and take satisfaction in doing it well. In the past that may have been true in this country, but rarely any more. The boss has to instill that spirit of professionalism.

The repercussions of slipshod garden work are cumulative. Rows planted crookedly in a moment of carelessness cannot be cultivated efficiently and will require hand weeding for the entire growing season. Weeds that are allowed to go to seed one year will increase the weed problem for the next seven years. The quality of each job will affect the efficiency of the entire operation. Poor work must not be tolerated.

Along with quality production goes excellence of skills. Set work standards and stick to them. Most people have never learned the necessary bodily coordination needed to work well with simple tools. This lack of training and the consequent awkwardness result in making a job much more difficult than it needs to be. Show your helpers how it's done. They should be taught how to use garden tools just as carefully as they would be taught to play an instrument or speak a foreign language. Remember, any physical work is made easier by planning the job out beforehand, working at an efficient rhythm, and dividing the job up into attainable pieces.

Inspiring the Crew

An important facet of management is attitude. Management must care about labor's satisfaction. Many people will come to work because they are interested, so encourage their involvement. Explain not only what the job is but where it fits into the overall scheme of things and why it is important. If someone is starting in the middle of a process, take a moment to explain it fully so they can see both the beginning and the end. Not only will they be more interested when they understand the rationale for their efforts, but once they see the whole picture they will be able to suggest improvements in the system. Very often a beginner has seen things that I have missed because I was no longer looking at the job from a fresh perspective.

Finally, one last suggestion for dealing with outside labor. As I have said, the farm family is its own best labor force because they are motivated. Think for a moment — why? Because they love what they are doing, because it is creative and satisfies a creative urge, because farming is necessary and fulfilling work, because quality is important, and good growers take pride in producing a quality product. Whatever the reason, the bosses must convey a sense of that to outside workers. Don't hesitate to be inspirational and enthusiastic. If it is the magic of transforming a tiny seed into daily bread, then say so. If it is the joy of providing customers with truly nourishing food that they can trust, talk about it. Not everyone will share the same motivation, but enthusiasm is contagious. Spread it about.

Firing Workers

There are times when it will be necessary to fire someone. Do it nicely, but don't put it off. There is nothing more frustrating than making do with uninterested and unmotivated workers. One determined griper can ruin the experience for everyone else. Nip it in the bud quickly. If there are valid gripes, they should be dealt with fairly and openly. But beyond that, be firm. Some people seem to enjoy complaining. I prefer not to have them around.

A farm can't do without labor. The trick is to do well with it. If outside labor can't be counted on, don't set up a system that relies on it. When outside labor is necessary, use the natural advantages of the farm to attract people who want to be there.

Chapter *5* MARKET STRATEGY

ESTABLISHING A MARKETING STRATEGY IS ONE OF the first steps in a successful vegetable operation. Which crops? How much to grow? Ready when? Sold to whom? The key to success in marketing is to pay careful attention to one considerable advantage of the small producer—high-quality crops.

The European Lesson

In the early days of my own marketing education, I had the opportunity to visit many small farms in Europe. I learned a great deal there. The farmers I visited were successful first of all because they worked hard. Second, they succeeded because they worked intelligently. They took advantage of their strengths and minimized their weaknesses. For example, they diversified in order to spread their production, income, and family labor over a longer season. They chose agricultural enterprises that fit together spatially or temporally. That is, the preceding crop would fertilize the succeeding. The periods of heaviest work did not come all at once. They succeeded because they had access to modern production technologies scaled to their operations. But most important of all, they were economically successful because they understood how to compete in the marketplace with the most valuable product they had to offer—quality.

Standardization in food does not exist in Europe on the scale it does here. Regional and varietal differences are treasured. Quality in food is demanded as much as is quality in other products. In Europe, small growers are encouraged to produce a more carefully nurtured, high-quality product. What does that quality consist of? Many factors: Truly fresh produce. The tastiest and most tender varieties. The most careful soil and cultural practices needed to grow the crop correctly. The widest selection. The longest season. The personal touch. All are criteria where a small farmer producing for a local market has a great advantage over bulk-grown, trucked-in foodstuffs. The European farmers' success lies in concentrating on the areas in which the small farm excels.

Quality from Within

The benefits are enormous. I have noted over the years that many people feel uncomfortable about hustling a product, about putting on the hard sell, and so forth. Those people can calm their fears right now. If their product is good, necessary, and really first-class, then they never need worry about finding customers. The negative image many people carry of "salesmen" stems from the association of that profession with unwanted, unneeded, shoddy, poorly made, frivolous products that logically require fast talking and other unsavory skills to sell. Good growers should understand that they are not in that category. Theirs is a first-class product; it is produced locally without polluting the environment; it saves energy because the food doesn't have to be transported across the country; the production of it has stimulated employment and strengthened the local economy. A quality product always benefits the buyer as well as the seller. And that is how transactions between human beings should be, a mutually beneficial two-way exchange.

Ideas need to be sold, too, especially those ideas that are fundamental to good farming. Therefore, this chapter deals with more than just selling a product. It also deals with caring. Quality is the result of the skill of the producer coupled with care. Experience will provide the skills, but caring must come from within. Many customers may not be aware of real quality. The public is not always well informed about agricultural practices and their effect on the quality of food. So it is the grower who must care about his agricultural practices and their repercussions, even though there may be no one forcing him to. Giving a damn and doing what you believe is right are rewards in themselves. In the long run, producing a poor or deceptive product, or a less-good-than-you-can-do product, is harder on the producer than on the consumer. The consumer may only encounter it once or twice. The producer has to live with it all the time.

Real Carrots   Even though the consumer may be adept at distinguishing quality in manufactured goods, this perceptiveness does not always extend to food crops because he or she often has no standard for comparison. To most people, a carrot is a carrot is a carrot. Well, to tell the truth, it isn't. And the difference is not just looks. Carrots can take up large quantities of pesticide residues when they are grown in soils that contain them. Carrots grown in soil with a low pH take up more lead, cadmium, and aluminum. Unbalanced soluble fertilizers modify plant composition. The lack of minor elements, limited by poor soil conditions, inhibits protein synthesis. There is definitely a "biological value" in food plants that is hampered or lost by inadequate soil fertility and growing conditions.

For the most part, scientific evidence on the subject of food's biological value is contradictory and incomplete. It remains one of those areas where people are intuitively conscious of differences once they experience them, but tests for those differences are inadequate. There are documented differences in food quality as affected by growing conditions but not enough to constitute "absolute proof"—as if absolute proof is ever possible with any biological concept. Perhaps we aren't wise enough to know what to look for. But the sensible consumer doesn't always wait for science. The consumer has generally led science rather than followed it. I remember watching meticulous French customers shopping for vegetables in a rural village. Their standards, which had been honed by generations of awareness, were very high. If "a carrot is a carrot is a carrot," you could not have proved it by them.

Other ideas are spreading as well. Agricultural chemical technologies are under heavy criticism. Consumers are demanding safer food and more control over additives and residues. The idea is dawning that food must be judged not by its cosmetics but by its composition. The public is aroused because of a sense that the system they have been taught to rely on has betrayed them, and will probably continue to betray them.

That system, which is composed of the regulatory agencies of the government—the Environmental Protection Agency, the USDA, and the Food and Drug Administration—has compiled a dismal and embarrassing record of failure with regard to safeguarding the public. Stories to that effect appear in the media every day. Pesticides or additives sworn to be absolutely benign one day are banned as hazardous the next. Scientists upon whose knowledge we depend to make those decisions disagree vehemently among themselves over the safety of agricultural practices vis-à-vis the health of the consumer, the pollution of our water supplies, and the long-term productive capacity of the soil. But the consumer is no fool. The disturbing evidence can no longer be ignored. Something is amiss and whether there is "absolute" scientific proof or not a groundswell has begun. The king has no clothes and the public, by doubting the adequacy of the regulatory agencies, has begun to make independent decisions to seek safer food.

We may seem to have wandered off the subject of marketing strategy, but not in practical terms. Quality is the lynch pin of a small-scale grower's business. Once consumers realize that certain producers *care*, that they are *sincere* and that their word and their produce are *dependable*, they will patronize them faithfully. I ran a market garden in Maine from 1968 to 1978 in a very unlikely location. The farm was six miles from a numbered highway (and the last three miles were dirt road). Marketing problems? I had none. Our produce *set* the quality standard and we always had more demand than we could meet. Once a reputation for "real" food is established, there is no better advertising or marketing program. The market, as they say, will take care of itself.

Chapter *6* PLANNING AND OBSERVATION

When I began farming full-time on my own land in Maine, I was extremely fortunate to have as friends and neighbors Scott and Helen Nearing. The Nearings taught me a wide range of economic survival skills, but none were so important as *planning* and *observation*. The Nearings demonstrated those two valuable skills at their best.

They were careful planners and organizers of the work to be done and the crops to be grown, and always sought out the most efficient way to accomplish any task at hand. They were without a doubt the most practically organized country people I have ever met. In fact, I remember marveling that Scott was the one nonagenarian I knew with plans for what future farm project he would be working on ten years hence.

Farming on Paper

I soon learned to plan ahead much more efficiently than I ever had, to set out the whole year's work on paper during the winter months and thus have a good grasp well in advance of what resources I would need, where they would come from, how I would acquire them, and how much time I could allot to each task. I organized a notebook into sections for each vegetable crop, for every year in the different rotations I was trying out, for fertilization records on each field, and so forth. There is no way to match the value of organizing and planning beforehand.

The Nearings were masters of observation. They meticulously recorded all the bits and pieces of data gleaned out of day-to-day farm activities — from what variety of lettuce wintered over best to what combination of ingredients made the most effective compost for peas. Some of their observations came from intentional comparative trials, but the majority came by chance from keeping their eyes open and training themselves to notice subtle differences where less perceptive observers would pass by unaware. In short, they never stopped learning and were wise enough to record what they noticed so it would be of use to them in the future.

Taking a cue from the Nearings, the first step, therefore, is to plan out your operation in detail. Let's go through this process step by step to figure out what crops to grow, in what quantities, and how to set it all up.

What To Grow

Depending on the market and the climate, the possibility exists to grow from 1 to 70 or so reasonably common vegetable crops. The 45 vegetables I consider the most promising are listed below and are divided into two categories, major and minor.

Major		Minor
Asparagus	Onion, bulb	Celeriac
Bean	Onion, scallion	Chicory
Beet	Parsley	Chinese cabbage
Broccoli	Peas	Collards
Brussels sprouts	Pepper	Dandelion
Cabbage	Potato	Eggplant
Carrot	Pumpkin	Endive
Cauliflower	Radish	Escarole
Celery	Rutabaga	Fennel
Chard	Spinach	Kohlrabi
Corn	Squash, summer	Leek
Cucumber	Squash, winter	Mache
Garlic	Tomato	Okra
Kale		Salsify
Lettuce		Shallot
Melon		Turnip

One way to begin deciding which vegetables to grow is to write down in chart form any information that will help organize your planning. For example, I might begin by compiling a chart of the months when different vegetables could be available for sale if they were grown in my area. That chart should include the potential for extended availability of these crops if the growing season is supplemented by the protection of walk-in tunnels, the greater protection of a heated greenhouse, or out-of-season sales from a storage building. (For a discussion of the whole range of season extension possibilities, see Chapter 19.)

A chart of the potential availability of crops for sale in my area, mid-Vermont, might look like the following chart.

AVAILABILITY OF MAJOR CROPS FOR SALE

Outdoor ▇▇▇▇ Protected ▨▨▨▨ Greenhouse ▭▭▭▭

Crop	J	F	M	A	M	J	J	A	S	O	N	D
Asparagus					Protected	Outdoor	Outdoor					
Bean						Protected	Outdoor	Outdoor				
Beet					Protected	Protected	Outdoor	Outdoor	Outdoor	Outdoor		
Broccoli							Outdoor	Outdoor	Outdoor	Outdoor	Outdoor	
Brussels sprout									Outdoor	Outdoor	Outdoor	Outdoor
Cabbage							Outdoor	Outdoor	Outdoor	Outdoor		
Carrot	Protected	Protected	Protected		Protected	Protected	Outdoor	Outdoor	Outdoor	Outdoor	Protected	
Cauliflower							Outdoor	Outdoor	Outdoor	Outdoor		
Celery					Greenhouse	Protected	Outdoor	Outdoor	Outdoor	Protected	Protected	
Chard					Protected	Protected	Outdoor	Outdoor	Outdoor	Protected	Protected	
Corn							Outdoor	Outdoor	Outdoor			
Cucumber				Greenhouse	Greenhouse	Protected	Outdoor	Outdoor	Outdoor			
Garlic								Outdoor	Outdoor	Outdoor		
Kale							Outdoor	Outdoor	Outdoor	Outdoor	Outdoor	
Lettuce	Greenhouse	Greenhouse	Greenhouse	Protected	Outdoor	Outdoor	Outdoor	Outdoor	Outdoor	Protected	Protected	
Melon						Protected	Outdoor	Outdoor				
Onion, bulb							Outdoor	Outdoor	Outdoor	Outdoor	Outdoor	Outdoor
Onion, scallion			Protected	Protected	Protected	Protected	Outdoor	Outdoor	Outdoor	Protected	Protected	
Parsley			Greenhouse	Greenhouse	Protected	Protected	Outdoor	Outdoor		Protected	Protected	
Parsnip				Outdoor							Outdoor	Outdoor
Peas						Outdoor	Outdoor	Outdoor	Outdoor	Outdoor		
Pepper					Greenhouse	Protected	Outdoor	Outdoor	Protected	Protected		
Potato							Outdoor	Outdoor	Outdoor	Outdoor	Outdoor	
Pumpkin									Outdoor	Outdoor		
Radish			Greenhouse	Protected	Protected	Outdoor	Outdoor	Outdoor	Outdoor	Outdoor	Protected	
Rutabaga									Outdoor	Outdoor	Outdoor	
Spinach					Protected	Protected	Outdoor	Outdoor	Outdoor	Protected	Protected	
Squash, summer					Greenhouse	Protected	Outdoor	Outdoor				
Squash, winter									Outdoor	Outdoor		
Tomato					Greenhouse	Greenhouse	Protected	Outdoor	Outdoor	Greenhouse	Greenhouse	

AVAILABILITY OF MINOR CROPS FOR SALE

Legend: Outdoor █████ Protected ▒▒▒▒▒ Greenhouse □□□□□

Crop	J	F	M	A	M	J	J	A	S	O	N	D
CELERIAC									█	█		
CHINESE CABBAGE					█	█	█	█	█	█	█	
COLLARDS									█	█	█	
DANDELION				█	█	█	█					
EGGPLANT							▒	█	█	▒		
ENDIVE					▒	█	█	█				
ESCAROLE					▒	█	█	█				
FENNEL							█	█				
KOHLRABI									█	█		
LEEK									█	█	█	
MACHE	▒	▒	▒	▒						█	█	▒
OKRA							█	█	█			
SALSIFY									█	█	█	
SHALLOT									█	█	█	
TURNIP									█	█	█	

Then, depending on whether I wanted to grow just seasonally or for an extended market, I would have an idea which crops could be available and when. The advantage of compiling this kind of information is that it stimulates thinking. It might suggest a specific course of action, such as a degree of specialization, perhaps. Certain other crops can be made available year-round. In many markets year-round production can help keep customers or acquire restaurant contracts. A look at the chart shows that many salad crops fit the year-round production plan. A chart for specialization in salad crops would look like the following.

The "A" crops are the most potentially lucrative for the grower, but they are also the most expensive to produce.

They need higher temperatures requiring more heating costs and a more professional greenhouse, one that is taller and stronger for trellising. They also are not actually year-round crops, although they are long-season. Only the most specialized producers plan on harvesting before April and after November.

The "B" crops can be grown in simpler tunnel greenhouses at lower temperatures. Some, such as mache, parsley, scallions, spinach, and carrots, can be grown as fall crops with no supplementary heat at all. They can be harvested all at once before real cold sets in, or over a good part of the winter by providing just enough heat to keep them from freezing. The decision depends on your market.

The most basic year-round greenhouse crop is lettuce. It is always in demand. Excellent varieties for winter production are available through the specialist seed catalogs. If the grower uses an adapted variety, lettuce can be grown at low temperatures and winter harvesting can be planned on a regular schedule.

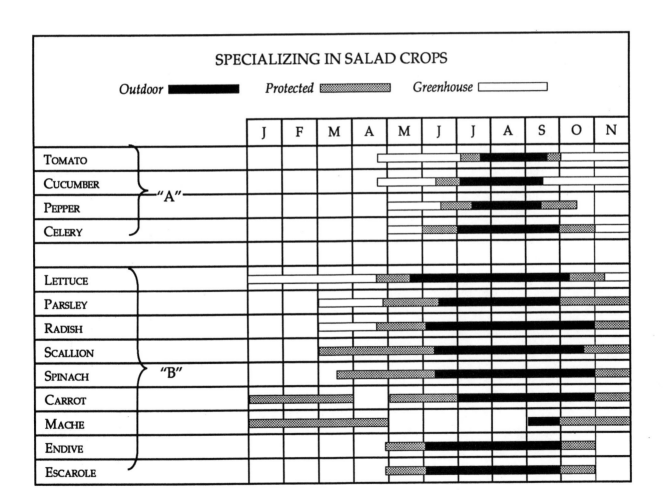

SPECIALIZING IN SALAD CROPS

Outdoor ▮ Protected ▨ Greenhouse ▭

Production Size This is a function of a number of other factors. How much land is available? How fertile is it? How many workers are involved? What kind of equipment is on hand? As I said earlier, I consider five acres of intensive production to be the upper limit. The decision about the size of a production cannot be made in a vacuum. The relationship of size to all of the production and marketing factors must never be forgotten.

The market garden layout will obviously be determined by the lay of the land, but there are some general suggestions that are applicable almost everywhere.

Subdivision No matter what size the field, it should be subdivided. One-hundred-foot sections are the ideal size for the scale of machinery to be used. A 5-acre field, sectioned off, might look like this:

Ideally, the field will slope to the south. The rows run across the field. Each row is 100 feet long. The paths in between, which allow for access and turning a walking tractor/tiller at the end of each row, are from 5 to 10 feet wide.

There are some solid reasons for subdividing. Ease of access, of calculating input and production information, and of general organization are just a few. The most important reason is management. Subdivision makes it easy to keep an eye on everything. Care is the key, and nothing must be neglected. Subdivision helps to get the grower and his attention to every part of the operation. The crop that could easily be forgotten in the middle of a large field is more likely to receive care in a smaller space. No matter what the shape of the growing area it should somehow be divided into workable sections.

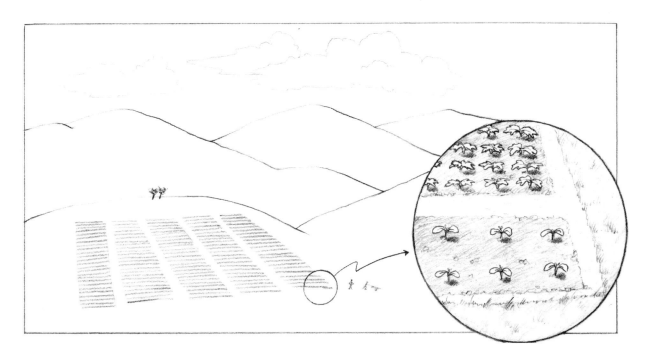

Layout and Crop Spacing

The divisions above must now be progressively subdivided again. Just as a country is easier to comprehend when it is divided into states, counties, and towns, a garden is more comprehensible as sections and strips and rows. Each section in the illustration above is 100 feet by 200 feet, or ½ acre. A strip is a part of a section 100 feet long by 5 feet wide. There are 40 strips side by side in each section.

Only 4 feet of the strip width is planted to crops. The remaining 1 foot is used as an access path. Foot traffic should be confined to these paths in order to avoid soil compaction in the growing area. The row spacings used for various crops follow, accompanied by drawings from a worm's-eye view. Thinking in terms of strips helps to make the production system more flexible. Any strip can be planted after harvest to a succession crop or to a green manure independently of the rest of the section.

4-inch row spacing
10 rows per strip

Radish, spinach, mache, green manure. These are planted with the 5-row seeder (see Chapter 8)

12-inch row spacing
4 rows per strip

Carrot, beet (fresh), celery, chard, garlic, lettuce, onion, parsley, spinach, celeriac, chicory, Chinese cabbage, dandelion, endive, escarole, fennel, kohlrabi, leek, shallot, turnip

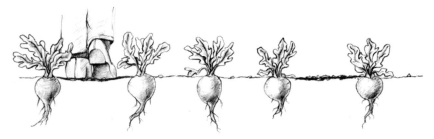

18-inch row spacing
3 rows per strip

Beet (storage), kale, rutabaga, collards, salsify, parsnip

30-inch row spacing
2 rows per strip

Bean, broccoli, Brussels, cabbage, cauliflower, corn, cucumber, peas (low), pepper, potato, tomato (staked), eggplant

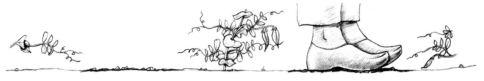

60-inch row spacing
1 row per strip

Asparagus, peas (tall), tomato (flat), melon, squash (summer)

120-inch row spacing
Every other strip

Pumpkin, squash (winter)

Getting Good Seed   So many factors are important in vegetable growing that there may be disagreement with the values I ascribe to some of them. But I doubt if anyone will dispute the importance of good seed. Without high quality seed, all the other activities are moot.

The grower will first be concerned with varieties (or cultivars, as they are also called). At the start I suggest sticking with tried and true locally adapted varieties from a dependable regional supplier. After the first year or two, the grower should have enough experience about what works and what needs improvement to begin selecting from seed catalogs. With catalogs, it is mostly a case of learning to read between the lines. New seed varieties, no matter how highly praised, are always a risk. This is especially true with the commercial catalogs, which often select new cultivars for their ability to perform under conventional fertilizer/pesticide regimes. Growers will find as I have that the stable, older varieties often give more dependable results.

That is not to say that you should avoid trying something new. Just never abandon a dependable old variety without being sure about the quality of its replacement. I have always found it rewarding to read specialist and foreign seed catalogs and then conduct trial plantings of promising varieties and even new crops. I have discovered a small but important number of my favorites this way. The number I trial is small because the seed companies are also testing and trialing varieties from many sources with far greater resources than I possess. For the most part their results are thorough and dependable. There always exists, however, the pleasure of a new discovery made on my own, and I heartily recommend the practice of seeking and trying.

Below are some criteria that you may want to consider when selecting varieties:

Eating Quality   This is most important by far and includes the flavor, tenderness, and aroma of the vegetable, both raw and cooked.

Appearance   Color, size, and shape are also important but are second to eating quality.

Pest and Disease Resistance   This is useful where a problem exists; otherwise, choose a variety for its flavor and tenderness.

Days to Maturity   This is obviously an important factor in planning early and succession crops.

Storage   Suitability for long or short periods in storage.

Vigor   This includs quick germination and quick growth.

Performance   Does the variety have vigor under a wide variety of conditions?

Standability   This describes non-cracking tomatoes, non-splitting cabbages, and so forth.

Ease of Harvest   Carrots with strong tops are easier to pull, and beans held above the foliage are easier to pick.

Time of Harvest   Various cultivars can extend your growing season.

Frost Resistance and Hardiness   These are spring and fall concerns.

Day Length   There are short-day varieties for winter greenhouse production, and so forth.

Easy To Clean   Some leafy greens hold their leaves high to avoid soil splash.

Uncomplicated   This includes self-blanching cauliflower, non-staking tomatoes, and other convenient growers.

Easy To Prepare   This means long as opposed to round beets, round as opposed to flat onions, and so forth.

Adaptability   Many varieties winter over and provide early spring growth.

Nutrition   Some varieties have higher levels of nutrients.

Marketability   This includes specialty, ethnic, and gourmet varieties.

Quantity   Quantity is the next concern. How much of each variety should be purchased? Planting techniques will affect this decision. If a majority of crops are transplanted as this book recommends, the grower will be able to get by with far fewer seeds than would be needed if plants were to be sown directly. Information on quantities of seed needed for direct-sown crops is given in most seed catalogs. At the start one might want to purchase extra seed just to be sure. A new seeder or a new setting could easily plant twice the seeds calculated until it is calibrated correctly. Nothing is as discouraging as running out of seed on a perfect spring planting day. The cost of seed for field crops is a small expense in most cases, and a little extra is good insurance for the grower.

If there are specific varieties or crops that become important to the farm's production, it is a good practice to purchase an insurance packet of those seeds from a second supplier. This is especially important with succession crops. Along with the first planting of the standard seeds, plant seeds from the insurance packet. If all goes well the extra seedlings won't be needed, but if the standard seeds don't perform well the grower will be covered and know where to order new stock. Be sure to set up credit accounts with favored seed firms so seeds can be ordered by phone quickly if there are any problems during the year.

It is wise to be covered the same way when planning to use last year's seeds. Most of the time and for most varieties, year-old seeds that were stored properly (cool, dry, and dark) will work just fine. However, the savings are a false economy if a crop or a succession planting is lost because of seed failure. The grower should be sure to obtain each year's seeds as soon as possible. Never wait until the last minute. Early planting dates have a habit of sneaking up; before you realize it, spring is here. Whether you purchase seed from a mail order catalog or from a local supplier will depend upon personal preference. What is necessary in either case is dependability. A grower needs consistent quality and up-to-date information. If the seed stock for a certain variety is poor one year, it is important that the supplier informs its customers of this fact. Smaller growers are often not privy to this information, so it always pays to ask.

I suggest a further precaution. After a few years' experience, a grower should experiment with saving seed. For most crops the vigor and viability of seed grown under the careful cultural practices of this production system will far excel seeds that are purchased. I make this recommendation for another reason, too. I doubt that the direction of present-day seed breeding, selection, and genetic manipulation is favorable to the producer of high quality vegetables. Many older varieties are being abandoned or unnecessarily tinkered with. I now save seed from any open-pollinated varieties that I treasure for their eating qualities or excellent growth under my production methods. Seeds are the spark of the farm operation, and the more control the grower can exert the more dependable his system will be.

When To Plant   The date of harvest depends on the date of planting. The span of time between the two may be longer or shorter depending on the effects of day length, weather, the aspect of the land, the crops grown, and many other growth-related factors. Although control is possible with protected cropping (tunnels and greenhouses), the earliest and latest unprotected outdoor crops are still important. They cost less to produce and they include many crops that are not usually grown with protection.

Early and Late   The best information on your earliest and latest local planting dates will come from other growers, and not necessarily just the professionals. Good home gardeners are surprisingly astute about planting dates and other matters. More than once I have seen the experienced home gardener beat the pros to the earliest harvest. In truth, this is such a complex subject and one that can be influenced in so many ways that even the best growers are not doing all they could be doing. Without doubt the early outdoor production potential of many farms can be improved by paying attention to windbreaks, exposure, soil color, and other microclimate modifications.

As a further refinement there are specific cultural factors to take into account. Sweet corn, for example, is an important crop for most market stands, and earliness is what brings the customers. But the planting date of corn can be pushed back only so far because of the limits of temperature. Corn won't germinate reliably or at all if the soil temperature is below 55°F. Yet corn seedlings will grow at or below that temperature. That is the factor that is usually overlooked. Pre-germinating corn seed or transplanting corn seedlings may be worth considering. Remember, we are not talking about the whole corn crop, rather just a few days' worth to catch the earliest market. Corn can be transplanted quite successfully if it is grown in soil blocks (see Chapter 13).

Succession and Greenhouse Planting   If a grower wishes to harvest a crop such as lettuce progressively throughout the year, it may seem logical to plant every week to keep up the continuity of supply. The logic is only partially valid. There may indeed be 52 planting dates during the year, but they will not be at 7-day intervals. The season of the year affects plant growth because of light, temperature, day length, and so on. Planting dates must be adjusted accordingly. Although these dates will vary with the geographical region and lay of the land, certain general patterns can be used as a guide.

The maturity time for lettuce is doubled and tripled for plantings from September through February. The spacing of the planting dates must reflect that reality. In order to harvest lettuce every week from early November through April, Dutch research has determined that the following planting schedule is necessary:

September 1 to 10	sow every 3½ days
September 10 to 18	sow every 2 days
September 18 to October 10	sow every 3½ days
October 10 to November 15	sow every 7 days
November 15 to December 15	sow every 10 days

Other trials have shown that seed-to-harvest times can be speeded up if lettuce transplants are grown under artificial lighting for the first 3 weeks.

Outdoor production has similar variables. In my own experience in Maine, lettuce sown in a sun-heated greenhouse on March 1 and transplanted outside April 21 was ready for sale on about May 25, whereas lettuce sown April 1 in the same greenhouse and transplanted outside on May 1 matured on June 2. Remember, specific dates are only guidelines. I wish to stress the understanding of the concept and the general pattern. All growers need to compile information for the climate and conditions of their individual farms. In the long run trial and error will be the best teachers of specific planting dates. This is another area where keeping careful records can be so valuable to the success of your farm.

Despite all the best planning, climate is never consistent. Unusual extremes of heat and cold can make life difficult. One way to offset unpredictable weather is to grow more than one variety of any crop. The varieties would be chosen for their slightly different performance under similar growing conditions, thus allowing the grower to "blanket" the ideal maturity date. The dependability of the harvest is more assured by adding a comfortable flexibility that can absorb some of the shocks of climatic anomalies.

MAJOR CROPS: AN OVERVIEW

Crop	Quantity Consumed: Rank Order (USDA)	Greenhouse Production	Transplanted	Direct Seeded	Row	Plant
ASPARAGUS	17		√		60	24
BEAN	8			√	30	4
BEET	14			√	18	3
BROCCOLI	12		√		30	24
BRUSSELS SPROUT	12		√		30	24
CABBAGE	7		√		30	24
CARROT	9			√	12	1
CAULIFLOWER	12		√		30	24
CELERY	10	√	√		18	12
CHARD	18	√		√	18	6
CORN	4			√	30	12
CUCUMBER	6	√		√	30	12
GARLIC	20		√		12	4
KALE	7		√		18	12
LETTUCE	3	√	√		12	12
MELON			√		60	24
ONION, BULB	5		√		12	3
ONION, SCALLION	5	√		√	12	1
PARSLEY		√	√		12	6
PARSNIP				√	18	3
PEAS	11			√	60	2
PEPPER	15		√		30	12
POTATO	1			√	30	12
PUMPKIN				√	120	24
RADISH		√		√	4	2
RUTABAGA	19			√	18	4
SPINACH	13			√	12	3
SQUASH, SUMMER	16			√	30	30
SQUASH, WINTER	16			√	120	24
TOMATO	2	√	√		60	24

A Final Word   Another lesson I learned from the Nearings is the folly of working 7 days a week. There is a strong temptation when starting out in farming, without the benefit of parents and grandparents having done much of the preliminary work years before, to try to do it all right now. Working non-stop day after day is not the best way to achieve that goal. You soon get stale and lose the sense of joy and pleasure that made farming seem so desirable in the first place. Scott and Helen taught me the importance of pursuing something different, at least one day out of the 7, no matter how much work needs to be done on the farm. Even in the midst of the spring rush it always turns out that one day of change allows much more to be accomplished on the other days. Rest and reflection not only heal the body but help provide insight into how to get more accomplished with less work in the future so the same bind won't exist another year.

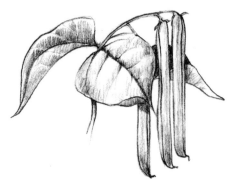

Chapter 7 CROP ROTATION

MOST DEPENDABLE AGRICULTURAL PRACTICES are ages old. Crop rotation is a good example. Descriptions of the benefits of rotating crops can be found in the earliest Roman agricultural writings. The Greeks and before them the Chinese were also well acquainted with the principles of crop rotation. A well-thought-out crop rotation is worth 75 percent of everything else that might be done, including fertilization, tillage, and pest control. In fact, I think this is a conservative estimate. Rarely are the principles of crop rotation applied as thoroughly as they might be in order to garner all of their potential benefits. To my mind, crop rotation is the single most important practice in a multiple-cropping program.

In a word, crop rotation means variety, and variety gives stability to biological systems. By definition, crop rotation is the practice of changing the crop each year on the same piece of ground. Ideally, these different crops are not related botanically. Ideally, two successive crops do not make the same demands on the soil for nutrients, nor do they share diseases or insect pests. Legumes will be alternated with non-legumes. A longer rotation before the same crop is grown again is better than a shorter rotation. And ideally, as many factors as possible will be taken into account in setting up the sequence.

Space and Time The key to visualizing crop rotations is to understand that two things are going on at once. Rotations are both spatial (crops move) and temporal (time moves). With both crop sequence and time to consider, there may be some initial confusion when considering complicated rotations. Hang in there.

A graphic representation of an 8-year crop rotation would look like the following. There are 8 sections with a different crop growing in each section. Now let's say we want to rotate these 8 crops so that A follows B, B follows C, and so on. Adding arrows to the picture indicates the direction of rotation. In each case the letters represent where the crop grows this year. The picture for the next year would follow the arrows one space over and have A growing where B grows this year, with H growing in A's old place. The following year would have A growing where C grows this year, and so on.

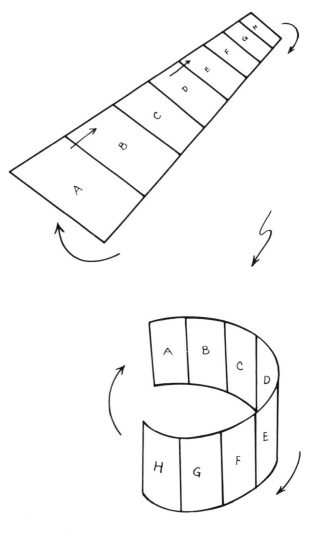

When planning rotations I use 3 by 5 index cards with the crop names written on them. Some of you may wish to use a computer to display your planning options. I move the cards around as I try to determine the ideal sequence for the number of crops involved. Let's see how that works. With 2 crops, there is no problem. Take corn and beans. Corn is growing this year where beans will be next year and beans are growing this year where corn will be next year.

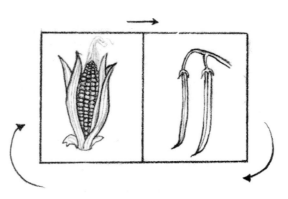

A 3-year rotation expands that concept. Once there are more than 2 crops, a new factor is involved — order. There are now 2 possible sequences. The index cards can be placed: corn/beans/squash or corn/squash/beans.

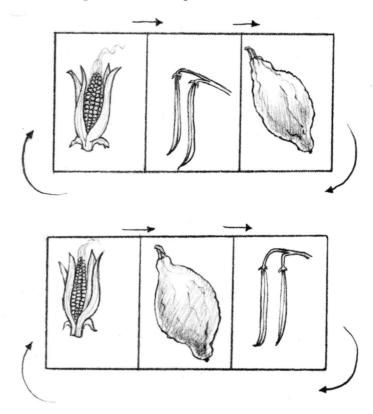

Notice that we are not concerned with the number of ways in which 3 items can be ordered (of which there are 6), but rather with the possible sequences. If we go to a 4-year rotation, there are 6 possible sequences. An 8-year rotation offers 5,040 sequences.

Why Bother?

Decisions, decisions. Why bother with crop rotation? Because there are so many benefits to the grower from setting up a rotational sequence that exploits every possible advantage. Corn, beans, squash, and other crops all take different nutrients out of the soil. All respond to diverse fertilization patterns. All are amenable to specific cultivation practices. All may affect or be affected by the preceding or succeeding crop. Whenever the crop or cultural practices of the current year can be chosen to benefit a future crop, there is reason for bothering. In fact, whenever there is a choice between one or more ways of doing a job, one of them is usually the best way. The determined grower will take the time to think things through to maximize every aspect of his production.

Time spent planning a rotation is never wasted. Not only will you learn a great deal about important biological balances on the farm, but the results will be so effective in halting problems before they occur that you may sometimes have to remind yourself that a lot is happening. Very often farmers fail to take full advantage of a well-planned rotation, because rotations don't have any computable costs and because they work so well at preventing problems that farmers are not aware of all the benefits. Those benefits are, in a sense, invisible.

Insect, Disease, and Weed Control

Rotations improve insect and disease control by managing the system to benefit the crop. Monoculture encourages many pest problems because the pest organisms specific to a crop can multiply out of all proportion when that crop is grown in the same place year after year. Pests are most easily kept in balance when the soil grows different crops over a number of years. A good rotation spaces susceptible crops at intervals sufficient to hinder the buildup of their specific pest organisms.

Rotations affect weed control in a similar way. The characteristics of a crop and the cultivation methods used to grow it may inadvertently allow certain weeds to find a favorable niche. A smart crop rotation will incorporate a successor crop that eradicates those weeds. Furthermore, some crops can work as "cleaning crops" because of the style of cultivation used on them. Potatoes and winter squash fit in this category because of the hilling practiced on the former and the long period of cultivation that is possible prior to vining for the latter.

Plant Nutrition

Rotations can make nutrients more available in a biological farming system. Some plants are more effective than others in using the less-soluble forms of plant nutrients. The residues of these nutrient-extracting plants will make the minerals more available to later, less effective plants in the next sequence of the rotation.

In general, plants of a lower order of evolution have been shown to be better feeders on less soluble nutrient sources than those of a higher order of development. Lowly plants—evolutionarily speaking—such as alfalfa, clovers, and cabbages, are more aggressive at extracting nutrients than more highly developed plants such as lettuce or cucumbers. Lettuce and cucumbers, I've found, don't feed well on less-soluble mineral nutrients. Thus, in my rotations, the choicest spot and the finest compost is always saved for the lettuce and cucumbers crops, and their exceptional quality has always repaid that care.

Manure

Rotations encourage the best use of organic soil amendments. Some crops (squash, corn, peas, and beans, for example) grow best when manure or compost is applied every year. Others (cabbages, tomatoes, root crops, and potatoes) seem to grow better on ground that was manured the previous year. Greens are in the former category with the caveat that the compost should be well decomposed. Obviously, a rotation that alternates manured crops with non-manured crops will allow a grower to take these preferences into account.

Soil Structure   Rotations preserve and improve the soil structure. Different crops send roots to various depths, are cultivated with different techniques, and respond to either deeper or shallower soil preparation. By changing crops each year, the grower can make use of the full depth of the soil and slowly deepen the topsoil in the process.

Deeper-rooting plants of both cash crops and green manures extract nutrients from layers of the soil not used by the shallow rooters. In doing so they open up the soil depths, leaving paths for the roots of other, less vigorous crops. Deep rooters also incorporate mineral nutrients from the lower strata into their structure, and eventually, when the residues of these plants decompose in the soil, those nutrients become available to the shallow rooters.

Yields   Rotations improve yields not only in the many ways discussed above but also in subtler ways. Some crops are helped and some hindered by the preceding crop. The possible reasons for this are numerous, but even after extensive study there is no general agreement on what exactly are the processes involved. Some causes for the beneficial influence of preceding crops on subsequent crops are:

- Increase in soil nitrogen

- Improvement in the physical condition of the soil

- Increased bacterial activity

- Increased release of carbon dioxide

- Excretion of beneficial substances

- Control of weeds, insects, and disease

The injurious effects of preceding crops, which I aim to avoid by careful rotation planning, are produced by:

- Depletion of soil nutrients

- Excretion of toxic substances

- Increase in soil acidity

- Production of injurious substances resulting from the decomposition of plant residue

- Unfavorable physical condition of the soil due to a shallow rooting crop

- Lack of proper soil aeration

- Removal of moisture

- Diseases passed to subsequent crops

- Influences of crops upon the soil flora and fauna

Patterns Despite a lack of agreement among researchers, certain patterns emerge from the studies that have been done on good and bad rotational effects:

- Legumes are generally beneficial preceding crops.

- The onions, lettuces, and squashes are generally beneficial preceding crops.

- Potato yields best after corn.

- For potatoes some preceding crops (peas, oats, and barley) increase the incidence of scab, where others (soybeans) decrease it significantly.

- Corn and beans are not greatly influenced in any detrimental way by the preceding crop.

- Liming and manuring ameliorate, but do not totally overcome, the negative effects of a preceding crop.

- Onions often are not helped when they follow a leguminous green manure.

- Carrots, beets, and cabbages are generally detrimental to subsequent crops.

These are merely patterns, not absolutes. Still, it is necessary to start somewhere, and these patterns have been discovered through research on the influence of preceding crops on subsequent crops and from my own and other farmers' experience. Since these patterns may be soil or climate specific, they are offered mainly to indicate the kinds of influences to which alert growers should attune their senses. Whether universal or applicable only to a specific farm, these bits of wisdom can be valuable to the farmer who learns to apply them.

One Percenters

Whereas the rotation guidelines presented earlier in this chapter qualify under the category of standard crop rotation "rules," the patterns above belong more in the category of "suggestions, hints, and refinements." The effect of any of them on improved yield, growth, and vigor may only be one percent, an amount that may not seem worth considering to some. What must be understood is that a biological system can be constantly adjusted by a lot of small improvements I call "one percenters." *The importance of these one percenters is that they are cumulative.* If the grower pays attention to enough of them the result will be substantial *overall* improvement. And best of all, these one percenters are free. They are no-cost gains that arise from careful intuitive management.

One percenters may not always provide measurable results, but they have a definite influence. I have learned to pay attention and try to make use of them. Sir George Stapleton, an English grassland specialist, referred to this approach as "competent ignorance." He was always aware of how much he did not know and how much science always misses, but he did not want that to limit his ability to act. I think that attitude is wise. Rather than not acting because we can't be certain, I suggest we try instead to apply what we hope we know. The grower should try to take as many intelligent actions as possible to incrementally improve his crops and then be attentive to what happens. Given our limited knowledge about all the interrelated causes and effects operating in the biological world, this seems to be the most productive attitude.

A Sample Rotation   Before deciding what crops the As, Bs, and Cs of those earlier illustrations stand for, we must first collect a good deal of information. Toward that end, let's set up a sample rotation for our 5-acre vegetable farm. The following things need to be considered.

Number of Sections   A crop rotation works best if the rotational sections are all the same size. That goal is not always easy on the large farm, where whole fields are involved, but it should be manageable with 5 acres of vegetables. For this discussion let us assume that we will be using 5 acres of land divided into 10 half-acre sections.

Number of Years   Just as two dozen crops don't necessarily mean a 24-year rotation, you should realize that 10 sections don't have to mean a 10-year rotation. Each section can be divided into 2, 3, or more separate and shorter rotational cropping plans. Possibly a legume-grass pasture could be included for a number of years in rotation. Each grower makes these decisions to suit his own situation. For now, let's say that the 10 sections will be managed as a 10-year rotation.

Number of Crops   In the example we are working with at the moment, all 24 major crops will be grown. To begin to get an idea of where to grow each crop in the rotational sequence, we need to divide up the crops, first by botanical classification.

Gramineae	*Cruciferae*	*Umbelliferae*
Corn	Rutabaga	Carrot
	Kale	Parsley
Amaryllidaceae	Broccoli	Celery
Onion	Cauliflower	Parsnip
	Cabbage	
Chenopodiaceae	Brussels sprouts	*Solanaceae*
Beet	Radish	Potato
Chard		Tomato
Spinach	*Leguminosae*	Pepper
	Pea	
Cucurbitaceae	Bean	*Compositae*
Squash, winter		Lettuce
Squash, summer		
Cucumber		

The reason for this division by vegetable families is the basis of one of the first principles of rotations—not growing the same crop or a related crop in successive years. Our list is a good start, but more information is needed. It might help to divide up the crops according to more general gardening categories:

Root Crops	*Vine Crops*	*Brassica Crops*
Beet	Squash	Broccoli
Carrot	Cucumber	Cauliflower
Onion		Cabbage
Parsnip	*Grain Crops*	Brussels sprouts
Potato	Corn	
Rutabaga		*Greens*
Radish	*Fruit Crops*	Lettuce
	Tomato	Spinach
Legumes	Pepper	Chard
Pea		Parsley
Bean		Celery
		Kale

Although this categorization mixes up the botanical divisions, it adds valuable new information. Since more than one crop will be growing in some sections, it helps to decide which crops have similar cultural requirements or which, such as greens, might need to be harvested together for a specific market.

Space for Each Crop The fact that 24 crops will be grown in a 10-section rotation indicates that some of the crops do not need as much growing area to meet market demand as others. And that leads to one of the most interesting of the rotation planning puzzles: how to meet the different needs of the market and still fit all of these disparate crops into a systematic crop rotation. The best place to begin is by deciding how much space or what percentage of the total cultivated area each crop needs in order to produce the right amount for market. We can determine those space requirements by creating 6 different categories, from the largest space needs to the smallest. From my experience, divisions for our 24 crops would look like this:

		More Space		*Less Space*	
6	5	4	3	2	1
Corn		Potato	Tomato	Lettuce	Onion
		Pea	Cauliflower	Pepper	Beet
		Winter squash	Broccoli	Carrot	Chard
				Summer squash	Parsley
				Bean	Celery
				Cabbage	Parsnip
				Spinach	Rutabaga
					Kale
					Radish
					Brussels
					Cucumber

Now the index cards come into play. Each card will represent a section of the rotation. Write each of the names of the left-hand crops (those requiring the most space) on a separate card (or 2 cards, in the case of larger crops like corn). Take a pair of scissors and cut up proportional sections of other cards to represent the smaller areas needed by the right-hand crops. More than one of the smaller-space crops will occupy the same rotational section. Next, tape a number of them together in the space of 1 card. Whenever possible, put crops that are in the same family or require similar cultivation conditions together. To begin with, the cards might look like this:

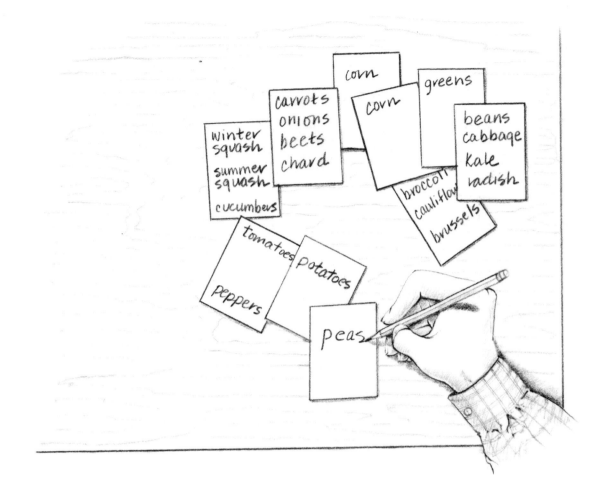

The Crop Rotation Game

At this stage, the arrangement and rearrangement of the cards is something like a board game. The rotation principles and patterns discussed earlier are the "rules." New rules are added as the grower becomes aware of them through experience, reading, and suggestions from other growers. The game begins by placing the cards on a flat surface and adjusting their positions to make up one rotational sequence or another. The aim is to determine if it is possible to grow all the crops desired on the land available and in the quantities necessary, while at the same time satisfying all the rules. The winner is the sequence that comes closest to the ideal pattern, one that optimizes as many of the beneficial aspects of a crop rotation that can be achieved with these specific crops.

So let's give it a try. The 2 corn crops should not be side by side. Put one in the middle of the rotation and one at the end, thus placing the corn crops as far from each other as they can be in a 10-year rotation. We know that potatoes yield best after corn, so put the potatoes in section 4. That naturally suggests a place for the tomatoes and peppers in order to create distance between them and the related potatoes.

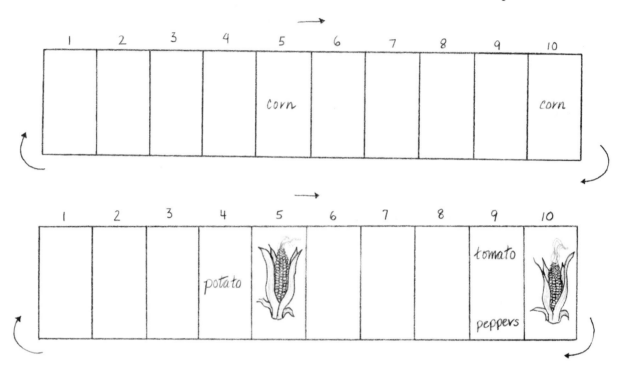

Since grain crops (corn) traditionally do well after legume crops (peas and beans), what if we precede the corn with the 2 legumes? Granted there are the cabbage family crops sharing the bean section, (and one of our patterns suggests that cabbages are negative preceding crops), but corn has been found to be the least affected by a preceding detrimental crop. Further, the corn field will likely be manured, helping to offset any negative effects.

Since beans are not affected too much by the preceding crop, let's put the often detrimental roots (carrots and beets) in front of them. Now a nuance can be considered. Onions have been shown to be a very beneficial crop before the cabbage family. We aren't growing enough onions to take advantage of that in whole sections, but they can still be effective depending upon where the crops are placed in a section. In this case we can grow the carrots and beets where they will be followed by the beans, and grow the onions, as much as possible, where they will be followed by the cabbage family. What the heck? They have to grow somewhere, so it might as well be where they have a chance of doing some good. And since those cabbage family crops are in the bean section, the other crucifers ought to be set apart from them. Section 7 would seem to be ideal.

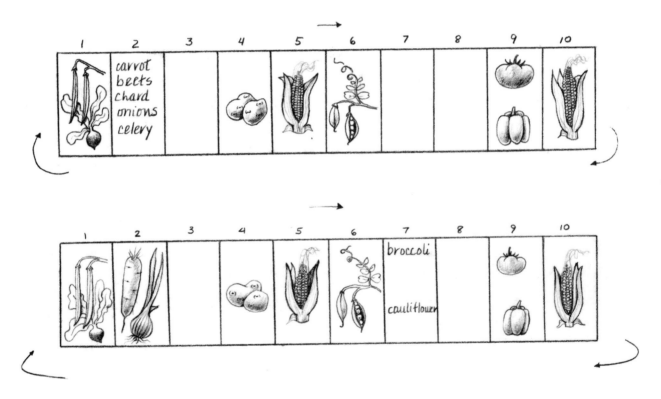

Now for the final 2 sections. Squash is a generally beneficial preceding crop, and it is well suited to growing with an undersown leguminous green manure (see Chapter 8). Since that green manure would be excellent before the broccoli-cauliflower section, let's put the squash card in section 8. By default, the greens go to section 3. Now let's see if this fits in with some of the rules we haven't considered yet. What about the crops that most benefit from manure or compost the same year it is applied? The ideal situation has those crops alternating with the others. Not bad. I would suggest that the manure for the corn in section 5 could be omitted since the pea crop will be finished early enough, even here in the cold part of New England, to allow a leguminous green manure to be seeded and get well established by the end of the growing season. When tilled under the next spring, the green manure should provide more than adequate nourishment for the corn crop to follow.

If manure and compost are in short supply, some selective decisions will have to be made. It would be nice to aim for a manure application at least 1 year in 3, but even that isn't vital. Instead, the grower has recourse to another management practice, the undersown green manures mentioned earlier. Those techniques will be discussed in the next chapter.

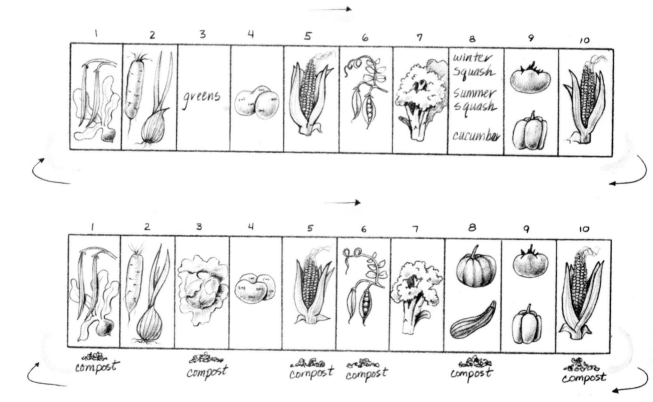

Multi-Year Crops There is no problem including in the rotation those crops that need to remain in the ground for more than 1 year. They are assigned as many sections as the number of years they are to grow. A 6-year rotation for 4 crops would look like this in year 1:

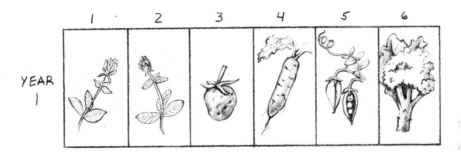

Let's say crop A is strawberries. In year 1, only section 3 would be planted to strawberries. The other sections could grow green manure or any other crop unrelated to B, C, or D. The strawberries in section 3 are now in their second year and cropping. Section 4 has just been planted to strawberries. Section 2 can be treated again as in year 1.

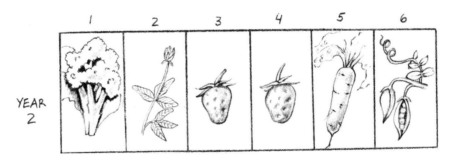

Now the rotation is off and running. The strawberries in section 3 will give a second crop this year before being turned under. The section-4 berries are in their first year of cropping, and the section-5 berries have just been planted.

The sequence continues in future years. If the "As" were a pasture or hay crop, the same system would prevail. One new section would be seeded each year and one old section would be tilled up and readied for the following crop.

Short Rotations

Not surprisingly, the actual result is often not as perfect as the ideal. When there is no way to run a longer rotation, you have to make the best of it. If a single crop dominates a large part of the production program, it may be necessary to repeat it every other year—or, as in the case of some greenhouse lettuce production, even twice a year. In these short-rotation situations, changes should be introduced at every opportunity. That even includes changing the variety of the crop. Any slight genetic difference should be exploited if it adds diversity to the cropping program. A succession crop sown after the main crop can help. A green manure can follow or be undersown (see Chapter 8). Mustard or rape, traditional cleansing crops for sick soil because they stimulate soil microorganisms, can be very effective as long as the dominant crop is not a fellow crucifer.

In other words, shoot for as great a variety of unrelated crops as possible in the span between related crops. Some growers advocate growing 2 consecutive crops (of, say, lettuce) followed by a longer break instead of alternating the crop with shorter breaks. I have not found that to be better, but I encourage a trial if the idea seems appealing. Other growers suggest that the more intensive the cropping, the more care must be taken to optimize all the growing conditions, especially by using extra soil-improving organic amendments like compost. I fully agree with that suggestion.

In some cases, no rotation at all is recommended. Many old-time growers insist that tomatoes do best if planted every year in the same spot. They even recommend fertilizing them with compost made from the decayed remains of their predecessors. I once grew tomatoes that way for 8 years in a greenhouse. In truth, they were excellent, and they got better every year. I do not grow field tomatoes that way now and cannot really defend my decision except to say that it is more convenient when they are part of the rotation. It could be that I am just uncomfortable about breaking the rules I have found to work so well with other crops. It could also be that I am unnecessarily limiting my options. I suggest that you try growing tomatoes (or any crop, for that matter) without rotation. Nothing is as stifling to success in agriculture as inflexible adherence to someone else's rules. With a little daring and imagination whole new vistas may open up. Remember, the aim of this farming system is independence, reliability, and sustainability. Any practices and attitudes that contribute to that goal should become part of the rule book.

A Tried-and-True Rotation

The 10-year rotation we just developed was meant as a teaching exercise. It may need refining for your operation. The 8-year rotation presented below is a good one to conclude with because it is one I have followed since 1982. It has been well tested. I have thought about modifying it countless times but never have. Its virtues always seem to outweigh its defects, although that isn't to say it can't be improved. I'm sure it can. But it has been a dependable producer and I offer it here as a tried-and-true example of a successful rotational sequence that incorporates many crop benefits.

The goal of this particular rotation is to grow 32 vegetable crops in adequate quantities to feed for a year the community of 60-some people who eat daily in the Mountain School dining hall. Since we have found that we can feed 40 people per acre, the rotation below represents 1½ acres of land. The salad crops not included here are grown in a separate small salad garden close to the kitchen.

Potatoes follow sweet corn in this rotation because research has shown corn to be one of the preceding crops that most benefit the yield of potatoes.

Sweet Corn follows the cabbage family because, in contrast to many other crops, corn shows no yield decline when following a crop of brassicas. Secondly, the cabbage family can be undersown to a leguminous green manure which, when turned under the following spring, provides the most ideal growing conditions for sweet corn.

The Cabbage Family follows peas because the pea crop is finished and the ground cleared by August 1, allowing a vigorous winter green manure crop to be established.

Peas follow tomatoes because they need an early seed bed, and tomatoes can be undersown to a non-winter-hardy green manure crop that provides soil protection over winter with no decomposition and regrowth problems in the spring.

Tomatoes follow beans in the rotation because this places them 4 years away from their close cousin, the potato.

Beans follow root crops because they are not known to be subject to the detrimental effect that certain root crops such as carrots and beets may exert in the following year.

Root Crops follow squash (and potatoes) because those two are both good "cleaning" crops (they can be kept weed-free relatively easily), thus there are fewer weeds to contend with in the root crops, which are among the most difficult to keep cleanly cultivated. Second, squash has been shown to be a beneficial preceding crop for roots.

Squash is grown after potatoes in order to have the two "cleaning" crops back to back prior to the root crops, thus reducing weed problems in the root crops.

Chapter ❧ 8 GREEN MANURES

NOT ALL CROPS ARE FOR SALE. GREEN MANURES are grown not for cash but to contribute to the care and feeding of the soil. A green-manure crop incorporated into the soil improves fertility, but the eventual benefits are far greater than that.

Low-Cost Returns Green-manure crops help protect against erosion, retain nutrients that might otherwise be leached from the soil, suppress the germination and growth of weeds, cycle nutrients from the lower to the upper layers of the soil, and — in the case of legumes — leave to the following crop a considerable quantity of nitrogen. Other contributions of a green manure are improved soil structure, additional organic matter, enhanced drought tolerance, and increased nutrient availability.

The value of green manures has been appreciated since the earliest days of agriculture. It should hardly be necessary to extol their virtues here, yet the situation is similar to that of crop rotation. The full potential of green-manure use is still under-appreciated and unexploited. The overall advantage of green manures is that they are a management benefit like crop rotation. These are farm-generated production aids that give an excellent return from management at little or no cost. Granted the seeds for a green-manure crop may have to be purchased, but their inclusion in the crop rotation yields benefits far exceeding their small cost. When green manures are included in the overall soil-management program, the combination of green manures and crop rotation can result in a truly unbeatable vegetable production system.

Growing green manures has traditionally been viewed as an either/or situation. You grew either a paying crop *or* a green manure. If the use of green manures means replacing a cash crop, then the lack of interest in them is understandable. There are other options. But first, let's review the general benefits of green manures.

Free Nitrogen

Leguminous green manures are a most economical and inexpensive source of nitrogen. The nitrogen is produced right where it is needed—in the soil. In fact, when leguminous green manures are used effectively and levels of organic matter are maintained, there rarely is a benefit from any additional application of nitrogen. The symbiotic process by which leguminous plants fix nitrogen from the air is dependent upon a number of factors for its success. The soil pH should ideally be between 6.5 to 6.8. The proper rhyzobium bacteria for the specific legume must be present. An innoculant should be applied if there is any doubt. Innoculants for specific legumes can be purchased from farm stores or seed catalogs along with seeds. A soil test for molybdenum (Mo) and cobalt (Co), both known to be important catalysts for symbiotic nitrogen fixation, is often a worthwhile investment.

Humus

Every little bit of organic matter added to the soil helps add to the all-important store of humus. Humus, the end product of organic-matter decay in the soil, is the key to soil structure, nutrient availability, moisture supply, and the biological vitality of the soil. Some forms of residues are more long lasting than others. Very young, sappy, green growth will stimulate a lot of activity in the soil but will not contribute much if anything in the way of lasting humus. Old, dry residues take longer for the soil processes to digest but are more valuable in building humus reserves. A 2- or 3-inch growth of recently sown oats or clover is an example of the former. Brown, frosted, and dried-out corn stalks would be at the other end of the scale. A lush green manure is probably better mowed and left to wilt for a day before being incorporated into the soil to help slow down what could be a too-rapid decomposition. The tough, mature crops will decompose faster if they are chopped or shredded before they are incorporated in the soil. Most of the green-manure crops that we will be concerned with fall somewhere between these extremes.

Stable Nutrients

Plant nutrients can be lost from unprotected soil. During fall, winter, and early spring, when commercial crops are not in the field, the growing green-manure crops will not only hold the soil against erosion, but their roots will capture and use available plant nutrients that might otherwise be leached away. Prevention of this waste is considered to be so important on most small European farms I visited that they think of the harvesting operation as having two inseparable parts: first the harvesting of the crop, and second the seeding of the land to a winter green manure. Seeding is done as soon as possible after harvesting.

In addition to the nitrogen nodules on the roots of legumes, green manures provide further contributions to the mineral nutrition of subsequent crops. The green-manure plants themselves, once decomposed by soil organisms, provide the most direct contribution. An indirect contribution results when the process of decomposition aids in making further nutrients available. Decaying organic matter can make available otherwise insoluble plant nutrients in the soil through the actions of decomposition products such as carbon dioxide and acetic, butyric, lactic, and other organic acids. Carbon dioxide is the end product of energy used by soil microorganisms. Increasing the carbon dioxide content of the soil air as a result of the decomposition of plant residues increases the carbonic acid activity, thus speeding up the process of bringing soil minerals into solution.

Soil microorganisms are also stimulated by the readily available carbon contained in the fresh plant material, and their activity results in speeding up the production of ammonium and nitrate. Even soils naturally high in organic matter, such as peats or mucks, are improved by the incorporation of a green-manure crop, which makes them more biologically active.

Biological Subsoilers The deep-rooting ability of many leguminous green-manure crops also makes them valuable as "biological subsoilers." Where soil compaction exists, deep-rooting green manures can bring a startling improvement in subsequent crops solely by penetrating and shattering the subsoil with their roots. This opens up the soil, permitting the crop roots to more easily reach lower soil levels, where they find greater supplies of water and nutrients. Studies have shown a considerable improvement in drought resistance and crop yields following lupins, sweet clover, alfalfa, and other tap-rooted green manures.

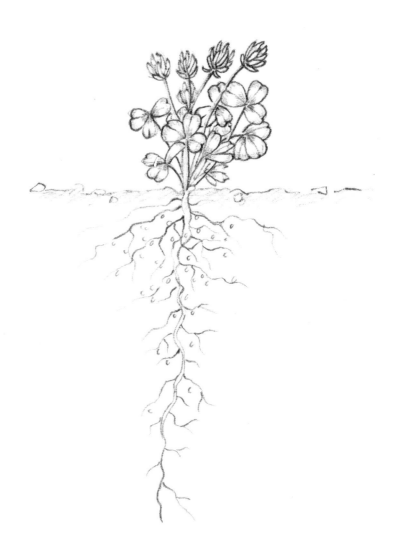

Over-Winter Green Manures

There are three ways in which green-manure crops can be managed: as over-winter crops, main crops, and undersown crops. Green manures can be sown for over-wintering after a market crop has been harvested. For example, in the crop rotation at the end of Chapter 7, a leguminous green manure could be sown after pea harvest and would occupy the ground until it was tilled in the following spring prior to planting cabbages. The other choice would be to plant a second market crop after the peas. In many cases that might be desirable, but the benefit from a wintered-over legume that provides ideal growing conditions for next year's crop is a strong incentive for growing it.

Main-Crop Green Manures

In this case the green manure occupies ground during the growing season in place of a market crop. If extra land is available, this is a highly recommended practice, and when the green-manure crop can be grazed by livestock, it serves a double purpose. If a grower prefers to put all the land into market crops, however, a choice must be made between losing the future benefits of the green-manure crop to the potential income from a market crop. Since this is a choice that usually goes against green manures, often at the expense of the soil, I recommend a third management option, one that allows the grower to have a leguminous green-manure crop and the cash, too: that option is known as undersowing.

Undersown Green Manures

Undersowing, also known as overseeding or companion seeding, is the practice of growing a green manure along with the market crop. When done correctly, undersowing provides the best of both worlds. It is established practice in small-grain growing. The clovers or other legumes are sown with or shortly after the wheat or oats, for example, and grow slowly in the understory until the grain crop is harvested. In vegetable growing this practice is not common, to the best of my knowledge, and only recently has begun to be seriously considered.

The advantage of undersowing is that the green-manure crop is already established at harvest time. In our northern New England climate, winter rye is the only green manure that can be seeded after fall harvest. A legume cannot be established that late in the season. Since in my experience legumes are the most beneficial green manures, I try to use them whenever possible. The only way I can do that without taking land out of cash-crop production is to undersow them.

Timing Crops and Green Manures   The practice of undersowing is something like planting desirable weeds between the crop rows. In a way that is very similar to the relationship between weed competition and crop growth, the effect of the undersown plant—the deliberate weed—upon the crop plant depends upon the age of the crop. Weeds can overwhelm young crops if they both start at the same time. Weed research has shown that crops will do fine if they have an adequate head start. If most crops are kept weed-free for the first 4 to 5 weeks after establishment, later competition from low-growing weeds will have little effect on them. If we interpret that correctly, then the best crops for undersowing would be low-growing, and the best sowing date for green manures would be 4 to 5 weeks after the establishment of the crop plants. My experience bears that out.

Where timing is important, there is a tendency to err on the safe side. Why not wait 6 weeks or more before undersowing the green manure just to be sure? The problem is that the balance is tipped too far in the other direction. Since the undersown "weed" is deliberate, I want to be sure it grows. If I wait too long before undersowing, the crop plants will be large enough to overwhelm the green manure. The trick is to undersow when the crop plants are well enough along not to be adversely affected by the undersowing, but not so well established as to hinder growth of the undersown green manure.

How does this timing work out in actual practice? Here in Vermont, where our springs are cool and crops such as corn, beans, squash, and late brassicas are not planted or set out until June 1, I find the 4th of July to be just about perfect, year in and year out, as the date for undersowing those crops. Obviously, later crops or succession crops will have their own dates. In all cases, the 4- to 5-week delay has proven to be a reliable yardstick.

Before Undersowing   Successful undersowing requires a clean, weed-free seed bed. Sowing the green manure is no different from sowing the crop: when seeds are planted into a weedy mess they become the seeds for failure. I have often thought that another side benefit of undersowing is that it motivates the grower to pay attention to clean cultivation right from the start simply because there is one more reason to do so. Like any problem "nipped in the bud," weeds are easiest to control early in the season. The clean seed bed prepared for undersowing is a by-product of early weed control. At least three cultivations should be made prior to undersowing, the last one just a day or two beforehand.

The goal of the grower is to provide every opportunity for the undersowing to get well established without weed competition. Unless the garden has a lot of weed pressure, the canopy of the undersowing will join with the crop canopy to keep later weeds from germinating. The few that do pop through should be pulled before they go to seed. Occasional forays down the rows will keep these competitors from becoming a problem.

Seeding the Undersown Crop I have seeded undersown crops both by broadcasting and drilling, and I emphatically recommend drilling. If the undersown crop is broadcast in the standing market crop, there is no way to cover all the seeds to ensure their establishment and germination. In a hot, dry spell the green manure can be a total failure. When I use a cultural practice I want to be able to depend on its performance. If the undersown crop is drilled between the crop rows with either a single- or multi-row drill, the seeds are planted at the proper depth, in contact with moist soil where they are much more certain to germinate.

The single-row drill is the same garden seeder I use for corn, carrots, and peas. It is equipped with an appropriate plate for whatever green-manure seed I am planting. The multi-row drill consists of 5 of these single-row seeders bolted together side by side with common axles and a common push bar. That gives the tool a total width of 20 inches, which fits nicely between the 30-inch row at which corn, beans, and brassicas are planted.

When using the multi-row model, all 5 hoppers can be filled with either the same seed or different seeds. Each hopper can be fitted with its own seed plate. Under some conditions, the grower might want to alternate rows of different legumes or legumes and grasses.

A Few Examples The garden is most easily visualized as a series of long strips 5 feet wide and 100 feet long. Forty-eight inches of that width is given over to the crops and 12 inches is used as an access path. For crops such as carrots, onions, and lettuce planted in 12-inch rows, there are 4 rows side by side with a 12-inch spacing.

The 1-row seeder can be used to drill 3 rows in the path. A single undersown row can be drilled between each crop row. In this case I usually sow dwarf white clover in the paths. White clover or biennial sweet clover can be used between rows of onions or carrots. The rows spaced at 18 inches are similarly undersown, with 3 rows in the path and 1 row between the crops.

For the 30-inch spacing at which corn, beans, brassicas, and so on are planted, the 5-row drill is used. One pass is made down the center between each crop row. Depending on the crop, dwarf white clover, sweet clover, red clover, hairy vetch, and soybeans have all worked well between these crops.

In the crops spaced at 60 inches (tomatoes and melons, for example) two passes are made with the 5-row drill. Dwarf white, red, and sweet clover are all good choices here.

At the widest spacing, 120 inches for pumpkins and winter squash, everything except a strip about 2 feet wide on either side of the row is drilled (four passes with the 5-row drill). My favorite undersown crop for squash and pumpkins is biennial sweet clover.

Thinking It Through

Sowing dates and equipment for undersown green manures should be as well thought out as those for the cash crops. Sowing dates should be marked on the calendar. The seeds should be ordered ahead. The equipment should be quick, in good working order, and simple to use.

At the end of this chapter is an illustrated flow chart that shows what my crop rotation and undersown green manure recommendations look like when they are combined. Obviously, green manures are most effective when they are considered as an important component part of the crop-rotation planning.

There is another parallel between green manures and crop rotation that should be noted. Variety in green manures is as important as variety in the market crops. Because green-manure plants also have different faults and virtues that affect the soil and following crops in different ways, green manures should be "rotated" to include as many different varieties as possible.

In studying the green-manure chart, you will note that 6 of the 8 rotational plots are undersown, a seventh is sown to legumes after early harvest, and only 1 — potatoes — is seeded to rye after fall harvest. The ground is never bare. The soil is always growing either a market crop or next year's fertility. For much of the summer it is growing both!

Which Green Manures?

My choices of green-manure crops for different uses are:

- With tall crops—sweet clover, vetch, red clover, or alsike clover

- For sod-like cover—dwarf white clover

- For resistance to foot traffic in picking—dwarf white clover or vetch

- Before potatoes—soybeans or sweet clover

- Under corn—soybeans, sweet clover, or red clover

- Between rows of root crops—sweet clover or dwarf white clover

- Soil protection that will winterkill—spring oats or spring barley

- For the latest fall planting—rye or winter wheat

In the milder European climate, mixtures of green-manure seeds are sown after harvest to provide late fall grazing. In parts of Germany these mixes of species for a green manure are known as *Landesberger Gemenge*. A Landesberger mix commonly consists of 2 legumes, a grass, and a cabbage family crop. When a field of Landesberger is ready for fall grazing it looks like a tossed salad for livestock.

Sample mixtures might include:

- Oats, red clover, field peas, and mustard

- Wheat, white clover, purple vetch, and rape

- Rye, ladino clover, winter vetch, and oil radish

In order to become well established they should be sown at least 6 weeks before the first fall frost.

Green-Manure Review

Green-manure varieties and combinations are endless and are not limited to the ones listed here. The varieties mentioned here worked for me as I developed the biological production technologies for my particular soil and climate. Instead of talking about specifics that are so often regional, I want to emphasize principles that are more nearly universal—not only because different parts of the country require different green manures but because there are no hard-and-fast rules. Although it is possible to present the broad outline of a biological system inside a book, the fine-tuning that goes on within that outline is the province of the grower. The best innovations and improvements usually come from the grower and not from any chart or list, no matter how complete it supposedly is. Whatever an expert does or does not say should not limit your options. The more active a grower becomes in taking charge of perfecting the system proposed here, the more independent, reliable, and sustainable his own system will become.

Below is a list of considerations when choosing green-manure crops:

- Time of seeding—Early, late, intercrop, undersown, over-winter, year-round?

- Establishment—The ideal crop is easy to establish and grows rapidly.

- Time of incorporation into the soil—How mature is the green manure? What is the following crop, seed, or transplant? Legumes turned under in fall lose 70 percent of added nitrogen but only 38 percent when turned under in spring. With a winter-killed green manure it may be possible to transplant the spring crop directly without incorporating the green-manure residues into the soil.

- Rotational fit—The green manure should not share diseases with the crop plants.

- Feed value—When a green manure serves as animal feed, manure is deposited on the soil, and fertility is enhanced even more.

- Soil microorganisms—Rape, for example, stimulates the biological activity of the soil. Soybeans improve scab control in potatoes.

- Beneficial insects—Some green manures can serve as nurse crops for useful insects. This is an emerging field of knowledge with much to be learned!

- Cost—Is the seed expensive? Can it be easily produced on the farm? Will the crop yield both seed *and* feed? Will a less costly seed be as effective if it is managed properly?

Undersowing Legumes

Considerations when choosing an undersown legume:

- Shade tolerance

- Ability to grow with the crop

- Effects, including competition, on this year's crop

- Beneficial effects on next year's crop

- Erosion control

- Winter hardiness (In some situations a crop that winter-kills is preferred to avoid having a vigorous residue in the way of an early spring sowing)

- Weed control (Rapid growth and broad leaves are a plus)

Green Manures in Rotation

Undersown green manures can be used extensively within the 8-year crop rotation shown at the end of the previous chapter. The following sequence has worked out very well in practice. The two-page illustrated flow chart shows how all the pieces can fit together.

Potatoes cannot be undersown easily if the cultivation method used is hilling. I have grown potatoes without hilling by planting at a depth of 6 inches and filling the furrow partly at first, then completely after the potatoes emerge. Vetch can then be planted as an undersown legume. If the green manure is to be established following the potato harvest, winter rye is probably the best choice as a green manure.

Sweet Corn is undersown to soybeans because research shows a soybean crop almost totally inhibits potato-scab organisms in the soil. The soybeans also grow well in the understory of the corn and provide excellent weed suppression.

The Cabbage Family is undersown to sweet clover, which is one of the best leguminous green manures to turn under for next year's corn crop. It grows well under the cabbage family because it is a tap-rooted crop that does not seem to interfere with the more shallowly rooted brassicas.

Peas are not undersown but are followed by a mix of clovers as soon as the peas can be cleared. This combination of legumes grows until it is turned under the following May, by which time enough nitrogen has been fixed to ensure a splendid crop of brassicas.

Tomatoes are undersown to oats or some other non-winter-hardy grass crop. Certain grasses have been found to be excellent preceding crops for legumes such as peas, since they produce an allopathic effect that suppresses grasses and other weeds, but not legumes. It is important to choose a non-winter-hardy cultivar so there will not be a mass of fresh green growth in the spring to impede early soil preparation and planting of the pea crop.

Beans are undersown to winter vetch. It is a dependable preceding green-manure crop for tomatoes.

Root Crops are undersown to dwarf white clover (both in the paths and between the rows) because it will grow in the crop understory and because it provides good erosion protection for the soil over winter.

Squash is undersown to sweet clover in the empty strips between the squash rows. Beets, carrots, and other root crops grow very well following sweet clover. The onion crop, on the other hand, has always grown best with no preceding green manure, so the onions are planted in the strips that were occupied by the squash plants themselves.

Following: Crop rotation and green manure flow chart

PLOT	Jan	Feb	Mar	Apr	May	Jun	Jul	Aug	Sep	Oct	Nov	Dec	Jan	Feb	Mar	Apr

YEAR 1 · YEAR 2

Plot 1: beans / white clover — vetch — vetch

Plot 2: roots / sweet clover — white clover

Plot 3: squash / rye — sweet clover

Plot 4: potatoes / soy beans — rye

Plot 5: corn / white clover — soy beans

Plot 6: cabbage family / vetch — white clover

Plot 7: peas / Oat stubble — vetch

Plot 8: tomatoes / vetch — oats

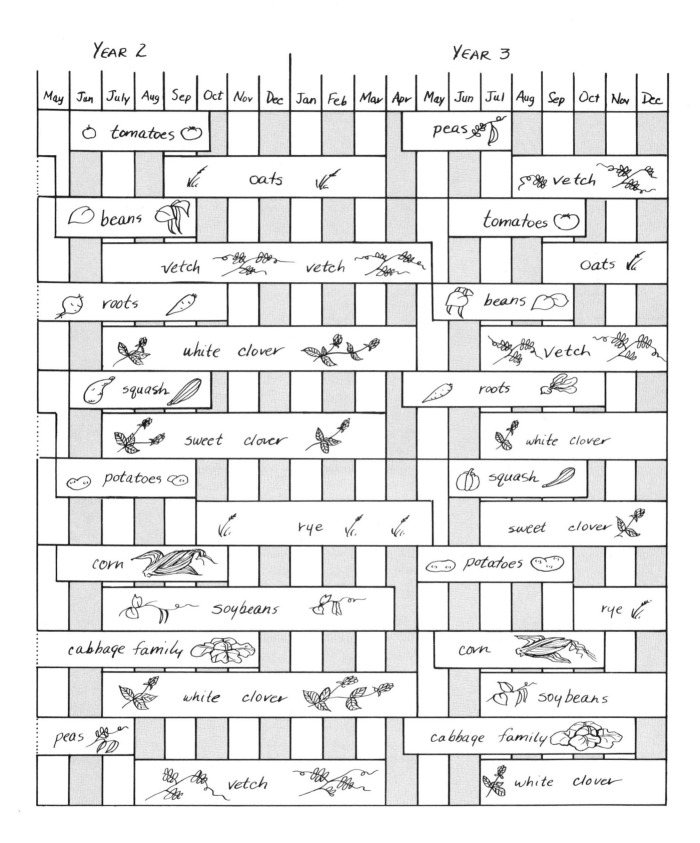

Chapter 9 TILLAGE

TILLAGE IS THE GENERAL TERM FOR SOIL PREPA-
ration in agriculture. It includes working the soil; incorporating lime, fertilizers, and manures; turning under green
manures and crop residues; and any other mechanical processes involved in preparing the land for raising crops. The
traditional implements are the plow, the disc, the harrow,
and occasionally the subsoiler. Plowing with a moldboard
plow is the method popularly associated with farming. In the
process of plowing, the soil layers are turned over, either
wholly or partially, depending on the adjustment of the
plow. Since this operation alone does not produce a suitable
planting surface or sufficient mixing action to fully incorporate fertilizers or organic materials, supplementary operations are necessary.

In order to come closer to the ideal of tillage, plowing is
commonly followed by discing and harrowing. The ideal is
to loosen the soil; incorporate air, organic matter, and fertilizers; and remove weeds in order to prepare a clean seedbed.
As a result of tilling, the air, moisture, temperature, chemical,
and biological levels of the soil are modified. The intent is to
optimize their effects on the growth and development of the
crops.

Tillage operations are divided into those that work the soil
deeply and those that work it shallowly. Deep tillage can go
down as much as 2 feet. Shallow tillage disturbs no more
than the top 6 inches of the soil, and preferably only the top 3
to 4 inches.

Deep Tillage   More and more scientific studies are pointing to sub-surface soil compaction from plow pans and wheel traffic as a serious problem in crop production. The subsoiler is the original tool for deep-soil tillage, which ideally loosens the lower soil layers and breaks up hard pans and compaction layers without inverting the soil or mixing the subsoil with the topsoil. In addition, deep tillage can aerate the soil to a considerable depth, improving drainage and increasing rooting depth and the amount of soil nutrients for the roots, and initiating a process of topsoil deepening, which greatly increases the fertility of the soil.

The Chisel Plow   For our purposes the chisel plow is more effective than the subsoiler. The chisel plow dates from the 1930s, when it was conceived as a soil-conserving alternative to the moldboard plow. The chisel plow consists of a strong metal frame bearing a series of curved, soil-penetrating shanks (chisels) about 2 inches wide and 24 inches long that can be fitted with different tips. When pulled through the ground, the chisels penetrate to depths of up to 16 inches, but they do not turn over the layers like a moldboard plow. Rather, they simply lift and loosen the soil and break up hardpan and compacted soil.

This is not a small-scale implement. Using it once a year for deep tillage involves renting a tractor or hiring an operator. The latter is the simplest and most economical way to go if you live in an area where the services and equipment are available. If not, the solution might be for a group of growers to collectively purchase a small chisel plow and hire a tractor to pull it. If rocky land is involved, the tractor should have a front loader to help in collecting and removing rocks.

Many growers believe a chisel plow is suitable only for rock-free soil. In my experience that is not the case. I have used a chisel plow on both stone-free land in Texas and fairly rocky land in Massachusetts and Vermont. It performed well in both cases. In fact as a tool for preparing New England soil for vegetable growing it is invaluable. The chisel plow finds rocks and brings them to the surface. You can then remove them by rolling them into the tractor bucket on the next pass.

There is no need to despair if you find it isn't possible to get a chisel plow. There are other options. The hand tool suggested below and certain biological techniques will also do the job. The more attention you pay to improving pH, drainage, and organic matter while minimizing compaction, the less you'll need mechanical deep tillage. I do, however, recommend the chisel plow as an extremely valuable tool in the *initial years of creating a fertile soil* for vegetable growing.

After the first years, though, you should be able to gain the same tillage effect with the roots of green manures. Deep-rooting green manure crops (alfalfa, sweet clover, lupines, soybeans, and red clover) are very effective at improving conditions in the subsoil. The deep rooting not only improves the soil physically by loosening it but also increases its fertility by bringing up more nutrients from the lower strata. The root channels remain long after the green manure has decomposed. They measurably help improve the soil's porosity and water-holding properties as well as prevent future pan formation.

The Broadfork

This two-handled deep tillage tool is known by different names, but broadfork comes as close to describing it as any other. Like most agricultural tools its genesis surely dates far

back in agricultural history. It consists of a 2-foot-wide spading fork with a 5-foot-long handle at either side of the fork. The teeth on the fork are spaced 4 inches apart and are about 12 inches long.

I first encountered the tool in the 1960s as the "Grelinette," after a farmer from France named Grelin. During the 1970s copies of the Grelinette began to appear in altered designs. As is often the case when a farmer builds a tool that is then redesigned by an engineer, Grelin's original design is superior to the copies. Certain nuances of Gerlin's design are

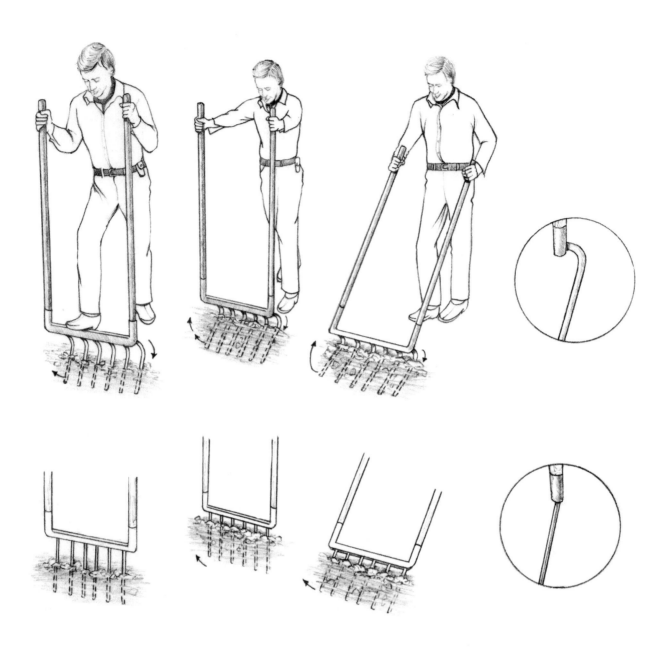

missed because they are appreciated only through constant use and are not apparent on the drawing board. The copies, which were often fabricated entirely of metal to make them stronger, have a number of flaws.

First, the all-metal construction makes the tool too heavy. Granted that one can occasionally break a wooden handle, I much prefer working with a pleasant tool and being inconvenienced occasionally by a broken handle than working with a cumbersome tool all the time. A second mistake in the copies is the use of straight tines attached to the bottom of the cross bar. In the original Grelinette the tines are designed with a parabolic shape and curve down from an attachment point at the back of the cross bar. This difference is the key. The parabolic curve of Grelin's original design works with an easy rolling motion. As the handles are pulled the tines curve under and lift the soil easily. With straight tines, a prying rather than rolling motion is used and you must muscle the soil upwards with brute strength.

Using the Broadfork   The broadfork is held with the handles tilted slightly forward of vertical. It is pressed into the soil as far as possible by stepping on the cross bar, then the two handles are pulled back toward the operator in an easy rocking motion. The broadfork is then lifted from the loosened soil, the operator steps backwards 6 inches, and the maneuver is repeated. The tool is comfortable to use and makes the work pleasant.

How large an area can be managed with a broadfork? It is certainly scaled for use in commercial greenhouse vegetable production. I have used it outdoors on areas up to one acre without feeling too much strain. The work can also be divided into sections and done only as needed prior to planting different crops. Anyway, there is no need to do every square foot. Just going down the row for widely spaced crops such as winter squash is sufficient. If the broadfork is used selectively during the planting season, even a two-acre garden is not unreasonably large for this tool. Some crops respond more than others. Sweet corn, root vegetables, and crops with extensive root systems such as tomatoes are greatly benefited by deep tilling.

The broadfork should be used prior to surface tillage, and preferably during the previous fall for sections of the rotation where the earliest crops will be planted. As with any tool it should be used with the eyes open: if there appears to be no difference in crop response, or a difference is apparent only on certain crops, then adjust when, how much, or how often you use the broadfork.

Advantages of Deep Tillage

- Breaks up soil compaction.
- Provides soil aeration.
- Aids the soil structure.
- Improves drainage.

- Extends crop-rooting depth.

- Deepens the range of soil nutrients available to plant roots.

- Helps deepen the topsoil, which greatly increases soil fertility.

Disadvantages of Deep Tillage

- Custom operators with chisel plow equipment may be hard to locate.

- A group of local growers may not exist to purchase a chisel plow collectively.

- In some soils the broadfork may be impractical on far less than two acres.

Solutions

- The rotary tiller can be used as deeply as possible as long as not too much subsoil is brought to the surface.

- When deep rotary tilling, you must be sure to mix extra organic matter with the soil to encourage an improved soil structure.

- Establishing the ideal biological soil conditions that favor bacteria and earthworms will improve soil structure and depth over time. Important practices include crop rotations, green manures, addition of organic matter, pH between 6 and 7, and adequate mineral nutrients.

Shallow Tillage

Shallow tillage is the preparation of the top few inches of soil. I recommend the rotary tiller for shallow tillage. It has many advantages over the traditional plow, disc, and harrow. First, it does the work of all three conventional implements in one operation. Second, it does the work at a speed that makes it considerably more efficient overall. And third, it does the job better.

The Rotary Tiller   In rotary tillage the soil is prepared by means of specially shaped soil-working blades (tines) which are rotated by a powered axle. A rotary tiller mixes and incorporates fertilizers, plant residues, and organic amendments (manures and composts) uniformly throughout the tillage depth and leaves them in contact with the greatest number of soil particles. This thorough mixing distributes organic materials and assures the availability of minimally processed fertilizers.

The low-solubility mineral fertilizers I recommend in this book work best when they are mixed well throughout the soil rather than banded or layered. They then have the greatest contact with the soil acids and microbiological processes that make the soil nutrients available for use by plants.

The rotary tiller most easily incorporates manures, composts, and other soil amendments when they are spread on the surface of the soil before tilling. The relative density between the soil and the amendments affects how thoroughly the mixing can be accomplished. Mineral fertilizers, which tend to have the same density as soil particles, can be mixed in most uniformly. When organic materials are mixed in, the lighter stuff tends to remain higher in the soil profile while the heavier material goes in more deeply. The ability of the rotary tiller to mix both organic and mineral amendments uniformly throughout the soil profile is an important feature of this tool. It increases the fertility and biological activity of the soil that is so necessary to the establishment of a viable biological system.

There is evidence that the rotary tiller—or, for that matter, any soil-tillage equipment—can be detrimental if it is overused. The effect of rotary tilling on the soil is like using a bellows on a fire: it speeds up the combustion process. Extra aeration of the soil hastens the decomposition of organic matter, which can be good or bad depending on when it is done.

Spring tilling can have a beneficial effect. Early in the season the soil is cool and may well profit from tilling to help warm it up and dry it out. Later in the season, most of the soil will be undersown to green manures. When there is an early green manure, or when there are residues of a preceding crop to till under before a late crop, the extra air and thorough mixing will help decompose the residues faster and make the soil ready for planting of the following crop sooner.

The Walking Tractor

A walking tractor is a two-wheeled power source. The rotary tiller in this system is powered by a 12- to 14-horsepower walking tractor. The tiller width should be 26 inches. This equipment will give you enough power to do an excellent tilling job under almost all conditions. The walking tractor also has the flexibility to be equipped with a wide range of other implements such as seeders, rollers, mowers, hillers, pumps, and harvesters if the farm operation requires them. All are available from the walking tractor manufacturer, but very often a grower can adapt the necessary implements from other sources. A walking tractor is my choice for the power unit in this small-scale operation for a few reasons. It is much less expensive than a four-wheel tractor. It is smaller and easier to work with when modifications or repairs are needed. It is much easier to learn to operate. The walking tractor has long been the small farmer's best power source.

Of course life might seem easier sitting on top of a powerful four-wheel tractor equipped with a large rotary tiller. But the economics would not be the same. A well-built 12- to 14-horsepower walking tractor with a 26- to 32-inch-wide tiller can be purchased new for a price that would purchase little more than the tiller for a large tractor. This same walking tractor/tiller also serves as the cultivator for more than half of the cropland in this system.

Obviously, if the farm already owns a four-wheel tractor and tiller, then by all means use it. The walking tractor/tiller is not *better* than a riding tractor, but it is perfectly adequate for the tasks you'll need it for. It is also affordable, nicely scaled, and less expensive to maintain.

Advantages of a Walking-Tractor/Tiller

Economics   The initial cost is much less, as are the operating costs.

Performance   Top-of-the-line models till as well as or better than many tractor-mounted tillers (except in old sod). These machines get the job done.

Flexibility   It is basically a power source on wheels and it adapts to many needs. It does the wide-row cultivation and pulls the hiller between potato rows. Implements such as a water pump or a rotary mower can be run off the same unit.

Simplicity   It is much easier to operate than a tractor, which means inexperienced helpers can quickly learn to use it, too.

Maintenance   It is far less overwhelming and complicated than a tractor when repairs are needed. With its approachable scale, you will soon feel confident about making home repairs.

Lighter   It creates no soil compaction and leaves no deep wheel ruts.

Smaller   It is far more maneuverable and less head land is required to turn it at the ends of the rows.

Tillage: The Future

Now that I've presented my best options for deep and shallow tillage, what about the possibility of reducing tillage, or eliminating it altogether? I think the idea is worth serious consideration. For one thing, any change that cuts a grower's expenses in soil preparation is worth trying. I have used a non-tillage (or, more accurately, a *surface cultivation*) system for the past three years in my greenhouses and I believe it produces superior results. Instead of digging, tilling, or using other conventional soil preparation methods, we shallowly hoe the greenhouse soil clear of weeds and crop residues and add a new layer of compost to the surface prior to planting the next crop. The encouraging result is that after three years the soil structure is better than I have ever seen it.

Could this idea work in the field on the scale of a commercial market garden? Could it work where, as in this system, extensive use is being made of green manures? The answers to those questions are still a few years down the road, but I am presently experimenting with field-scale surface cultivation in a green manure system, and I am confident that the concept is workable. Whether the answer lies in using specially designed cultivators to clean the surface or in growing winter-killed green manures that are easily brushed aside in the spring, or some of both, is yet to be seen. Despite my success over the years in creating fertile soils with the mechanical tillage systems described in this chapter, the direction in which I am now moving is toward minimizing mechanical solutions in favor of biological solutions that mimic the healthy natural structure of undisturbed soil.

Chapter 10 SOIL FERTILITY

The main problem of permanent fertility is simple. It consists, in a word, in making sure that every essential element of plant food is continuously provided to meet the needs of maximum crops; and of course any elements which are not so provided by nature must be provided by man.

—CYRIL HOPKINS

I LEARNED MY FIRST IMPORTANT LESSON IN SOIL fertility from the United States Department of Agriculture, albeit by default on their part. It happened in 1966 when I began growing vegetables on rented land in New Hampshire. Since I had limited farming experience at that time, I eagerly read everything I could find on the subject. The USDA, in an article about fertilizer nutrients in agricultural production, stated unequivocally that nitrogen was nitrogen and phosphorus was phosphorus. They said that it did not make any difference to the plant where the nutrient came from. Nitrogen from manure and nitrogen from a bag of store-bought fertilizer were the same. To me, that was welcome news indeed.

I was not aware at the time that the reason for these pronouncements was to discredit the organic farmers who claimed that manure or compost produced superior plants. In my naiveté, what I saw was a chance to save some money. I would not have to buy fertilizers! Just down the road was a horse farm with huge piles of rotted manure that the farmer was *giving* away, even delivering free to anyone who wanted it. Chicken manure, which the article said was high in phosphorus, was available from another neighbor. I figured that if the USDA experts said there was no difference between the elements in manure and those in store-bought fertilizer, that was good enough for me. I went with the manure and started a couple of acres of vegetables with what I assumed was the assurance of the USDA that everything would work out just fine.

And work out fine it did. During the three years I farmed that place, I had the best vegetables anywhere around. Not only that, but they got better every year. In fact, the old timers were coming and asking the new kid how he did it rather than the other way around. Obviously, soil fertility was a function of a number of factors, and they did not have to be chemically processed or cost a lot of money to work.

When I did need to purchase nutrients, I continued to take the USDA at their word that elements were elements. I purchased unprocessed minerals such as rock phosphate. In the long run they were less expensive. Because since they weren't water soluble and subject to leaching, enough could be applied at one time to last a number of years. The lesson: food for plants does not need to be prearranged in a factory. Nutrient availability is a result of biological and chemical soil processes that are stimulated by agricultural practices I learned to use and trust—crop rotations, green manures, and animal manures. This biological system comes full circle. Each practice aids another, and the result is synergistic.

Building the Soil

To build a fertile soil, 5 amendments should be supplied as raw materials.

Organic Matter   Compost or manure applied at the rate of 20 tons per acre every other year.

Rock Phosphate   A finely ground, natural rock powder applied every 4 years (quadrennially). There are 2 forms—hard rock phosphate containing 33 percent P_2O_5 and colloidal

phosphate containing 22 percent P_2O_5. I prefer the colloidal, but other growers will make an equal case for the hard rock.

Greensand Marl An ancient sea bed deposit containing some potassium, but principally included as a broad-spectrum source of micronutrients. Applied quadrennially.

Limestone Rock A ground rock containing calcium and magnesium used to raise the soil pH. Sufficient lime should be applied to keep the pH within the range of 6.2 to 6.8.

Specific Micronutrients Elements such as Zn, Cu, Co, Bo, Mo are needed in very small quantities but are absolutely essential for a fertile soil. They will usually be adequately supplied if the grower has paid attention to pH and organic matter. The need for supplemental application of micronutrients is best gauged by careful soil tests and grower observation. In many cases boron is the one most likely to need amending. Obviously, if a soil test indicates that one or the other of these is already well supplied, that supplement will not be needed.

Two Ways To Fertilize

Although this is a chapter on soil fertility, I am first going to discuss philosophy. That may be unconventional, but it is crucial to an understanding of the supplements recommended above. There are two basic philosophical approaches to fertilization.

Feed the Plant Directly This involves using soluble fertilizers so the nutrients are "predigested" for plant use without the need for the natural soil processes.

Feed the Soil and Let Soil Processes Provide for the Plant This involves creating and maintaining the optimal conditions of a fertile soil under which a healthy soil-plant economy can exist.

In the former case, the farmer provides plant food in a "predigested" form because the soil processes are considered inadequate. A symptom—poor plant growth—is treated by using a temporary solution—soluble plant food. In the latter case the farmer makes sure that the soil processes have the raw materials needed not only to be adequate, but exceptional. The cause of poor plant growth—lack of sufficient plant food in the soil—is corrected by providing the soil with the raw materials needed to produce that plant food.

Natural Processes

Although we are dealing with agricultural techniques, we can't ignore the patterns of thinking that lead toward choosing one agricultural technology over another. These thought patterns stem from different points of view about the "natural system" that governs plant growth. Some questions:

- Are natural processes so inefficient that we can do better by taking over their roles, even though the energy cost of such a choice is high? Or can natural processes provide all that we need if we work to enhance them?

- Is it wise to rely on a crop production system that is totally dependent on purchased materials involving great cost, supply networks, and safety considerations over which the farmer has no control? Or is it preferable to create a farm-generated system that relies on minimal quantities of off-farm products and maximum enhancement of the soil's inherent fertility?

- Is it acceptable to add only enough nutrients to "get a crop"? Or is it more worthwhile to try and provide all the known and unknown nutrients and growing conditions to allow the plants to grow at their optimum?

I have encountered many responses to these questions. There are always some growers who say, "Natural processes and growing optimum be damned. I just want to grow the crop with the least possible effort and deal with any problems later." Unfortunately, later problems, when they occur, are not limited to low yields, but involve insects, diseases, and poor crop quality. Other "purchased products" (pesticides, fungicides) are then used to deal with the new problems. Since agricultural systems are interconnected, one action leads to another and one problem begets a subsequent problem.

My own position on these issues is that I simply do not know enough to tamper with the natural system, and I have no desire to do so. I am an admirer of the intricate cyclical systems of the natural world, and I prefer to study them in order to make *less* work for myself, not more. Even if I thought I knew everything, I would rather let it be done for me by the real experts. The real experts in this case are all the processes that take place in a fertile soil—the interrelated activities of bacteria, fungi, dilute soil acids, chemical reactions, rhizosphere effects, and countless others we are unaware of.

My attitude toward the natural world is one of respect for a marvelously efficient system. If I attempt to feed the plant directly, I am in effect deciding that I can do a better job. On an infertile soil, where the system is working poorly, maybe I can. But on a fertile soil the system can do a better job on its own. Therefore, my responsibility as a farmer is to add to the system the ingredients necessary to support a fertile soil. Those basic raw materials are organic matter and minerals in the form of powdered rock.

The annual purchase of soluble fertilizers locks the farmer into someone else's system. Remember that I am interested in independence, reliability, and sustainability. Soluble fertilizers are like the ideal industrial product which, as defined by a cynical old economist, is one that "costs a dime, sells for a dollar, wears out quickly, and leaves a habit behind." So don't buy finished products. Buy the few raw materials that cannot be farm produced, and let the soil processes finish the job. Not only does that policy make good sense agronomically, it is also the most successful, most practical, and most economical approach.

How It All Works

Let's say we start with an infertile soil. If we take the off-farm approach and add soluble fertilizers, a good crop can usually be grown. The soil serves merely as an anchor for plant roots and the majority of the food for plant growth is provided by the fertilizer. The soil remains infertile, however, and the fertilizer application will have to be repeated for every crop. The situation is similar to helping a student by providing the answers to the test. The result may be a good grade, but the help will have to be given every time.

If, on the other hand, the second approach is chosen, we try to create a fertile soil by adding those ingredients that distinguish a fertile from an infertile soil. The fertile soil will then do what fertile soils do—grow exceptional crops. To continue our student-teacher metaphor, this second process is like providing the student with the raw materials of knowledge (good books and study habits) so the student can develop the ability to excel on exams without help. I think most readers will agree that this second approach is the preferable choice in education. It is also the best choice for plant nutrition.

Feeding the Soil

The things that turn an infertile soil into a fertile soil are minerals and organic matter. If these are provided the soil can excel on its own merits. Instead of a temporary crutch that must be provided time after time, a process is established that becomes self-sustaining. A fertile soil, like an educated mind, is a cumulative process, and with care it is capable of continuous improvement.

There are two sources of nutrients for the soil: the remains of previously living organisms that make up the organic matter, or humus, and the finely ground rock particles that constitute the mineral portion of the soil. Plant nutrients from both sources are made available through the actions of the biology and chemistry of the soil.

Organic Matter

For best quality and best growth, vegetables require the richest soils of all farm crops. And that richness has to be real. Not stimulants, but what British farmers so aptly call "a soil in good heart." Organic matter is the key to "heart" in a soil. The best book I ever read on farming was not technically about farming. Selman Waksman's classic text, *Soil Microbiology*, dealt with the life in the soil. That book influenced my approach to soil fertility more than any other source. Waksman wrote from the point of view of one who had studied all the different life processes in the soil and how they affect nutrient availability and plant growth. His information opened my eyes to the marvelous world of living organisms under our feet and to the importance of *organic matter* for the well-being of that world. The quantity and quality of organic matter is the foundation for the microbiological life in the soil. This microbiological life grows and decays, solubilizes minerals, and liberates carbon dioxide as part of its life processes.

Organic matter also opens up heavy soils to make them more easily workable and binds a sandy soil so that it holds water better. In short, the organic matter portion of the soil is more than simply a source of plant food and physical stability. It is also the power supply, so to speak. Organic matter is the engine that drives all the biological (and some of the chemical) processes in the soil.

Although raw organic materials such as crop residues can be added directly to and can be digested by the soil, it is often better to compost them in a heap. Sheet composting in the soil involves biological processes that preclude crop growth for a period averaging two to four weeks or more, depending on how resistant to decay the material is. In an intensive vegetable growing system that "soil time" would be better spent growing the next crop. For example, where early peas are to be followed by a succession planting, I will remove the pea vines to a compost heap rather than turn them under. The next crop can then be planted or transplanted immediately.

I have the highest regard for composted organic matter as a long-term soil builder. The crumbly, dark, sweet-smelling product from a heap of assorted plant residues mixed with straw is the finest compost of all. Well-made compost has been shown to have plant-growing benefits far in excess of its simple "nutrient analysis" and to be an active factor in suppressing plant diseases and increasing plant resistance to pests.

Animal manure is also one of the staples for soil improvement in vegetable growing. Manure can either be produced on the farm or purchased in truckloads from neighboring farms or stables. It may be given away or sold. Either way, you will usually pay for the trucking. Large quantities of manure should be formed into windrows for composting. These windrows are 6 to 8 feet wide, 4 feet high, and can be any length. The top should be flat or slightly sloped. A shady spot is best to avoid the drying effect of the sun. For best composting, the manure must be moist but not wet. A hose sprinkler can be laid across the top to add moisture in dry weather.

It has long been assumed that organic agriculture and use of manure as fertilizer were synonymous. That is not the case. It is organic matter (and not necessarily manure) that is so vital for soil improvement. Once it has decomposed in the soil or the compost heap, almost any addition of organic matter can be as effective as any other. That includes autumn leaves, straw, plant wastes, spoiled hay, or other locally available materials. Further, the green manures and cover-crop rotations discussed earlier are equally viable methods for adding organic matter to the soil in lieu of using off-farm supplies. Composted manure is a wonderful soil improver. By all means use it. But if manure is not available, you can plan your soil-improvement practices around many other sources of organic matter.

Minerals

The mineral nutrients we are adding—limestone to keep the pH in the most favorable range for biological activity, colloidal phosphate to supply phosphorus, and greensand for a broad range of micronutrients plus some potassium—are raw materials for the soil. Colloidal phosphate and greensand are considered to be unavailable sources in a "feed the plant" system because they are not highly water soluble. But in practice their nutrients are made available for plants as a by-product of the soil's biological processes, which are stimulated by the cultural practices—high levels of organic matter, adequate moisture, soil aeration, green manures, crop rotations—mentioned so often in this production system.

To optimize the growth of crops, a grower must first optimize the workings of the biological "factory" in the soil. That is just what is done by all the cultural practices mentioned above. I can't stress enough the vital interrelations involved in this process; how much the benefits of these cultural practices are cumulative and synergistic; how much one makes another one work better. The cyclical concept is reaffirmed. No matter what the topic, we return again and again to cycles because a sound biological system is a cyclical system.

Why Do It This Way?

But why do it this way? Why not just use water-soluble chemical fertilizers? Because plant quality is dependent on a balanced availability of nutrients. The advantage of using the basic rock minerals in their natural form is that they are made available by the biological fertilizer factory of the soil at the rate plants need them. The two systems are harmonious. They evolved together. The correlation between availability of nutrients and their use by growing plants is a function of soil temperature, air temperature, moisture levels, and diurnal variation. Both plant and soil processes are affected simultaneously. During warmer, moister periods, plants grow better and nutrients are made available faster.

Thus, with natural rock minerals there are no problems from an excess supply of a soluble nutrient that can upset the mineral balance of the plant. Since there are no excesses, there is similarly no leaching of soluble nutrients such as nitrogen and potassium, which can be washed out of the soil to the detriment of the ground water and the farmer's pocketbook. Phosphorus doesn't leach out easily like nitrogen and potassium but rather becomes tied up in a soil that hasn't been programmed to release it. Either way, when water-soluble nutrients are used to "feed the plant," they do not contribute to a lasting soil fertility.

Other Rock Powders

Since the major ingredient of soils is finely ground rock particles from which bacterial action and plant roots extract mineral nutrients, some agriculturists have proposed amending the soil with rock powders other than lime, phosphate rock, or greensand. The suggestion makes sense.

Finely ground rock powders (usually waste products from quarrying operations) add to the soil a material that approximates the composition of highly fertile, unweathered "young" soils. Soil scientists classify soils as young, early maturity, late maturity, and old. Young soils provide large amounts of essential plant nutrients because easily acquired minerals from fresh surfaces (the unweathered primary mineral particles) are abundantly available. In older soils the weathering has already either partially or totally taken place, and the nutrients are no longer being liberated in such abundance, if at all. According to experimental work that has been done on this subject, a number of factors determine the performance of rock powders as soil amendments. These are the type of rock, the fineness of grind, the type of soil, and the type of plant.

Type of Rock   The first important variable is the type of rock. Over the years, trials have been conducted with volcanic dusts and pumices, granites, feldspars, and basalts, among others. Certain volcanic products have shown promise. Some granites have proven high in usable potassium, and biotite was the best of the feldspars. But the most researched and recommended have been the basalts.

The basalts are well-balanced rocks from the point of view of supplying soil nutrients. Basalts weather more easily than granites because they contain less silica and more calcium and magnesium. Soils derived from basalts are rich in clay and iron oxides and are usually very fertile. Basalt dusts are produced in large quantities as a result of trap-rock crushing operations, and at present they are a by-product looking for a use. European rock powder research has focused on basalt dusts in recent years, and they are used as an amendment in certain European biological farming systems. I suspect that in the future other rocks may also be appreciated as slow-release carriers of specific nutrients. An ideal product may someday be formulated that consists of a tailored blend of many different rock powders.

Fineness of Grind   The second most important effect on the ability of rock powders to supply nutrients to plants is the size of the particles. The finer the grind, the greater is the surface area of rock particles from which nutrients can be extracted. You can get an idea of the importance of particle size from the following statistic: a pound of average rock in a solid cube would have a surface area of about 30 square inches. But when ground to a 300-mesh powder (very fine), the surface area is increased to some 16 million square inches.

30 square inch surface area

16 million square inch surface area

Feeding Power The activities of a plant's root system through contact with the mineral particles of the soil constitutes its "feeding power." This is another factor in determining the availability of nutrients from less soluble sources. Studies have shown that plants of the lower order of evolution botanically have a better ability to extract less soluble minerals from rock sources than those plants that are more highly developed. Examples of strong feeders are cotton, okra, apples, peaches, berries, roses, alfalfa, clovers, kale, cabbage, cauliflower, and radishes. Some weaker feeders are cucumbers, lettuce, sunflowers, grasses, and mints.

It would seem logical, then, to use the rock powders to fertilize those crops and green manures that have been shown to utilize them effectively and then turn the crop residues and green manures into the soil to make their nutrients available for subsequent crops.

Cool-Weather Cures There are times of generally unfavorable growing conditions when the grower may want to use a temporary stimulant for plant growth. Let's take one common example. It is usually true that using soluble nitrogen or phosphorus to get plants growing in a cool spring may increase the bulk of the crop. Research has shown, however, that other nutrients are also immobilized by cool conditions and are unavailable to plants. The increase in bulk is an increase in quantity without quality because the composition of the plant is imbalanced. Where a grower wants to stress food quality as a marketing tool, nutrient imbalance is unsatisfactory.

If growing conditions are inadequate, then that is where the improvement should be made. The answer to cool conditions is to cure the problem by providing climatic protection such as walk-in tunnels or low covers for early crops. In the warmer conditions created by this protection, the natural soil-nutrient mobilization processes will be able to function without artificial stimulation.

For field crops such as corn, where climatic protection is not practical, I recommend two valuable human attributes — patience and confidence. Patience, because all will turn out well in the end, and confidence because it is often difficult to persevere when at first things look bad. Although the corn in a chemically fertilized field may be taller and greener early in the season, I guarantee that the corn from the biologically fertile soil will equal or surpass it by harvest.

It is a little bit like getting up in the morning. We can begin the day with some sort of stimulant or drug in order to "get going," but we pay the price later on through fatigue and continued reliance on the stimulant. Or we can accept the normal rate of mobilization of human energy that eventually results in a dependably productive day. There are a number of "natural" products on the market (liquid seaweed is one) that claim to offer plant stimulation without producing an imbalance. These products appeal to our human inclination to look for the "magic bullet," a secret potion that will make everything work better. In my opinion these products have mostly a psychological benefit. They make the grower feel more secure because something has been done whether it works or not. I have never thought they were the answer. In most cases, a grower would be better off spending that money to build up long-term soil fertility.

Natural Reserves

In many cases the use of mineral amendments may not be necessary. If the soil has adequate trace elements or if the manure is from animals fed a trace-mineral supplement, the micronutrient concern may be avoided. I do, however, recommend having some soil tests and tissue analyses made initially just to be sure. If the field has been heavily fertilized with superphosphate for many years past, there will usually be sufficient residual phosphorus for many years to come. Although the potassium content of the greensand is useful, it may not be necessary if manure is available. Further, the average agricultural soil has natural potassium reserves of from 20,000 to 40,000 pounds of potassium in the top 6 inches of each acre. Since I consider the usable soil depth for root feeding to be 24 inches, and since the subsoil is equally rich in potassium reserves, the aggregate amounts are considerable.

Sandy soils do not contain as much native potassium, so they should be treated differently. But even these will often have adequate stores of potassium if they are considered to a depth of 24 inches. Sandy soils may need heavier applications of organic amendments both initially and on a maintenance basis, not only to raise their potassium level but also to improve their structure and water-holding ability. Ways to provide extra organic matter for the farm at low cost, no cost, or even at a profit are suggested in Chapter 20. Obviously, any outside sources of free organic material such as autumn leaves or manure from stables and race tracks should be investigated.

In some cases it might be a good idea to include an extra year or two of a small grain undersown to clover in the rotation if only to bale the straw for a humus-building soil amendment. Or, 3 years of alfalfa might be included in the rotation and the 4 cuttings per year fed to livestock, composted, used as a mulch, or added directly to the soil and tilled in. On soils of lower initial fertility or on excessively sandy soils, one or more of these extra steps will be needed. The technique can vary as long as the goal is clear: long-term dependable fertility, not short-term plant stimulation.

Maintaining a Fertile Soil

A most important point to understand when following a "feed the soil" philosophy is that it is not necessary to apply every single year the amount of fertilizer required by the crop. Under a long-term approach, once a fertile soil has been established, it only needs to be maintained for plants to grow well. Obviously in order to maintain and hopefully to continue to improve the fertility of the soil, enough nutrients should be added to at least replace what is lost through erosion, leaching, and the sale of crops. If green manures are employed as assiduously as I recommend, though, there will be minimal losses from erosion and leaching, since the green manure roots will both hold the soil and use nutrients as they become available.

Once a truly fertile and productive soil has started to function, all that is necessary is to replace the equivalent of what leaves the farm in the produce that is sold. For example, if a farmer wishes to grow corn, the entire amount of the nitrogen (N), phosphorus (P), and potassium (K) necessary for the corn crop does not need to be applied each crop year. Adequate levels of these nutrients are available in the soil as a consequence of cultural practices and the quadrennial application of minerals.

How is that possible? Well, once a workable crop rotation is established, not only is the high level of fertility in the soil ready for the corn crop, but the preceding brassica crop was undersown to a legume—sweet clover—which will be turned under for the corn. The crop residues from the brassica crop are also incorporated (they account for over 75 percent of the crop mass that grew), and the quadrennial phosphate, greensand, and lime applications are all up to date. If there is manure or compost available, that will more than complete the package, but it is not absolutely necessary. I guarantee a first-class corn crop.

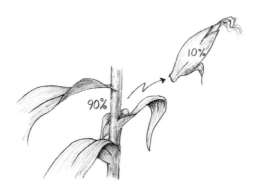

To look at it from another point of view, all that will be removed and sold from the corn crop are the ears. They represent less than 10 percent of the total nutrients in the corn plant. The rest of the plant is returned to the soil. If one calculates the amounts of P and K physically removed from the farm by the sale of corn, it would amount to approximately 17 pounds of P and 19 pounds of K, given an average 4-ton-per-acre yield. The cabbage crop preceding the corn, if it gave an average yield of 20,000 pounds per acre, would have removed about 6 pounds of P and 50 pounds of K.

Taking those two heavy feeders as representative crops, let us assign 12 pounds of P and 35 pounds of K as the average removed from each acre of land each year. That amounts to 48 pounds of P and 140 pounds of K removed every 4 years. Our quadrennial mineral fertilization, which consists of ½ ton of colloidal phosphate containing 80 pounds of P and 1 ton of greensand containing 140 pounds of K (in addition to the micronutrients), makes up for those withdrawals. Supplement those figures with the 40 tons of manure that may have been applied over the same 4 years—manure containing an additional 200 pounds of P and 400 pounds of K—and it is obvious that the soil is gaining both biological and mineral fertility.

The other major nutrient that hasn't been mentioned thus far, nitrogen, I do not consider to be in short supply. Nitrogen is available from the leguminous green manures, from crop residues, from nitrogen fixation, and as a component of the animal manures. Those sources are sufficiently nitrogenous to cover all demands.

BIOLOGICAL AND MINERAL ACTIVITIES OF THE SOIL

1. The majority of plant nutrients are most available between the pH range of 6.2 to 6.8.

2. Soil microbial life is most active within that pH range.

3. The nitrogen fixation by legumes and bacteria is also most effective within that pH range.

4. Most soils contain immense reserves of potassium, which become available if the soil is biologically active.

5. Organic matter is the power that makes all soil processes work.

6. Many trace elements are crucial not only to the optimum functioning of both the symbiotic and non-symbiotic nitrogen-fixation processes, but also to the quality of the crops grown.

7. Finely ground rock powders (usually waste products of the rock-crushing industry) can be valuable soil amendments in a biologically active soil. European farmers who have explored these concepts consider basalt rock to be highly effective.

8. The more finely ground the supplemental rock minerals, the greater their surface area and the more effectively their nutrients can be liberated by bacterial action in the soil.

9. The most complex systems are the most stable. For example, the best compost is a broad mixture of ingredients. A compost of varied plants, weeds, garden wastes, and manure is better than one made only of barley straw or pine sawdust.

Self-Sustaining Soil Fertility

I arrived at these "feed the soil" concepts over many years of observing how best to grow plants and conduct the business of agriculture. But they are not new. Nor am I their only advocate. The ideal of sustainable soil fertility has been understood for ages and expressed by many writers. Perhaps the most forceful champion in this century was Cyril G. Hopkins, Chief Agronomist and eventually Director of the Illinois Agricultural Experiment Station from 1911 to 1919.

Hopkins had his own "feed the soil" philosophy, which he called "The Illinois System of Permanent Agriculture." He advanced his ideas both in his best-known book, *Soil Fertility and Permanent Agriculture*, and in many experiment station publications. As Hopkins understood it, the fertility of the soil could be maintained with limestone, phosphate rock, and organic matter. I'll let him state the case in his own words:

> For practically all of the normal soils of the United States . . . there are only three constituents that must be supplied in order to adopt systems of farming that, if continued, will increase, or at least permanently maintain, the productive power of the soil. These are *limestone, phosphorus,* and *organic matter.* The limestone must be used to correct acidity where it now exists or where it may develop. The phosphorus is needed solely for its plant-food value. The supply of organic matter must be renewed to provide nitrogen from its decomposition and to make available the potassium and other essential elements contained in the soil in abundance, as well as to liberate phosphorus from the raw material phosphate naturally contained in or applied to the soil.
>
> The real question is, shall the farmer pay ten times as much as he ought to pay for food to enrich his soil? Shall he buy nitrogen at 45 to 50 cents a pound when the air above every acre contains 70 million pounds of free nitrogen? Shall he buy potassium at 5 to 20 cents a pound and apply 4 pounds per acre when his plowed soil already contains 30,000 pounds of potassium per acre, with still larger quantities in the subsoil? Because his soil needs phosphorus, shall he employ the fertilizer factory to make it soluble and then buy it at 12 to 30 cents a pound in an acid phosphate or "complete" fertilizer when he can get it for 3 cents a pound in the fine-ground natural rock phosphate, and when, by growing and plowing under plenty of clover (either directly or in manure), he can get nitrogen with profit from the air, liberate potassium from the inexhaustible supply in the soil, and make soluble the phosphorus in the natural rock phosphate which he can apply in abundance at low cost?

Prices may have changed, but the basic truths about long-term soil fertility and economic independence for the farmer are as clear now as they were then.

The efforts of Cyril Hopkins serve as a metaphor for independent truths up against an advertising and sales blitz that tries to pretend the truths don't exist. The result of more than a half century of fertilizer salesmanship is that no one remembers Cyril Hopkins. The soil fertility truths that he championed, although they were understood for generations, have been forgotten so long that they are now regarded as some sort of revolutionary heresy.

Hopkins was well aware of that possibility. He wrote numerous experiment station bulletins encouraging farmers to realize that no salesman was going to tell them about these ideas because there was so little to sell. He warned them that the large fertilizer manufacturers were concerned first and foremost with selling and only secondarily with farming. He predicted that the manufacturers would push their products endlessly until farmers forgot how well agriculture could work with a bare minimum of purchased materials. Well, Cyril Hopkins may have lost that struggle and been momentarily forgotten, but the truth of "permanent soil fertility" is still right there in the earth for those who care to look.

SOIL AMENDMENT RECOMMENDATIONS

Initial application (applied prior to year one)

For a soil initially of low fertility:

50 tons/acre manure or compost
2 tons/acre colloidal phosphate
2 tons/acre greensand

For a soil initially of medium fertility:

35 tons/acre manure or compost
1½ tons/acre colloidal phosphate
1½ tons/acre greensand

For an initially fertile soil:

20 tons/acre manure or compost
1 ton/acre colloidal phosphate
1 ton/acre greensand

In all cases add adequate limestone to maintain a pH of 6.5

Maintenance application (applied in years 2, 6, and so on)
½ ton/acre colloidal phosphate
1 ton/acre greensand
limestone as required

Maintenance application (applied every other year)
20 tons/acre manure or compost

GROWING AN ACRE OF CORN: TWO APPROACHES

Feed the Soil

Soil fertility is understood as a biological process. Once established, fertility can be maintained and improved by crop rotations that include legumes plus the addition of mineral raw materials.

Only the actual quantity of nutrients that leave the farm in stock or crops sold need to be purchased as inputs to maintain fertility. Nitrogen is not a purchased input because it is supplied by symbiotic and non-symbiotic processes.

Inputs are purchased in their least processed and least expensive form. Nutrient solubility and availability is considered to be a natural function of the biological processes in a properly managed soil.

Any feed brought onto the farm is calculated on the plus side of the input ledger. On average, 75 percent of the nutrient value of feed consumed by animals is returned in the manure as a nutrient input to the farm.

Sustainable

Feed the Plant

Soil fertility is understood to be an imported commodity. It is supplied by fertilizer inputs from off the farm, which are calculated in terms of so and so many hundred pounds of fertilizer applied to "create" the crop.

All the nutrients (N, P, K, Ca, Mg) known to be required to "create" one acre of corn (roots-tops-grain) are purchased as inputs each year. Nitrogen is a very important purchased input.

Inputs are purchased in their most processed and most expensive form. Nutrient solubility and availability is considered to be an industrial function of the chemical processes in a fertilizer factory.

Any feed brought onto the farm is calculated solely as a feed expense and is not credited for its manurial value. Animal manure, in general, is treated as a problem rather than as an asset.

Nonsustainable

Chapter
⚜ 11 DIRECT SEEDING

THE AIM OF SEEDING IS TO PLACE THE VEGETABLE seeds directly in the ground where they are to grow. The key tool for this process is a *precision seeder*. The perfect precision seeder will plant any size seed at any desired spacing and at the proper depth with reliable accuracy.

Since seeds come in so many different sizes and shapes, this is no easy task. Many seeders work well only with round seeds or those (pelleted seed) that have been made round by coating them with a clay-like material. Although pelleted seeds are easier for many seeders to handle, they do not always germinate well. They are also more expensive and are available in only a limited number of varieties. Frequently, the varieties of greatest value to the small-acreage grower (by virtue of flavor, tenderness, texture, storage, specialty market, and so forth) are not the commercial bulk-shipping varieties and are not available as pelleted seed.

The seeders most desirable for my production system are those that will handle naked seed. This is made easier if the seed can be bought "sized" — that is, separated by small increments into lots of identical dimensions. Sized-seed lots also germinate evenly and grow with equal vigor for, with most crops, these qualities correlate with seed size. Thus, crop uniformity and harvest predictability are further returns from a sized-seed lot.

Although many vegetable producers direct-seed the majority of their crops, I recommend direct seeding only those that are not practically or economically feasible to transplant. These are the tap-rooted crops (carrot, parsnip); the low-return-per-square-foot crops (corn, pumpkin); the easily drilled crops (pea, bean); and the fast-growing crops (radish, spinach). My reasons for broad-scale reliance on transplanting are outlined in the next chapter. One result of this preference is that it simplifies the direct-seeding system to fewer crops. The right choice of precision seeder is then the key to planting those crops as effectively as possible.

Precision Seeders There are a number of one-row, hand-pushed precision seeders available.

Fluid Seeder The seeds are pre-germinated and mixed with a carrier gel in which they are squeezed out into the seed furrow with a fair degree of precision. Fluid seeding is principally of value with a slow-germinating crop like carrot, or one, like corn, that won't germinate in cold soil in order to get the earliest outdoor harvest from a spring seeding. That virtue alone, though, is probably insufficient reason to justify the cost and complications of a fluid seeder.

Vacuum Seeder Although single-row vacuum seeders are pushed by hand, the vacuum mechanism is powered by a battery. The seeds are picked up individually by a rotating series of vacuum pipes fitted with special tips. As each pipe rotates past the seed-drop tube, the vacuum is removed and the seed falls to the soil. These seeders are reliably accurate with small seeds but are probably too expensive and high-tech for the requirements of a small-scale system.

Belt Seeder In this design a moving belt with seed-sized holes passes under the seed hopper and carries the seeds over to a seed-drop tube. Spacing is determined by the number of holes in the belt. A special belt is required for each size of seed. These models are very popular with vegetable growers but are highly reliant on pelleted seeds for best results.

Cup Seeder A disk mounted with a series of small individual cups (different sizes for different seeds) rotates through the seed hopper picking up individual seeds and then dropping them one by one as the cups pass over the seed tube. Spacing is determined by adjusting the speed of rotation of the cup

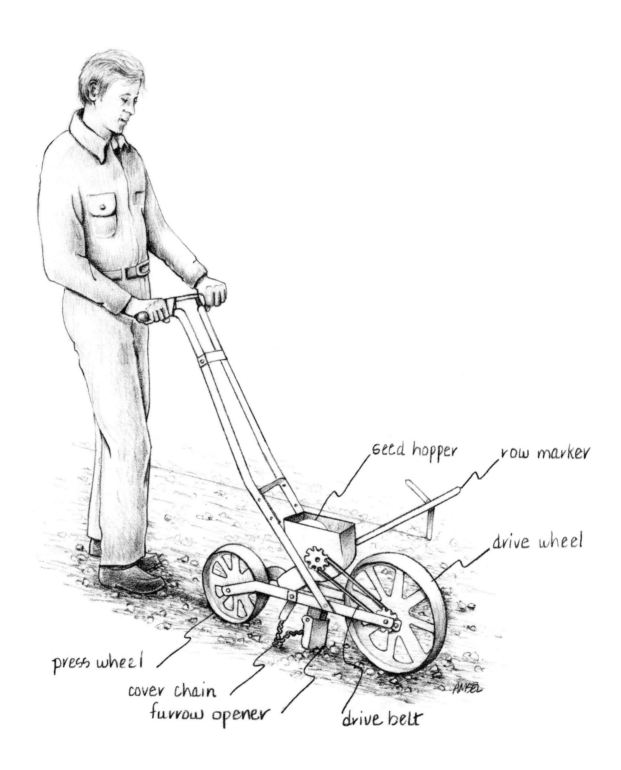

seed hopper

row marker

drive wheel

press wheel

cover chain

furrow opener

drive belt

disk. This is the best of the four types of seeders mentioned so far, since cups are available for almost any size seed, and this model works very well with naked seed. Unfortunately, it costs around $1,000 and cannot handle corn or pea seed.

Plate Seeder At present this is the best design for our needs on the grounds of flexibility and price. A notched plate is mounted to rotate on one side of the seed hopper. The notches, which are either cups, holes, or depressions formed along the edge of the plate, pick up individual seeds as the plate turns. Spacing is determined by the number of notches on the seed plate. The seed carried by the plate passes next to a hole in the wall of the seed hopper and falls through into the seed tube. The seed plates are made of plastic, and a dozen different types are available to handle every size seed. You can also purchase blank plates and drill or cut them to deal with specific seed sizes and spacings.

Desirable Features

A good one-row, hand-pushed precision seeder has certain features:

- *It is easy to push in a straight line.* This is crucial for ease of cultivation. Straight rows can be mechanically cultivated right up to the seedlings, saving a prodigious amount of hand weeding.

- *It gives precise seed placement.* Good seeds cost money and waste is expensive. Ideally, there should be no thinning required. When seeds are dropped where they are to grow and at the optimum spacing for best growth, the result is higher quality produce. Overly crowded plants grow poorly and are slower to mature.

- *It allows accurate depth adjustment.* Depth of planting affects germination, emergence, and early growth. The adjustment and maintenance of the necessary depth must be dependable. It is incumbent upon the grower to provide a smooth seed bed without hummocks and hollows if the best results are to be obtained.

- *It is easy to fill and empty.* In a multi-crop system many different seeds are involved. The seeder should be designed so that the seed hopper is easy to fill and easy to empty of excess seed. Changing from one size cup, plate, or belt to another should not involve extra tools or complicated procedures.

- *It is flexible and adaptable.* For a wide range of seeds, there needs to be a wide range of adjustments possible for seed size, seed spacing, and depth of planting. There should be no problem in making or obtaining special size cups, plates, or belts for the grower's needs.

- *There is a visible seed level and seed drop.* Nothing is more frustrating than to seed a crop and then find out that the seeder was not functioning correctly or that the seed supply ran out part-way through. In the best models of precision seeders, the operator can clearly see whether the seeds are dropping and how many are left.

- *It includes a dependable row marker.* The next row is marked by an adjustable marker arm while the previous row is being seeded. It is important to keep the rows spaced evenly. When rows are arrow straight and equidistant, between-row cultivations are much faster. The blades on the cultivator can then be set for the exact row width and the cultivator used with the assurance that there are no sections out of line.

Using the Seeder

It is good policy to calibrate the seeder before using it for all the different seeds and other adjustments involved. This is most easily done by measuring the circumference of the driving wheel (let's say it is 36 inches). Turn the wheel a number of times (say 3) by hand, with the seed hopper filled. The number of seeds that drop out of the seed tube (say 54) are the number that would be planted in 3 (revolutions) times 36 inches (circumference), or 108 inches of linear travel; 108 inches divided by 54 seeds is a seeding rate of 1 seed every 2 inches. If that is the desired seeding rate, then note the cup, plate, or belt number on the seed packet for future reference. If not, make an adjustment and go through the process again.

Fudge Factor

Now, just because it is possible to place a single seed at the precise spacing you desire, that doesn't always mean it should be done. Germination percentages must be considered. Seeds are sold with the germination percentage print-

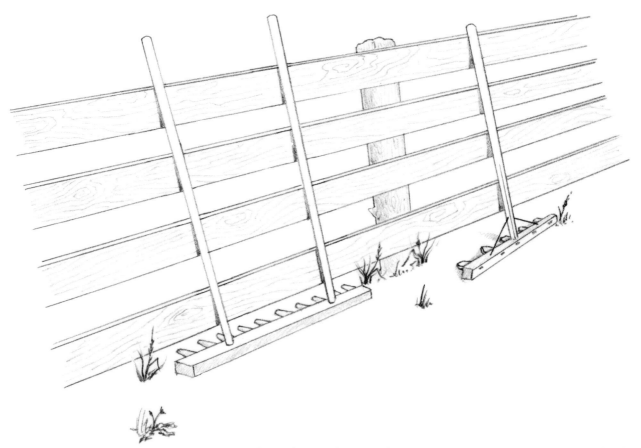

ed on the package, which was determined by a controlled laboratory test. Field germination will usually be less. Allowing for a fudge factor of 50 to 100 percent is wise when planning seeding rates. For example, if you want to end up with a plant such as rutabaga every 4 inches, the seeder could be set to drop a seed every 2 inches. Less-than-perfect germination will do some of the thinning for you. Further thinning is quickly done with a hoe, because the seeds will be evenly spaced and not in a thick row or clump.

Marking   When seeding, a string should be stretched tightly to guide the first row. All subsequent rows will be marked with the row-marker arm on the seeder. Be sure to aim the seeder as straight and true as you can with each pass. When hand seeding, the string or tape measure will need to be reset for each row. For larger areas, an adjustable rolling marker or marker rake can be used.

Hand Seeding

Hand seeding is used for the cucurbit family—cucumber, pumpkin, summer squash, and winter squash. These are relatively large seeds that can be easily picked up with the fingers. The quantities and areas to be planted are not excessive for hand seeding. Under poorer soil conditions these crops will benefit from being planted on small, soil-covered mounds of compost or manure for an extra fertility boost.

DIRECT SEEDING CHART

Crop	Machine Seeded	Hand Seeded	Spacing (inches)		Also Transplanted
			Plant	Row	
BEAN	√		4	30	√
BEET	√		3	18	√
CARROT	√		1	12	
CHINESE CABBAGE	√		12	12	√
CORN	√		12	30	√
CUCUMBER		√	12	30	√
KOHLRABI	√		6	12	√
PARSNIP	√		3	18	
PEA	√		2	30 or 60	√
POTATO		√	12	30	
PUMPKIN		√	24	120	√
RADISH	√		2	4	
RUTABAGA	√		4	18	
SPINACH	√		3	12	√
SWISS CHARD	√		6	12	√
SUMMER SQUASH		√	24	60	√
WINTER SQUASH		√	24	120	√

Chapter 12   TRANSPLANTING

TRANSPLANTING IS THE PRACTICE OF STARTING seedlings in one place and setting them out in another. In this way large numbers of young seedlings can be grown in a small area under controlled cultural conditions before they are taken to the field. Transplanting has traditionally been used for those crops (celery, lettuce, onion, and tomato) that regrow roots easily. These crops don't suffer much from being transplanted, although they obviously grow better the less their roots are disturbed. Transplanting is also of value for many crops (cucumber, melon, and parsley) that are less tolerant of root disturbance, but it must be conducted in such a way that the plants hardly know they have been moved. The best transplant system is one that does not disturb the roots, is uncomplicated, can be mechanized, and is inexpensive. In my opinion, *soil blocks* are the system that best fits those requirements.

Greenhouse to Field

Transplanting should be understood as three separate operations: *starting, potting on,* and *setting out.*

Starting involves its own three subdivisions—type of containment, soil mix, and controlled climate. The seeds are sewn in some sort of prepared bed or container. The container usually holds a special soil mix or potting soil. This mix differs from garden soil by being compounded of extra organic matter and drainage material so the seedlings will thrive despite the confined conditions. A controlled climate is provided by growing the plants in a greenhouse, hotbed, cold frame, or sheltered area to enhance early growing conditions for the young seedlings.

Potting on means transferring the seedlings from the initial container to a larger container with wider plant spacing. With soil blocks, this isn't always necessary from a practical point of view, except with those crops that are grown for a longer time or to a larger size before being set out. Potting on is always valuable from the perspective of the highest plant quality, however, since only the most vigorous of the numerous young seedlings are selected.

Setting out is the process of planting the young plants in the field or in the production greenhouse where they are to grow. The greater the efficiency with which this transfer can be accomplished, the more cost effective transplanting becomes as a component of vegetable crop production.

A Sure Harvest

Transplants assure the grower of crops throughout the growing season at the times and in the quantities required. A seed sown in the field is a gamble; a healthy 3- to 4-week-old transplant set out in the field is an almost sure harvest. Transplanting is the most *reliable* method for obtaining a *uniform* stand of plants with a *predictable* harvest date.

Transplanting is *reliable* because the grower has better control over the production environment. The germination and emergence variables that can be so unpredictable in the field are more certain in the greenhouse. The crops are *uniform* because there are no gaps in the rows. No land is wasted from a thin stand due to faulty germination. Vigorous transplants set out at the ideal plant density for optimum yield have a very high rate of survival. The harvest is *predictable* because the greatest variability in plant growth occurs in the

Direct Seeding

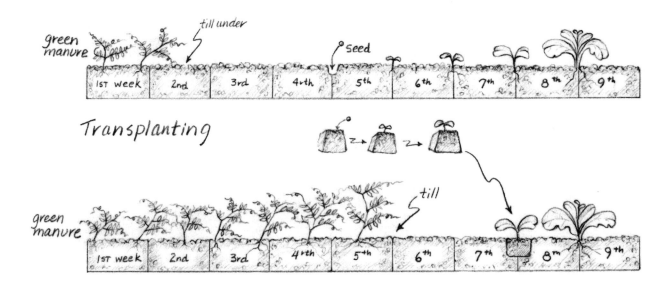

Transplanting

seedling stage. Once they are past that stage, an even maturity and a dependable harvest can be counted on.

It is far easier to lavish extra care on thousands of tiny seedlings in a small space in the greenhouse than over wide areas in the field. During the critical early period of growth, when ideal conditions can make such a difference, the grower can provide those conditions with less labor and expense in a concentrated area. Transplanting also allows for far more productive use of a green manure program to maintain fertility. Whereas many direct-seeded crops germinate poorly in a soil containing newly incorporated green manure residues, transplanted crops can thrive and grow quickly. (In the early stages of decomposition, compounds are formed which inhibit seed germination.) Thus, green manures can be left to grow longer before setting out transplants. Rather than having to turn under a green manure the recommended 3 to 4 weeks before a seeded crop, green manures can be left to grow until 2 weeks before a transplanted crop. Depending on the age of the transplant, that can increase the growth period of the green manure by up to 5 weeks. Under these conditions, green manures are a viable option before many early crops.

Cheating Weeds and the Weather

When crops are sown in the field, weeds can begin germinating at the same time or even before. Direct-seeded crops may also need to be thinned, and they must contend with in-row weeds while young. Transplant crops start out with a 3- to 4-week headstart on any newly germinating weeds because the soil can be tilled immediately prior to transplanting. Further, since transplants can be set out at the final spacing, they do not require thinning and are much easier to cultivate for the control of any in-row weeds that may appear.

Transplants can measurably increase production on the intensively managed small farm, because they provide extra time for maturing succession crops. This is done by starting the succession crop as transplants 3 to 4 weeks before the preceding crop is to be harvested. Immediately after harvest, the ground is cleared, the plants are set, and the new crop is off and growing as if it had been planted 3 or 4 weeks earlier (which, of course, it was). The result is the same as if the growing season had been extended by 3 to 4 weeks. Transplanting allows less land to be used more efficiently for more production.

Earlier maturity is another obvious advantage. Plants started ahead inside and set out when the weather permits have a head start and will mature sooner than those seeded directly. In many cool climates, tomatoes, melons, peppers, and others are only successful as transplanted crops.

Transplanting Methods

In earlier days, vegetable growers relied heavily upon *bare root* transplants, seedlings dug up from a special bed or outdoor field and transplanted with no attempt to retain a ball of soil around the roots. Uniform results and good survival rates are more difficult to achieve with this method. Most of the fine root hairs that supply the plant with water are lost upon uprooting. This reduces the absorbing surface of the root system and markedly delays the reestablishment and subsequent growth of the plants. This "transplant shock" can be avoided by moving plants without disturbing their fragile root systems.

Many types of containers have been used to keep the root ball intact—clay pots, plastic pots, peat pots, wood or paper bands, wooden flats, plug flats, and others. The plants and soil are either removed from the container before planting or are planted outside, container and all, if the pot (peat pot, paper band) is decomposable. Unfortunately, most contain-

TRANSPLANT CHART

Crop	Optimal Spacing (inches)		Transplant Age in Weeks	Also Direct Seeded
	Plant	Row		
BEET	4	12	3–4	√
BROCCOLI	24	30	4	
BRUSSELS SPROUTS	24	30	4	
CABBAGE	18–24	30	4	
CAULIFLOWER	18–24	30	4	
CELERY	12	12	8	
CELERIAC	12	12	8	
CHINESE CABBAGE	12	12	3	√
CORN	12	30	2–3	√
CUCUMBER	12	30	3	√
EGGPLANT	24	30	8	
KALE	12	18	4	
KOHLRABI	6	12	3–4	√
LEEK	8	12	4–8	
LETTUCE	12	12	3–4	
MELON	12	60	3	
ONION, BULB	3	12	4–8	
ONION, SCALLION	1	12	4–6	
PARSLEY	6	12	6	
PEA	2	30 or 60	3	√
PEPPER	12	30	8	
SPINACH	3	12	2–3	√
SUMMER SQUASH	24	60	3	√
SWISS CHARD	6	18	3–4	√
TOMATO	24	60	8	

ers have disadvantages. Peat pots and paper bands often do not decompose as intended and inhibit root growth. They are also expensive.

Traditional wooden flats grow excellent seedlings, but some of the seedling roots must be cut when removing the plants.

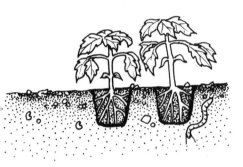

Individual pots of any type are time consuming and awkward to handle in quantity. The plug-type trays that contain individual cells for each plant solve the handling problem by combining the individual units. But they share a problem common to all containers—root circling. The seedling roots grow to the wall of the container and then follow it round and round.

Plants whose roots have circled do not get started as quickly after they are put in the field. An attempt has been made to improve on this situation by designing the tray cells with a hole in the bottom for air pruning, but root-circling can still occur in the rest of the cell.

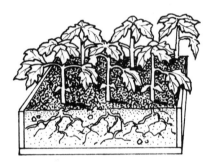

Fortunately, there is a "container" better than all of the above. That container—the soil block—is the subject of the next chapter.

Chapter 13 SOIL BLOCKS

IT IS ALWAYS SATISFYING TO FIND A NEW TECHnique that is simpler, more effective, and less expensive than what existed before. For the production of transplants, the "soil block" meets those criteria. The Dutch have been developing this technique for some 70 years, but the history of the idea of growing plants in a cube of "soil" goes back 2,000 years or more in Central American agriculture. A related technique is the old market gardener's practice of using 4- to 5-inch cubes of inverted sod for growing melon and cucumber transplants.

How Soil Blocks Work

A soil block is pretty much what the name implies—a block made out of lightly compressed potting soil. It serves as both the container and the growing medium for a transplant seedling. The blocks are composed entirely of potting soil and have no walls as such. Because they are pressed out *by* a form rather than filled *into* a form, air spaces provide the walls. Instead of the roots circling as they do upon reaching the wall of a container, they fill the block to the edges and wait. The air spaces between the blocks and the slight wall glazing caused by the block form keep the roots from growing from one block to another. The edge roots remain poised for rapid outward growth. When transplanted to the field, the seedling quickly becomes established. If the plants are kept too long in the blocks, however, the roots do extend into neighboring blocks, so the plants should be transplanted before this happens.

Despite being no more than a cube of growing medium, a soil block is not fragile. When first made, it is bound together by the fibrous nature of the moist ingredients. Once seeded, the roots of the young plant quickly fill the block and ensure its stability even when handled roughly. Soil blocks are the answer for a farm-produced seedling system that costs no more than the "soil" of which it is composed.

Advantages

The best thing about the soil-block system is that everything that can be done in small pots, "paks," trays, or plugs can be done in blocks without the expense and bother of a container. Blocks can be made to accommodate any need. The block may have a small depression on the top in which a seed is planted, but blocks can also be made with a deep center hole in which to root cuttings. They can also be made with a large hole in which to transplant seedlings. Or they can be made with a hole precisely the size of a smaller block, so seedlings started in a germination chamber in small blocks can be quickly transplanted on to larger blocks.

Blocks provide the modular advantages of plug trays without the problems and expense of a plug system. Blocks free the grower from the mountains of plastic containers that have become so ubiquitous of late in horticultural operations. European growers sell bedding plants in blocks to customers, who transport them in their own containers. There is no plastic pot expense to the grower, the customer, or the environment. In short, soil blocks constitute the best system I have yet found for growing seedlings.

The Soil-Block Maker

The key to this system is the tool for making soil blocks—the soil-block maker or "blocker." Basically, it is an ejection mold that forms self-contained cubes out of a growing medium. Both hand and machine models are available. For small-scale production, hand-operated models are perfectly adequate. Motorized block-making machines have a capacity of over 10,000 blocks per hour, but they are way overscaled for a five-acre vegetable farm.

There are two features to understand about the blocker in

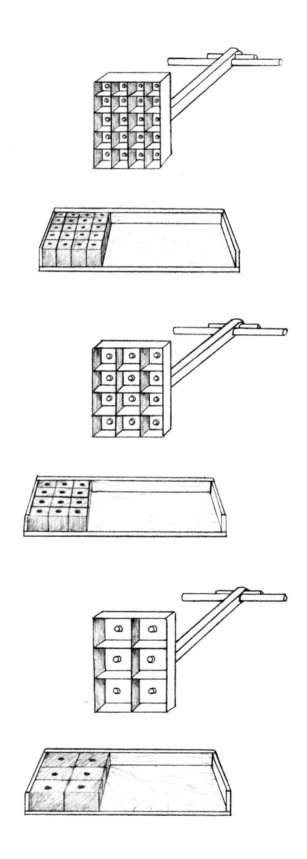

order to appreciate the versatility of soil blocks: the size of the block form and the size and shape of the center pin.

The Form

Forms are available to make ¾-inch blocks (the mini-blocker), 1½-inch blocks, 2-inch blocks, 3-inch blocks, and 4-inch blocks (the maxi-blocker). The block shape is cubic rather than tapered. Horticultural researchers have found a cubic shape to be superior to the tapered-plug shape for the root growth of seedlings.

Two factors influence choice of block size—the type of plant and the length of the intended growing period prior to transplanting. For example, a larger block would be used for early sowings or where planting outside is likely to be delayed. A smaller block would suffice for short-duration propagation in summer and fall. The mini-block is used only as a germination block for starting seedlings.

Obviously, the smaller the block the less potting mix and greenhouse space is required (a 1½-inch block contains less than half the volume of a 2-inch block). But in choosing between block sizes the larger of the two is usually the safer choice. Of course, if a smaller size block is used, the plants can always be held for a shorter time. Or, as is common in European commercial blocking operations, the nutrient requirements of plants in blocks too small to maintain them can be supplemented with soluble nutrients. The need for such supplementary fertilization is an absolute requirement in plug-type systems because each cell contains so much less soil than a block. The popular upside down pyramid shape, for example, contains only ⅓ the soil volume of a cubic block of the same top dimension.

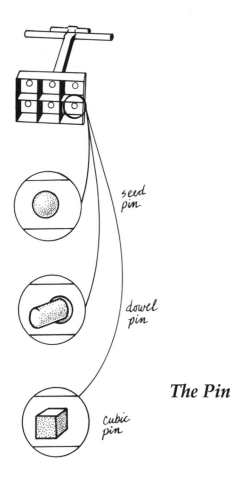

seed pin

dowel pin

cubic pin

My preference is always for the larger block, first because I believe it is false economy to stint on the care of young plants. Their vigorous early growth is the foundation for later productivity. Second, I prefer not to rely on soluble feeding when the total nutrient package can be enclosed in the block from the start. All that is necessary when using the right size block and soil mix is to water the seedlings.

Another factor justifying any extra volume of growing medium is the addition of that organic matter to the soil. If lettuce is grown in 2-inch blocks and set out at a spacing of 12 by 12 inches, the amount of organic material in the blocks is the equivalent of applying 5 tons of compost per acre. Since peat is more than twice as valuable as manure for increasing long-term organic matter in the soil, the blocks are actually worth double their weight in manure. Where succession crops are grown, the soil-improving material added from transplanting alone can be substantial.

The Pin

The pin is the object mounted in the center of the top press form plate. The standard seed pin is a small button that makes an indentation for the seed in the top of the soil block. This pin is suitable for crops with seeds the size of lettuce, cabbage, onion, or tomato. Larger seed pins are used for melon, squash, corn, peas, beans, and any other seeds of those dimensions. Other pin types are dowel or cubic shaped. A long dowel pin is used to make a deeper hole into which cuttings can be inserted. Cubic pins are used so a seedling in a smaller block can be potted on to a larger block. Cubic pins make a cubic hole in the top of the block into which the smaller block is placed. Pins are easily interchangeable.

Blocking Systems

The ¾-inch block made with the mini-blocker is used for starting seeds. With this small block, enormous quantities of modular seedlings can be germinated on a heating pad or in a germination chamber. This is especially useful for seeds that take a long time to germinate because a minimum of space is used in the process.

Mini-blocks are effective because they can be handled as soon as you want to pot on the seedlings. The oft-repeated admonition to wait until the first true leaves appear before transplanting is wrong. Studies have shown that the sooner

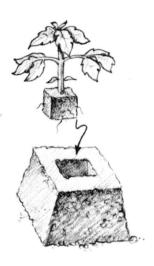

young seedlings are potted on, the better is their eventual growth.

The 1½-inch block is used for short-duration transplants of standard crops (lettuce, brassicas) and as the seed block for cucumbers and melons by using the large seed pin. When fitted with a long dowel pin it makes an excellent block for rooting cuttings.

The 2-inch block is the standard for longer duration transplants. When fitted with the ¾-inch cubic pin, it is used for germinating bean, pea, corn, or squash seeds and for the initial potting on of crops started in mini-blocks.

The 3-inch block fitted with a ¾-inch cubic pin offers the option to germinate many different field crops (squash, corn, cucumber, melon) when greenhouse space is not critical. It is also an ideal size for potting on asparagus seedlings started in mini-blocks.

The 4-inch block fitted with a 1½- or 2-inch cubic pin is the final home of cucumber, eggplant, melon, pepper, and tomato. Because of its cubic shape, it has the same soil volume as a 6-inch pot and can grow exceptional plants of these varieties to their 5- to 8-week field transplant age.

Other Pin Options

In addition to the pins supplied with the blocker, the grower can make a pin of any desired size or shape. Most hard materials (wood, metal, or plastic) are suitable as long as the pins have a smooth surface. Plug trays can be used as molds and filled with quick-hardening water putty to make many different sizes of pins that allow the integration of the plug and block systems.

Blocking Mixes

When transplants are grown, whether in blocks or pots, their rooting area is limited. Therefore the *soil* in which they grow must be specially formulated to compensate for these restricted conditions. For soil blocks, this special growing medium is called a blocking mix. The composition of a blocking mix differs from ordinary potting soil because of the unique requirements of block making. A blocking mix needs extra fibrous material to withstand being watered to a paste consistency and then formed into blocks. Unmodified garden soil treated this way would become hard and impenetrable.

A blocking mix also needs good water-holding ability because the blocks are not enclosed by a non-porous container. The bulk ingredients for blocking mixes are peat, sand, soil, and compost.

Peat   *Peat* is a partly decayed, moisture-absorbing plant residue found in bogs and swamps. It provides the fiber and extra organic matter in a mix. Two types are used. *Brown peat* is the standard peat moss. All brown peats are not created equal, however, and quality can vary greatly. I recommend the premium grade. *Black peat*, also called dark-peat humus or "terre noire" by Canadian manufacturers, is a more highly decomposed product from the lower layers of a bog. It holds more moisture than the brown peat and gives "body" to a block.

Sand   *Sand* or some similar granular substance is useful to "open up" the mix and provide more air porosity. A coarse sand with particles having a ⅛- to 1/16-inch diameter is the most effective. I prefer not to use pearlite or vermiculite as many commercial mixes do, because they are too light and tend to be crushed in the block-making process. There is a manufactured granular additive, calcined clay, which is superior to coarse sand and not as heavy. It provides the best aeration and moisture-holding properties. Unfortunately, calcined clay is significantly more expensive and not as easy to obtain. Whatever the coarse product involved, adequate aeration is a key to successful plant growth in any medium.

Soil and Compost   Although most modern growing mediums no longer include any real soil, I have found both soil and compost to be important for plant growth in a mix. Together they replace the "loam" of the successful old-time potting mixtures and give superior results. In combination with the other ingredients, they provide stable sustained-release nutrition to the plants so there is no need for supplemental feeding.

Compost is the most important ingredient. It is best taken from 2-year-old heaps that are fine in texture and well decomposed. The compost heap must be carefully prepared for future use in potting soil. I construct the heap with 4- to 6-

inch layers of mixed garden wastes (outer leaves, pea vines, or weeds) covered with a sprinkling of manure or topsoil and 2 inches of straw. The sequence is repeated until the heap is complete. The heap should be turned once the temperature rises and begins to decline so as to stimulate further decomposition. When breakdown is completed, the heap should be covered with a tarp. I strongly suggest letting the compost sit for an additional year (so that it is 1½ to 2 years old before use); it is well worth the trouble. The better the compost ingredient, the better the growth of the plants will be. The exceptional quality of seedlings grown in this mix is reason enough to take special care when making a compost. Compost for blocking mixes must be stockpiled the fall before it is used so as to have plenty on hand.

Soil refers to a fertile garden soil that is also stockpiled ahead of time. I collect it in the fall from land off which onions have just been harvested. I have found that seedlings (onions included) seem to grow best when the soil in the blocking mix has grown onions. I suspect there is some biological effect at work here, since crop-rotation studies have found onions (and leeks) to be highly beneficial preceding crops in a vegetable rotation. The soil and compost should be sifted through a ½-inch mesh screen to remove sticks, stones, and lumps. The compost and peat for the extra-fine mix used either for mini-blocks or for the propagation of tiny flower seeds are sifted through a ¼-inch mesh.

Extra Ingredients

Lime, colloidal phosphate, and greensand are added in smaller quantities.

Lime Ground limestone is added to adjust the pH of the blocking mix. The quantity of lime is determined by the amount of peat, the most acidic ingredient. The pH of compost or garden soil should not need modification. My experience as well as recent research results have led me to aim for a growing medium pH between 6 to 6.5 for all the major transplant crops. Those using different peats in the mix may want to run a few pH tests to be certain. However, the quantity of lime given in this formula works for the different peats that I have encountered.

Blood Meal I find this to be the most consistently dependable slow-release source of nitrogen for growing mediums. English gardening books often refer to hoof-and-horn meal, which is similar.

Colloidal Phosphate A clay material associated with phosphate rock deposits and containing 22 percent P_2O_5. The finer the particles the better.

Greensand (Glauconite) Greensand contains some potassium but is used here principally as a broad-spectrum source of micronutrients. A dried seaweed product can serve the same purpose, but I have discovered more consistent results with greensand.

The last three supplementary ingredients—blood meal, colloidal phosphate and greensand—when mixed together in equal parts are called the "base fertilizer."

BLOCKING MIX RECIPE

A standard 10-quart bucket is the unit of measurement for the bulk ingredients. A standard cup measure is used for the supplementary ingredients. This makes approximately 2 bushels. Follow the steps in the order given.

> 2 *buckets black peat*
> ½ *cup lime. MIX.*
> 2 *buckets coarse sand*
> 2 *buckets brown peat*
> 3 *cups base fertilizer. MIX.*
> 1 *bucket soil*
> 1 *bucket compost*

Mix all ingredients together thoroughly.

The lime is combined with the black peat because that is the most acid ingredient. Then the sand is added. The brown peat and base fertilizer are mixed in next. By incorporating the dry supplemental ingredients with the peats in this manner, they will be distributed as uniformly as possible throughout the medium. Next add the soil and compost, and mix completely a final time.

To use this recipe for larger quantities, think of it measured in "units." The unit can be any size as long as the ratio between the bulk and the supplementary ingredients is maintained. A "unit" formula would call for:

20 units black peat	20 units brown peat	10 units compost
⅛ unit lime	¾ unit base fertilizer	
20 units coarse sand	10 units soil	

Mini-Block Recipe

A different blend is used for germinating seeds in mini-blocks. The ingredients are finely screened through a ¼-inch mesh.

16	parts	brown peat
½	part	colloidal phosphate
½	part	greensand
4	parts	compost (well decomposed)

Sterilizing the Mix

In more than 20 years of using home-made mixes, I have never sterilized them. And I have *not* had problems. I realized early on that damp-off and similar seedling problems, which are usually blamed on unsterilized soil, are actually a function of cultural mistakes like over-watering, a lack of air movement, not enough sun, over-fertilization, and so forth. Good, fertile garden soil and well-prepared compost contain many organisms that benefit seedling growth. If you "sterilize" these ingredients you lose the benefits of a live mix without gaining the advantages that are achieved through proper seedling management.

Nitrogen Reaction

With certain crops (mostly the more delicate bedding-plant flowers) there may be a further consideration. Research has determined that where organic sources of nitrogen like blood meal are included in a mix, the mineralization of the nitrogen by biological processes and the consequent production of ammonia can inhibit plant growth for a period after the mix is made, especially if moisture and temperature levels are high. If you want to be assured this will not occur, the mix should be prepared well ahead of use. When the mix is stored for more than 3 months, that excess activity will subside, reactions will return to normal, and minor growth inhibition will no longer be a factor.

Moistening the Mix Water must be added to wet the mix to blocking consistency. The amount of water varies depending on the initial moisture content of the ingredients. On average, to achieve a consistency wet enough for proper block-making, the ratio of water to mix by volume will be about 1 part water to every 3 parts mix. A little over 2½ gallons of water should be added to every cubic foot of mix.

For successful block-making, be sure to use a mix that is wet enough. Since this will be much wetter than potting mixes used for pots or flats, it takes some getting used to. The most common mistake in block-making is to try to make blocks from a mix that is too dry. The need to thoroughly wet the mix is why the mix requires a high percentage of peat to give it the necessary resiliency.

Handling Soil Blocks Many large block-making operations set the newly formed and seeded blocks by the thousands on a plastic sheet on the floor of the greenhouse. When they are ready to go to the field, the blocked seedlings are lifted with a broad, fine-tined fork and slid into transport crates. These crates have high sides so they can be stacked for transport without crushing the seedlings. In lieu of these special crates, two other options are practical for small-scale production.

Simple 3-sided wooden flats work well for soil blocks. The inside dimensions are 18¾ inches long by 8 inches wide by 2 inches high. Three-quarter-inch stock is used for the sides and half-inch stock for the bottom. One flat holds 60 of the 1½-inch blocks, 36 of the 2-inch blocks, or 18 of the 3-inch size. These block flats are efficient to use in the greenhouse because the benches need to be no more than 2 by 4s spaced to hold two rows of flats side by side. Low-sided flats such as these are not stackable when filled with plants. For transport, a carrying rack with spaced shelves is required.

The flats have only 3 sides so the blocked seedlings can be easily removed from the open side one at a time as they are being transplanted in the field. The flat is held in one hand by the long side while blocks are quickly placed in holes in the soil with the other. Similar 3-sided flats (half as wide and only ¾ inch high at the sides) are used for mini-blocks. Since they are the same length as the others, they fit two to a space on the greenhouse bench for modular efficiency. Each of these flats holds 120 mini-blocks.

Bread Trays

When handling greater quantities of blocks, you can use the large plastic mesh bread trays seen in bread delivery trucks. They can generally be bought used at a reasonable cost from regional bakeries. Since the sides on these trays are higher than all except for the tallest seedlings, they can be stacked for transport. Bread trays vary in size, but on average each tray can hold 200 of the 1½-inch blocks and proportionally fewer of the larger sizes.

Results are excellent with bread trays. What with the open mesh sides and bottom plus the air spaces between the blocks, the roots of the seedlings remain poised at all 5 potential soil-contact surfaces. The bread trays are not as easy to handle for field transplanting as the smaller 3-sided flats, but they become manageable with practice.

Making Soil Blocks

The wet mix should be spread on a hard surface at a depth thicker than the blocks to be made. The block maker is filled by pressing it into the mix with a quick push and a twisting motion to seat the material. Lift the block maker, scrape off any excess mix against the edge of a board, and place the block maker on the 3-sided flat, the bread tray, the plastic sheet, a concrete floor, or other surface. The blocks are ejected by pressing on the spring-loaded handle and raising the form in a smooth, even motion. After each use the blocker is dipped in water to rinse it. A surprising speed of block production (up to 5,000 per hour using the 1½-inch floor model) will result with practice.

Seeding the Blocks

Each block is formed with an indentation in the top to receive the seed. The hand-made blocks are usually sown by hand. With the motorized blockers, the sowing as well as the block forming is mechanized. An automatic seeder mounted over the block belt drops one seed into each indentation as the blocks pass under it. These motorized models are too large and expensive for the small-scale grower, but if a group of growers get together, there is a role for one of them as a specialized seedling-grower. Small farmers always benefit from such cooperative arrangements and should consider participating whenever the opportunity arises.

Single-Plant Blocks

One seed is sown per block. There is a temptation to use two (just to be on the safe side), but that is not necessary. Germination is excellent in soil blocks because of the ease with which ideal moisture and temperature conditions can be maintained. The few seeds that don't germinate are much less of a problem than the labor to thin all those that do. Of course, if the seed is of questionable vitality it is worth planting more than one seed per block, but obviously it pays to get good seed to begin with.

Seeding can be done with the fingers for large seeds such as cucumber, melon, and squash. Finger seeding is also possible for small seeds that have been pelleted, although pelleted seeds are not easily available in most varieties, and naked seeds are commonly used. The small seeds can be most accurately handled by using a small thin stick, a sharpened dowel, a toothpick, or similar pointed implement. Seeds are spread on a dish. The tip of the stick is moistened in water and touched to one seed. The seed adheres to the tip and is moved to the seed indentation in the top of a block and deposited there. The solid, moist block has more friction than the tip of the stick, so the seed stays on the block.

Another obvious technique is to crease one side of a seed packet or use any other V-shaped container and tap out the seeds by striking the container with the fingers or a small stick. Commercial seeding aids are available that aim to either wiggle, click, or vibrate the seeds out one by one. Growers should try such aids to decide for themselves whether they are worth it. Whatever method is used, the seeding should be done carefully to ensure that the seeds are accurately planted in each block.

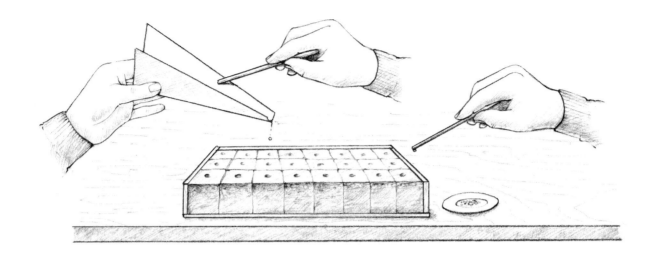

In practice, these planting techniques quickly become efficient and precise. Remember that for many crops the soil-block system avoids all intermediate potting on. Crops are started in the block and later go directly to the field. That savings in time alone is worth the effort required to become proficient at single seeding.

Germination

The seed in the indentation on top of the block should not be covered. Studies on seed germination emphasize that oxygen is important for high-percentage seed germination. Thus, even a thin covering of soil or potting mix can lower the germination percentage for most seeds. The same isn't true for outside planting because another key to germination—moisture—becomes limiting if the surface of the soil dries out on a sunny day. In the ideal conditions of a greenhouse, the moisture level can be kept high during the germination period by misting frequently with a fine spray of water. The third key to a high-germination percentage—heat—can best be provided by using a thermostatically controlled soil-heating pad under the blocks.

Multi-Plant Blocks

Although I have stressed the wisdom of sowing only 1 seed per block, there is an important exception to that rule—the multi-plant block. In this case 3 to 12 seeds are deliberately planted in each block with no intention of thinning. Many crops grow normally under multi-plant conditions, and transplant efficiency is enhanced by putting out clumps rather than single plants.

The concept of the multi-plant block is based on spatial rather than lineal plant distance in the field. For example, say the average ideal in onion spacing is 1 plant every 3 inches in rows 12 inches apart. Multi-plants aim at an equivalent spacing of 4 onions per square foot. The difference is that all 4 onions are started together in one block and grow together until harvest. Since it is just as easy to grow 4 plants to the block as to grow 1, there is now only one-quarter the block-making work and greenhouse space involved in raising them. A similar advantage is realized when transplanting them to the field. When 4 plants can be handled as 1, then only a quarter as many units need to be set out. Although bunched together, the plants will have extra space all around them. The onions grow normally in the clump, gently pushing each other aside, attaining a nice round bulb shape and good size.

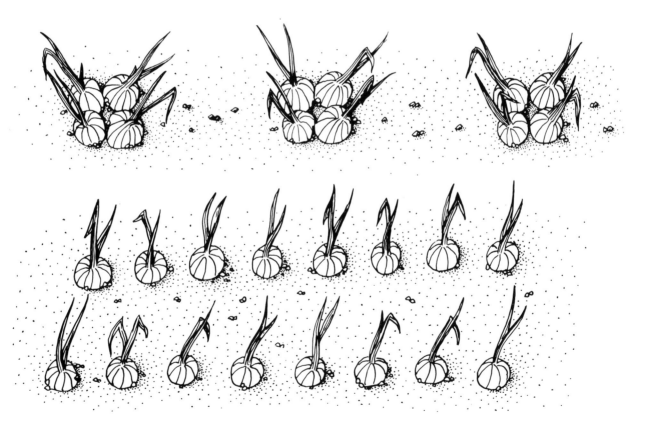

Not only bulb onions but scallions (green onions) thrive in multiple plantings. Scallions are seeded 10 to 12 per block and grow in a bunch ready to tie for harvest. Weeding between the plants in the row is no longer a chore, since the wider spaces allow for easy cross-cultivation with a hoe. Obviously, multi-plant blocks must be transplanted to the field a bit sooner (at a younger age) than single-plant blocks because of the extra seedling competition in the limited confines of the block.

Multi-plant blocks can be sown seed by seed or in bunches. For counting out seeds, one of the wiggle, click, or vibration seeders have a place here in speeding up the seeding operation at the sacrifice of some accuracy. For bunch sowing, tiny scoops or spoons or other small-volume measures can be fabricated by the grower to hold 6, 12, or whatever number of seeds. These are used to scoop up the seeds and dump them in each seed indentation. This method is not as accurate as counting, but it is a lot faster.

Multi-plant blocks are an efficient option for a number of crops. In my experience onions, scallions, leeks, beets, parsley, spinach, corn, pole beans, and peas have been outstandingly successful in multiple plantings. Spinach, corn, pole beans, and peas, which are rarely transplanted, even for the earliest crop, become a much more reasonable proposition when the transplant work can be cut by 75 percent. European growers claim additional good results with cabbage, broccoli, and turnips planted at 3 to 4 seeds per block.

MULTI-PLANT BLOCKS				
	No. of	Spacing (inches)		Block Size
Crop	Seeds	Plant	Row	(inches)
BEET	4	6	16	2
BROCCOLI	4	24	30	2
CABBAGE	3	24	30	2
CORN	4	30	30	3
CUCUMBER	3	30	30	3
LEEK	4	8	16	2
MELON	3	24	60	3
ONION, BULB	6	12	12	1½
ONION, SCALLION	12	12	12	1½
PEA	3	6	30	2
SPINACH	4	6	12	1½
TURNIP	4	6	12	1½

Watering   Blocks are made in a moist condition and need to be kept that way. Their inherent moistness is what makes them such an ideal germination medium. It is therefore most important that blocks are not allowed to dry out, which can result both in a check to plant growth and difficulty in rewetting. When blocks are set out on a bench or greenhouse floor, the edge blocks are the ones that are most susceptible to drying. A board the same height as the blocks placed along an exposed edge will help prevent this. Since the block has no restricting sides, the plants never sit in too much water. The block itself will take up no more water than it can hold.

To prevent erosion of the block, watering at first should be done gently with a very fine rose. If the rose is not fine enough, the mini-blocks should be misted rather than watered. Once the plants in blocks are growing, water can be applied through any fine sprinkler. Extra care in attention to watering is a general rule in successful block culture. It will be repaid many times over in the performance of the seedlings.

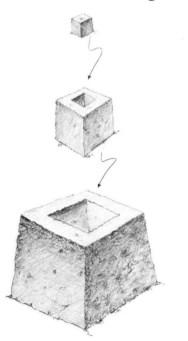

Potting On   Potting on is the practice of starting seeds in smaller blocks and then setting those blocks into larger blocks for further growth. Since most crops benefit from bottom heat to ensure and speed up germination, this practice makes efficient use of limited space in germination chambers or on heating pads. For example, 240 mini-blocks fit into the same space as only 36 2-inch blocks.

Potting on blocks is quickly accomplished in one-third the time required for potting on bare-root seedlings. The smaller block easily fits into a matching size hole in a larger block. The mini-blocks are usually potted on to 2-inch blocks and those, in turn, to 4-inch maxi-blocks.

The 2-inch blocks are easily potted on using the fingers. For the mini-blocks, some form of transplant tool for lifting the blocks and pressing them into the cavity will be useful. One of the best implements for this job is a flexible artist's pallet knife. It provides the extra dexterity necessary to handle mini-blocks with speed and efficiency.

Keep Them Growing   Potting on should be carried out as soon as the seeds have germinated in the mini-blocks and before the roots begin growing out of the small cubes. The less stress seedlings encounter the better. Crops like tomatoes and peppers need to be given progressively more space as they grow. They produce the best transplants when they are spaced enough so that their leaves never overlap those of another plant.

For ease of moving, the 4-inch blocks can be set on pieces of tile or shallow saucers and moved in that small "flat" as necessary. Or if they are set directly on a smooth surface, the best tool for handling them is a heavy duty kitchen spatula. It is easily slid under it, and the block can be safely lifted and moved. There is as much soil volume in a 4-inch maxi-block as there is in a conventional 6-inch pot. It grows a first-class tomato plant.

CHART OF SOIL BLOCK AND PIN SIZES

CROP	¾″	1½″	2″	3″	4″	PIN
BEAN		√√	√			L
BEET		√√	√			S
BROCCOLI		√	√√			S
BRUSSELS SPROUTS		√	√√			S
CABBAGE		√	√√			S
CAULIFLOWER		√	√√			S
CELERY	√√	→	√√			S → ¾
CELERIAC	√√	→	√√			S → ¾
CHINESE CABBAGE		√	√√			S
CORN			√√	√		L
CUCUMBER		√√			√√	S → 1½
EGGPLANT	√√	→	√√	→	√√	S → ¾ → 2
KALE		√√	√			S
KOHLRABI		√√				S

√√ = Recommended
√ = Alternate
→ = Potted on to

Standard Pin
L = Large
S = Small
Cubic Pin
¾″
1½″
2″

CHART OF SOIL BLOCK AND PIN SIZES (continued)

CROP	¾"	1½"	2"	3"	4"	PIN
LEEK		√	√√			S
LETTUCE		√√	√			S
MELON		√√	→		√√	L → 1½
ONION		√√	√			S
PARSLEY	√√	→	√√			S → ¾
PEA			√√			L
PEPPER	√√	→	√√	→	√√	S → ¾ → 2
PUMPKIN				√√	√	L
SPINACH		√√				S
SUMMER SQUASH		√√	→		√√	L → 1½
WINTER SQUASH				√√	√	L
SWISS CHARD		√√	√			S
TOMATO	√√	→	√√	→	√√	S → ¾ → 2

√√ = Recommended
√ = Alternate
→ = Potted on to

Standard Pin
L = Large
S = Small
Cubic Pin
¾"
1½"
2"

Chapter ❧ 14 SETTING OUT TRANSPLANTS

MOISTURE IS THE FIRST CONCERN WHEN SETTING out transplants. Soil block plants should be watered thoroughly before being put into the ground. At first, the amount of moisture in the block is more important to the establishment of the plant than the moisture level of the surrounding soil. The moisture level of the block allows the plant to send out new roots into the soil. Only after roots are established does the soil moisture become more important. Blocks should be very wet at the start and kept moist during the transplant operation. The carrying flats and transport rack should be shaded from the sun and shielded from drying winds.

The second concern is soil contact. The transplanted blocks must be placed lightly but firmly into the soil. Avoid air pockets and uncovered edges. If transplanting is to deliver all the benefits we've discussed, it must be done well. I recommend irrigating immediately following transplanting, not only to provide moisture. The action of the water droplets also helps to cover any carelessness when firming the plants in. Although the wet block planted into dry soil will support itself surprisingly well, it can eventually suffer from stress. Irrigation is stress insurance.

Consistent depth of setting is also important for rapid plant establishment, even growth, and uniform maturity. The blocks should be set to their full depth in the soil. If a corner is exposed to the air, the peat in the blocks can dry out quickly on a hot sunny day and set the plant back. On the

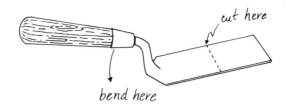

cut here

bend here

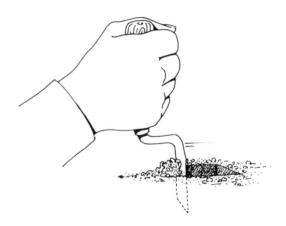

smallest scale, transplant holes are made with a trowel. There are a number of designs for soil block trowels, but my preference is for what I call the "dagger" style, which has an upright handle and a right-angle blade. It is jabbed into the soil and pulled back toward the operator to make a neat hole for setting the plant.

I make my own dagger-style model using a bricklayer's trowel with a 2- by 5-inch blade. I first cut off 2¼ to 2½ inches to shorten the blade then bend the handle down to below horizontal at about the same angle that it was above. I now have a very efficient transplant trowel for soil blocks. The same tool can be used to lift blocks from the flat, if desired.

When setting out plants, be sure to space them correctly. Accurate spacing not only makes optimum use of the land area but also improves the efficiency of all subsequent culti-

vations. Straight rows of evenly spaced seedlings can be cultivated quickly without the constant stopping and adjusting caused by out-of-place planting. The only way to assure accurate spacing is to measure. Stretching a tape or a knotted string is a perfectly reliable method (unless a strong wind is blowing), but it is also slow and tedious. A marker rake equipped with adjustable teeth for both lengthways and crossways marking is faster. A roller with teeth on it to mark all the plant sites in one trip is better yet.

The Studded Roller

For more efficient transplanting, the next idea is to combine the spacing and hole-making operations in one tool. If a marking roller is fitted with studs that are the size of the soil blocks, both jobs can be done at once. In newly tilled ground, this "studded roller" will leave a regular set of cubic holes in the soil.

A few design modifications can make this idea work even better. The marking studs should have slightly tapered sides (10°) to make a more stable hole. The roller should ideally be

11½ inches in diameter (you should be able to get a local metal working shop to make one for you). That gives it a rolling circumference of 36 inches. Then, if a number of stud attachment holes are drilled in the roller, plants can be spaced at 6, 12, 18, or 24 inches in the row. The roller can be made 24 inches wide, half the width of a standard planting strip, or the full 48-inch width. After the ground is tilled, one trip down and back with the 24-inch studded roller or a single trip with the 48-inch roller will prepare the entire strip for transplanting. The final step is simply to set the square block in the square hole. When placing the block, the soil should be lightly firmed around it with the tips of the fingers.

The above is an excellent system, one that I have used myself and have seen in operation on a number of European farms. It has just two small drawbacks. First, if the soil dries out between tilling and rolling, the holes will not form well. Second, the soil at the bottom and sides of the hole is compressed and could inhibit easy root penetration. These are minor points, but they make a difference. One improvement is to replace the blocks with small (2-by-3-inch) trowel blades. These are attached to the roller at a 15° angle toward the direction of travel. The rotation of the roller causes these "shovels" to dig small holes. Since the holes are scooped rather than pressed, there is no soil-compaction problem.

The next step is to improve the efficiency of the system from two trips over the field to one by combining tilling and rolling in one operation. This is done by mounting a 24-inch-wide roller with blocks as closely as possible behind the tines of the tiller. In this way the holes are formed immediately in moist, newly tilled soil. Compaction is avoided because the roller has become the back plate of the tilling unit. The soil, driven against it by the tines, is falling back into place at the same time the blocks are forming the holes. The roller is attached by arms hinged to the sides of the tine cover. Metal blocks welded on the bottom edges of the tine cover raise the roller when the tiller is raised at the end of the row.

With this one-pass tiller–hole-maker plus the convenience of modular plants in soil blocks, the small-scale vegetable grower now has a very efficient transplant system for all the crops in 1½-inch and 2-inch blocks. The larger blocks are transplanted into holes dug by hand. A two-handled post-hole digger is the best tool for setting out 3- and 4-inch blocks. One quick bite of the jaws leaves a hole the perfect size.

Chapter *15* WEEDS

I'M ALWAYS EAGER TO SEE NEWLY GERMINATED crop seedlings starting to poke through the soil. They are a sure sign that the growing season has begun. Tiny weed seedlings are another sure sign—a sign that weed competition is not far behind. I'm always quick to spot them and dispatch them while they're still small.

Weed Control

There are two conventional approaches to weed control—physical control or chemical control. Physical control involves cutting off the weeds (cultivation) or smothering them (mulching and hilling). Chemical control depends on the use of herbicides. In this production system, only physical control is recommended. I have too many objections to herbicides. For one thing, herbicide residues make it impossible to establish the undersown crops (the "deliberate weeds"), which are an integral part of the soil improvement program. There is also a great deal of evidence that herbicides have harmful effects on crop plants, weakening them and making them more susceptible to pests and diseases. But most important, herbicides pose so many known and unknown dangers. I believe that over the long run, all herbicides will be proven to be harmful to both growers and consumers.

Physical control, principally cultivation, is the weed-control method of choice here. Not only do I emphasize cultivation, but cultivation done with hand tools. First, let me stress that this is not the same old drudgery that farm children have always shirked. The tools I recommend are designed for the job and make it quick and efficient work.

A further emphasis in this system involves more than just the design and operation of the tool—it includes the approach taken by the weeder. Weed control is often considered the most onerous of tasks, and the reasons are obvious. Not only the tools, but also the *timing* is often a drawback. Too many growers consider hoeing to be a treatment for weeds, and thus they start too late. Hoeing should be understood as a means of prevention. *Don't weed, cultivate.*

Cultivation is the shallow stirring of the surface soil in order to cut off small weeds and prevent the appearance of new ones. *Weeding* is when the weeds are already established. Cultivation deals with weeds before they become a problem. Weeding deals with the problem after it has occurred. When weeds are allowed to grow large and coarse, the task becomes much more difficult. But weeds should not be allowed to become so large. They should be dealt with just after they germinate. Small weeds are easy to control, and the work yields the greatest return for the least effort. As well, small weeds have not yet begun to compete with the crop plants. Large weeds are competition for both the crops *and* the grower.

The Wheel Hoe

A wheel hoe combines a hoe blade with a wheeled frame to support the blade. It is the best cultivation tool for inter-row work on this 5-acre scale. There are two common styles of wheel hoe. One has a large-diameter wheel (about 24 inches) and the other has a smaller one (about 9 inches). Each style also has different means for attaching tools and handlebars to the frame. I have a strong preference for the small-wheel model. It works better.

I remember being told years ago that the advantage of the large-diameter wheel hoe was that it could roll easily over obstacles. My reaction was that if there were obstacles that size lying about the fields, I had more problems than the selection of a wheel hoe. The truth of the matter is that the design of the large-diameter wheel hoe is faulty. Human

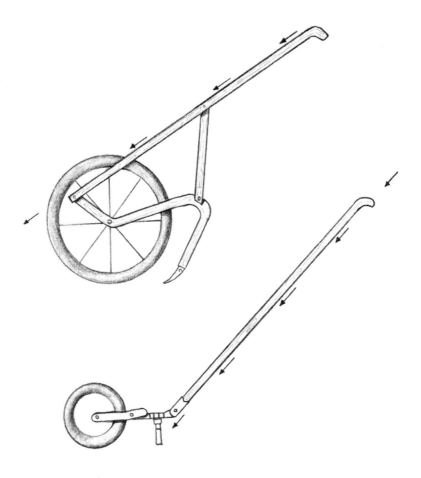

power is limited and shouldn't be wasted. In a well-designed tool, the force exerted by the operator is transferred directly to the working part. In the case of a wheel hoe, the working part is the soil-engaging tool, not the wheel. The low-wheel design transfers force much more efficiently than the high-wheel model. The drawings below illustrate the line of force in relation to each tool's structure.

The small-wheel model obviously allows the most efficient and direct transfer of force from the operator to the hoeing tool. Because the force is direct, a much higher percentage of the effort is applied to the cultivating blade. A further disadvantage of the high-wheel hoe is that a forward force is being used to manipulate a rear-mounted implement, thus causing torsional (twisting) forces to come into play that put even more strain on the operator. In sum, the low-wheel hoe is more accurate (easier to direct), less tiring (no force is wasted), and less cumbersome to use.

In recent years improvements have been made on this

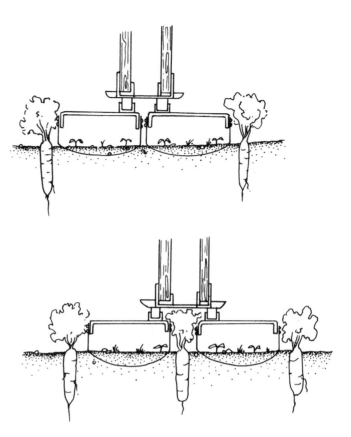

reliable tool. The heavy metal wheel of the old model, with its crude bushing, has been replaced by a lightweight rubber wheel with ball bearings. The original cultivating knives have been replaced by a far more efficient oscillating stirrup hoe which has a hinged action and cuts on both the forward and back strokes. When combined, these improvements result in the most efficient implement yet for extensive garden cultivation.

Oscillating stirrup hoes are available in widths from 6 to 14 inches. Wing models can extend the total cultivating width out to 32 inches. The wheel hoe can also be fitted with two wheels, allowing you to straddle the crop and hoe two rows simultaneously. As is evident from the drawings, the curved shape of the stirrup hoe blade cuts more shallowly next to the crop plants than in the middle of the row, thus sparing crop plant roots. The open center also allows rocks to pass through and even to be lifted up and out of the soil for later retrieval.

Stirrup hoes are double-stemmed, that is to say, they have a vertical support at each end of the blade. Because of this shape they are most effective when the crop is small or has only vertical leaves. To cultivate around and under the leaves of spreading crops, a single-stemmed hoe is necessary. Single-stem goose-foot and chevron-shaped hoes are available in widths from 5 to 10 inches.

Old-time wheel hoes were equipped with small plow attachments to turn a single furrow. I have never used one for plowing, but they are quite handy for burying the edges of plastic mulch and floating row covers. Wheel hoes can also be equipped with double-bladed plow bodies for furrowing or hilling up and with cultivating teeth for soil aeration.

Using the Wheel Hoe   A wheel hoe equipped with an oscillating blade makes for pleasant work. The operator walks forward at a steady pace while making smooth push-pull motions with the arms. The push-pull takes full advantage of the swinging action of the oscillating blade and keeps its

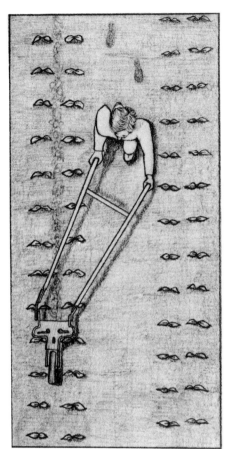

cutting edges free from debris. Accuracy along a row of seedlings is precise. The aim is gauged by focusing on one side of the blade (depending on whether the operator aims with the right or left eye) as it passes close to the row of seedlings. Ideally, the work should be done to a depth of only an inch or less.

A good wheel hoe will be adjustable at the front forks (A) to change the angle of attack of the blade, making it steeper for harder soils and shallower for light soils. The handles can be adjusted for the height of the operator (B). The height adjustment should be set so that the operator's hands are about waist level, and the forearms are parallel to the ground.

A further refinement makes the wheel hoe ideal for bed systems. Depending on the model, these tools are equipped with either a swivel joint or extension brackets through which the handles can be set at an angle off to one side. This feature allows the operator to walk alongside the direction of travel in order to avoid stepping on the newly cultivated soil. When crops are grown in a bed system, all cultivating can be done from the paths.

This blending of the old and the new in modern wheel hoes results in the most efficient hand-powered cultivating implement available. It permits a high level of cultivation accuracy (to within ½ inch of rows of newly germinating seedlings) in addition to great speed of operation.

With the precision seeder or the transplant roller described earlier, you can plant straight, evenly spaced rows. With the wheel hoe you can cultivate those rows right up to the seedlings. When used in combination, these systems do away with the major part of the labor previously required for thinning and hand weeding. The efficiency of these intermediate systems makes this scale of vegetable production just as competitive as large-scale, highly mechanized, and chemical-dependent systems.

The Long-Handled Hoe

The garden hoe that is well established in the public mind traditionally has a *wide blade*, a blade-to-handle angle of about 90°, and a *broadly curved shank* between blade and handle. The working edge of the blade is *offset* from the line of the handle. It is frequently a crude and heavy tool because it was designed for moving soil, digging, chopping, hilling, mixing concrete, and so on. It is this tool that has given hand

hoeing a bad name. A well-designed cultivating hoe, on the other hand, should have a *thin narrow blade*, a blade-to-handle angle of *70°*, a *slightly curved shank* between blade and handle, and have the working edge of the blade *in line* with the center line of the handle. This is a light and precise tool designed for a specific purpose—shallow cultivation. It is used as a soil shaver or weed parer rather than as a chopper or digger.

A number of considerations are important in hoe cultivation. It is undesirable to move excess soil, since this can bury seedlings or throw dirt on plants. The hoe blade should therefore be narrow and thin. The work must be accurate so as not to damage the plants. The sharp edge of the blade should therefore be intersected by the line of the handle. The work must also be shallow and not cut crop roots. The blade-to-handle angle must be set precisely. The technique is to skim, not chop, and the action should be fast and efficient, not tiring. The tool should be light, sharp, accurate, and easy to use.

Hand and Body Position   When using a hoe, the cultivator should be standing upright in a comfortable, relaxed position. The traditional bent-over position and resultant sore back is a consequence of the chopping hoe, not the cultivating hoe. Body position is determined by hand position on the handle. There are four possible hand positions on the hoe handle: both thumbs up, both thumbs down, both thumbs in, or both thumbs out. The last one is uncomfortable. The third is a compromise. The second one, with both thumbs pointing down the handle, is the conventional chopping-hoe position and results in bending the back. The first position is the way a cultivating hoe is held.

With both thumbs pointing up the handle, the cultivator can stand comfortably upright. This is not a new technique to learn, only a new application. Most people instinctively hold a broom or a leaf rake in the thumbs-up position. If one thinks of a cultivating hoe as a weed broom to be used with a

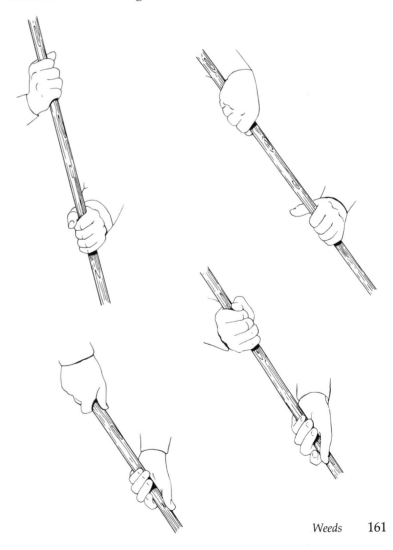

pulling or drawing motion, the hand position comes naturally. The hands are moved in unison to draw the hoe and are adjusted separately to idealize the working angle of the blade to the ground. These are very similar movements to those made by the hands and arms when sweeping or raking. With a little practice, the quick, accurate strokes that so effectively deal with weeds become second nature.

A Razor Edge

A dull hoe blade increases the work and lessens the efficiency of cultivating to a far greater degree than you might think. I have seen a number of estimates (depending, obviously, on how dull the hoe is), but I would say that even a moderately dull edge lessens efficiency by 50 percent. Like any edge tool designed for cutting, the working edge of a hoe (hand or wheel) must be sharpened. A number of different sharpeners will do the job, but I prefer a small file. It should be carried in the back pocket and used at regular intervals to catch the edge before it becomes dull. A hoe blade should be filed to a chisel shape so the cutting edge is closest to the soil.

Tool Weight

An average field worker using a cultivating hoe will make some 2,000 strokes in the course of an hour's work. A real go-getter might do twice that. In working with a wheel hoe, about 50 push-pull strokes will be made per minute, and the direction of the tool must be reversed at the end of each row. In any such repetitious work, the weight of the tool is an important consideration. If a tool weighs even a few ounces more than necessary, the effect of moving that weight over a day's work results in the unnecessary expenditure of a great deal of energy. A well-designed cultivating hoe should weigh no more than 1½ pounds. A modern wheel hoe should weigh no more than 15 pounds.

Wide-Row Cultivating

The widely spaced row crops are cultivated most efficiently with the tiller. The choice of row spacing when planting these crops is dictated by the adjustable dimensions of the appropriate tiller model. There should be 2 inches' clearance at least between the edges of the tiller and the crop rows. For example, a 26-inch-wide tiller carefully steered would be just able to cultivate rows planted at 30 inches. The depth skid for the tiller tines can be set so they run shallowly, ideally no more than 1 inch deep. For hilling potatoes, the wheels should be adjusted to the narrowest setting and the tilling attachment replaced with a furrower.

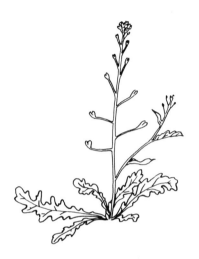

Long-Term Benefits

The emphasis on undersowing green manures in this production system obviously limits the period during which cultivation can be practiced. That is why cultivation must be done so well prior to the undersowing date. After that point the expanding leaf canopy of the crop progressively inhibits weed growth. When the additional low-leaf canopy of the undersowing is added, the inhibitory effect is more pronounced yet. The few weeds that do manage to grow, however, must be pulled. The grower should plan occasional forays through the garden for this purpose.

That exhortation may seem perfectionist, but with good reason. I remember reading an old grower's book, *Ten Acres Enough*, that was published in the 19th century. The author held a weed-free philosophy similar to mine and wryly noted that the neighbors thought he was wasting his time. His conclusion, on the other hand, was that the number of new weeds was smaller every year and that his diligence paid off in the long run. My experience is the same. I'm sure my neighbors also think I'm too thorough, but I haven't changed either. I want all aspects of my production system to operate at their best. I don't worry about the weed seeds in the soil at the start. They are a given. I concentrate on preventing those numbers from multiplying by not letting any that sprout go to seed. Since the undersown crop is a "deliberate weed" that benefits the system, it is the only weed I want. It may not be possible to attain perfection, but I will certainly approach a lot closer to that ideal if I try to prevent weeds from seeding.

System Benefits

One advantage of any system is the stability brought about by the practices involved. In a well-designed system the practices add to that advantage by complementing each other. For example, the two planting techniques presented in an earlier chapter aid in efficient weed control. The use of a precision seeder gives evenly spaced plants in straight, evenly spaced rows. That obviously adds to efficiency and ease of cultivation. Crops grown in soil blocks and transplanted into newly tilled soil solve a number of weed-control problems. First, the crops have a head start on the weeds, which are yet to germinate. Second, the crops are set at the desired spacing, thus reducing adjustments for in-row cultivation.

A Final Word

Throughout this book I have stressed the need for the grower to develop keen powers of observation. The use of hand tools in cultivating is an aid to keeping on top of day-to-day changes. An English naturalist once made a comment in reference to Robert Burns' poem, *To a Mouse, on Turning Her Up in Her Nest with the Plough, November 1785.* "Wee, sleekit, cow'rin, tim'rous beastie / O what a panic's in thy breastie! . . ." He said that in a modern age, the poem would not have been written because a driver of a tractor would not have noticed the mouse. The old horse farmer's advantages were not limited to mice and poetry. A grower with two feet in contact with the earth will notice more about the soil, the crops, and the general state of affairs than he could ever observe from the seat of a tractor.

Despite our modern motorized prejudices, hand tools, when designed correctly, are preferable for many operations. Good hand tools and techniques are not a step backwards. They are, together with the other practices I recommend, a step forward to a better vegetable farm.

Chapter *16* PESTS?

THE MOST RELIABLE TEACHER I'VE HAD THROUGH all my years of learning about farming has been my own insatiable curiosity. How do things work? Why do they work? Is this practice really necessary? Might there not be a better way? This attitude of persistent inquiry eventually opened up to me a whole new conception of the role of insects and diseases in agriculture.

Like most farmers, I did not find anything appealing about using pesticides. The idea of striving to create life-giving and nourishing food crops while simultaneously dousing them with deadly poisons seemed inherently contradictory. From the very first I sensed that chemical pest control was a blind alley. To me, the logical goal was simply to keep the pests from destroying the crops—and not necessarily by killing them. In fact, if the highly publicized problems with resistant insects and ineffective pesticides were any indication, trying to kill them was the least effective method in the long run.

Plant Vigor and Pests

As I considered these ideas, my curiosity about what was really happening led me on an interesting journey into an understanding of the natural world. From my earliest experiences in the garden I had noticed that pests and diseases were not consistent in their actions. The problem might be far worse at one end of the row than at the other. A certain pest would exist one place in the field and not in another. I began to notice two correlations. One was the seemingly obvious connection between how well I had prepared the soil (the cultural conditions) and the vigor of the plants. The second was the correlation between the vigor of the plant and its resistance to pests. When the plants were growing at their best, pests were a negligible problem. In short, it became more and more obvious that the better I prepared the growing conditions for the needs of the plants, the more resistant to insects and diseases the plants turned out to be.

To learn more about this concept, I spent many evenings in libraries reading through agricultural research journals. My observations in the garden were confirmed by the results of scientific studies I read about. Even though modern pest-control theory was preoccupied with killing pests, the opposite theory — that well-grown plants require no such protection against diseases and insects — was well established and backed up by hard data. For years studies had shown that excesses and deficiencies of primary or secondary nutrients caused imbalances that made plants susceptible to pests, and that such things as the improved root systems of plants in soil with ideal structure made them more pest resistant.

The practical application of this notion that *cultural practices affect plant health, which affects pest resistance* did not surface overnight. My increasing familiarity with the management of this approach took place during the years after I started farming in Maine. Learning all the ins and outs of creating ideal soil conditions to affect plant-pest relationships was a step-by-step process. The procedure was very simple. First, I would divide a field into strips. Each strip was fertilized or prepared differently. For a start, I tilled under manure, autumn leaves, seaweed, and compost, each in a different strip. Problem crops were planted *across* those four strips.

Where differences were noted, new trials were laid out. The following year saw strips of cow, horse, pig, and chicken manure, or beech, maple, oak, and ash leaves, or clover, vetch, buckwheat, and rye green manures. Soil that had been deeply aerated was compared with undug, mulched, or roto-tilled soil. I also sent off soil for testing to try to pinpoint the beneficial factors involved, and how I might duplicate them by other means. In short, I ran my own little experimental farm and developed techniques specific to its conditions. Every year crops grew better and I had fewer problems.

Plant-Pest Partnership

I was beginning to understand the intricacies of the plant-pest relationship, and the potential was exciting. It was clear that the biologically based production technologies that I favored (crop rotation, green manures, organic matter, slowly available nutrients, pH management) were instrumental in creating a more ideal mineral balance, soil structure, and root environment. Those conditions in turn were contributing to the plants' resistance to pests. There truly seemed to be a comprehensible system in the natural world, and I was enthralled by its potential.

Insects and disease, it turns out, are not accidental. They are not a whim of nature or happenstance. Insects and disease have a rhyme and a reason. They have their roles in the natural system, and they become destructive only when growing conditions are unfavorable to the crop. In effect, they are a well-planned, carefully designed reaction to the actions of the grower. If something goes wrong, the grower must realize that it is not nature's fault but that the blame lies closer to home. The grower has somehow failed in the performance of important duties — the correct preparation of the soil; providing balanced fertilization; ensuring optimum supplies of soil, air, and moisture; selecting a suitable variety; setting the best planting date; or some other contributing factor.

Insects and disease are not the only reactions to the grower's actions. Sometimes the plants are too big or too small, grow too fast or too slowly, yield abundantly or sparsely, are too tender or too tough. Similarly, the appearance and spread of pest problems are a function of the growing conditions.

As in any case where one is working within natural systems, there are occasional unforeseen irregularities that cannot be prevented easily. It rains for two months straight; temperatures are abnormally hot or cold; plants are grown under conditions against which they have no genetic potential for self protection; a plague of locusts blows in from the Sahara on the sirocco wind; or some other occurrence against which even the best-laid plans fall victim. Under normal conditions, however, when pest problems appear, my experience demonstrates that they are a function of something that could have been prevented by better preparation.

A Cause-Correction Approach

Now, thinking this way goes against our modern instincts. We much prefer to believe that it is not our fault but Nature's if the creepy crawlies eat the crops. It also runs counter to another instinctive human tendency—the love of quick solutions. Pesticides ostensibly satisfy that urge. They provide a quick but temporary cosmetic cure. By cosmetic, I mean that the symptom, the pest, has apparently been removed but the cause has not been corrected. By temporary, I mean that in the long run pesticides are counterproductive because they do not provide a fundamental solution. They do not prevent the problem from recurring. When the pests return they have to be treated again. The only dependable solution is one that aims at correcting the cause rather than removing the symptom.

There is a further benefit to the cause-correction approach. It is educational. A wise man once called insects and diseases the best professors of agriculture. Pests tell you when you are doing right by their absence and when you are doing wrong by their presence. By trying to understand the reason for their appearance a lot can be learned. There are many possible factors that might have contributed to the problem. If its solution requires no thought because it is something that can be purchased and applied without understanding the cause, then the chance to learn has been missed. If, on the other hand, the solution requires sitting down and thinking through the production practices of this particular operation to evaluate their weaknesses, then the result is a far deeper understanding of the causes and the courses of action that are open to do better next time.

Whether my success with cultural pest control can be ascribed to fortuitous circumstances, unintentional biological control, or some other phenomenon, I do not know. All I can say is that the idea works. My subsequent experience on three other New England farms confirms it. I have never found any need for pesticides once I figured out which cultural conditions were ideal for the crop.

There is still one crop-pest relationship that I haven't totally figured out—the potato and the potato beetle. But that is not surprising. These methods evolved while I was engaged in farming full-time with no resources other than my curiosity about the natural world and a conviction that there had to be a logical answer. I am equally confident that I will figure out this final puzzle in the years to come.

I am sure that readers unfamiliar with the idea may find it difficult initially to accept this concept of pest control through induced plant resistance. That reluctance is perfectly understandable. We have been brought up in a world where it is commonplace to attack our supposed "enemies" rather than to stand back and quietly determine whether they really *are* enemies in the first place. We tend to strike out directly, in an almost instinctive reaction to a perceived threat. Most of us have never been encouraged to think through the reasons why problems exist and what we might do to remove causal factors and thereby correct the problems on a more permanent basis.

Biological Diplomacy

This cause-correction approach to pests is fundamental to organic agriculture. The hard truth is that if you don't understand this approach, you won't be able to understand how organic agriculture really works, nor will you have any idea of its potential. Without this understanding, organic agriculture continues to be constrained by an imitative type of thinking that merely substitutes "organic" for chemical inputs. Too many organic farmers unconsciously accept the framework of industrial agriculture, while employing natural ingredients—blood meal for nitrate of soda, bone meal for superphosphate, rotenone instead of DDT. When done that way, organic farming works reasonably well because the new ingredients are more harmonious with the natural system than the old were. But it hasn't even scratched the surface.

What I am proposing is a totally revised way of thinking for the proper understanding of agriculture. We need to develop a biologically-oriented thinking that sees our agricultural efforts as *participatory* rather than as *antagonistic* vis-à-vis the natural world. It isn't a question of whether pesticides are undesirable or not. The fact is that they are totally superfluous. They were devised to prop up an agro-industrial framework that was misconceived from the start. When you abandon that framework, you can abandon its superficial thinking pattern. Don't start with industrial theory and try to "naturalize" it. Start on another plane entirely. Study the established balances of the natural world in order to learn how to nurture and enhance those balances for agricultural production. Pay attention to the existing framework of plant-pest relationships and learn how food production can be achieved through biological diplomacy rather than chemical warfare. The potential of such a new understanding is as yet undreamed of.

Chapter HARVEST
✿ 17

NOW THAT TIME AND EFFORT HAVE BEEN EXPEND-
ed to grow first-class, top-quality vegetables, there is one last
important step—harvesting. A good harvesting system involves more than just getting the crops out of the field. It
must also concentrate on preserving the high quality of the
produce until it reaches the customer. And it must do so
efficiently, both from a practical and an economic perspective. This is the grower's final exam. All efforts up to this
point can be wasted by a careless and slipshod harvesting
program.

Preserving Quality

Vegetable crops continue to respire after they are harvested.
That is to say, their life processes proceed as if they were still
growing. Unfortunately, since they no longer have roots in
contact with the soil to maintain themselves, harvested crops
have a limited keeping span. The length of time depends on
the individual crop, but the process involved is universal.
The higher the temperature, the higher the rate of respiration of the crop and the shorter the keeping time. The grower's aim is to slow respiration in order to maintain all the
quality factors—sweetness, flavor, tenderness, texture—that
have been achieved by careful attention to cultural conditions during growth. This is best achieved by picking the

crops efficiently and cooling them rapidly to slow down the rate of respiration.

There are two parts to the harvesting operation: the efficient organization of the actual harvest and the post-harvest treatment.

Tools and Equipment

Efficiency and economy of motion are important in all phases of the physical work of vegetable growing, but nowhere are they as vital as they are at harvest. Speed is essential. It keeps quality fresh and, as we have noted, quality determines the market. If the crop is grown well but is not harvested or handled properly, the earlier work was all for naught. Harvesting speed is initially a function of organization beforehand. The grower must assure that there are adequate tools—knives, baskets, containers—on hand. The key tool is a good harvest knife. Some growers prefer the California field knife with its large, broad blade. Others use shorter styles with a hook-shaped blade like a linoleum knife or a belt sheath knife with a 3-inch blade. In many cases, a choice of knife depends on the crop to be harvested. For example, I use a field knife for broccoli and cauliflower but a lighter knife for harvesting butterhead lettuce. I also like to have a wrist loop attached to the knife so it remains on my wrist even when I let go of it with my fingers.

Harvest baskets or crates are most efficient if they are of regular size and sturdy enough to be filled in the field and stacked for transport. For many crops, plastic crates with an open-mesh design are desirable because they can be dunked in ice water to quick-cool the produce. The truck, trailer, or harvest cart for collecting or transporting the produce must be suited to the job. A well-designed harvest cart will have the wheels and support legs spaced so they straddle the growing beds. For this system the wheels would be set on 60-inch centers. Heavy-duty cart wheels can be purchased from garden-cart makers. The wheel diameter should be at least 24 inches or more. The best "body" for the cart is a flat bed for holding crates. The pickers can then cut and crate produce directly onto the cart as they move down the row. This can be the same cart used for carrying flats of soil blocks during the earlier transplanting operation. It is imperative that temporary shade over the cart or a fine cool mist be provided until the harvested crops reach the permanent storage area.

Planning Harvesting involves a great deal of repetitive work. Repetitive work is made much easier and more pleasant when economy of motion is understood and an efficient working rhythm can be maintained. To satisfy those criteria you must evaluate the job from top to bottom. What is going to happen? How is it to be done? What hand and body motions are involved? Is it simpler from left to right or vice versa? It is always possible to find an easier, quicker, and more economical way to do a job. The benefits of such improvements are important in reducing drudgery for the farm crew.

Many studies have been done on simplifying farm work, especially harvesting.

- Eliminate all unnecessary work.

- Simplify hand and body motions.

- Provide a convenient arrangement of work areas and locations for materials.

- Improve on the adequacy, suitability, and use of equipment needed for the work.

- Organize work routines for the full and effective use of labor and machines.

- Involve the workers in the process. When people become more conscious of the way they perform work, their interest increases and their attitude toward the work changes. They begin to notice other things and make valuable suggestions for further improvements.

Minor Details Let's take tomato picking as an example. Studies have shown that the average worker does not need to work harder, but rather more efficiently. Comparative trials have demonstrated the difference in worker productivity that can result from very simple changes. A comfortable handle on the picking basket so it can be moved with one hand rather than two may seem like a small detail, but the increase in efficiency is considerable. Picking with both hands and keeping them close enough together so the eyes can control them simultaneously without moving the head speeds up the process. The hand motion itself is more efficient if two tomatoes are grasped instead of just one. Since 40 percent of the picker's time is spent moving the hands to the basket, the picking rate

can almost be doubled by learning the finger dexterity needed to pick two fruits at once. The technique is to pick a
tomato in each hand, shift the tomatoes back into the palm of
the hand, and pick a second tomato in each hand before
moving the hands to the basket.

The upshot of approaching the physical aspects of harvesting in such a planned and organized manner is not just
an increased speed of one particular task such as tomato
picking, but improved efficiency of all harvest work. Further,
once the grower and the harvest crew become aware of the
possibilities for making the harvest easier and more pleasant
by focusing on everything from individual motions to overall organization, the improvements carry over into other aspects of the farm day. Any work that can be done in less time
and with less effort is more pleasant and relaxing. Any time
spent thinking about and reorganizing for work efficiency is
time well spent.

Post-Harvest Treatment

The best and most complete information on post-harvest
treatment of all crops is contained in the excellent publications on the subject by the USDA. I have followed their
guidelines for many years, with great success.

Harvested produce should be neither immature nor over-mature, because in either case eating quality and storage life are impaired. Any non-edible portions such as carrot tops or extra cabbage leaves should be removed unless they are absolutely required for dressing up a sales display. Such large, leafy expanses present extra evaporative surface, hastening the water loss and loss of overall quality. The leafy vegetables that wilt the fastest, such as lettuce and spinach, should be harvested last and taken into cool storage immediately.

The first step after harvest is to precool the crops. Precooling refers to the rapid removal of field heat. Crops harvested early in the morning, before the sun warms things up, have less field heat to remove. Since any deterioration in crop quality occurs more rapidly at warm temperatures, the sooner field heat is removed after harvest, the longer produce can be maintained in good condition. Precooling can be done by immersion in or spraying with cold well water. The colder the better. A superior method, although it is more expensive, is to place crushed ice within containers in direct contact with the produce or spread over the top of it. Freezing units to make crushed ice sometimes can be bought used from restaurant suppliers.

After precooling, any produce to be stored should be kept cool in a spring house, root cellar, or refrigerated cooler. A temporary home-made "refrigerator" cooled by evaporating water can be set up quickly by using a fan to draw air through water-soaked cloth into the storage area. This will also increase the humidity around the stored crops. High relative humidities of 85 to 95 percent are recommended for most perishable horticultural products in order to retard softening and wilting from moisture loss. Since most fruits and vegetables contain between 80- to 95-percent water by weight, wilting can seriously lower quality.

At times it may be necessary to store different products together. In most cases this is no problem, but with some products there can be a cross-transfer of odors. Combinations that should be avoided in storage rooms are apples or pears with celery, cabbage, carrots, potatoes, or onions. Celery can also pick up odors from onions. Ethylene damage is another consideration. Lettuce, carrots, and greens are damaged when stored with apples, pears, peaches, plums, cantaloups, and tomatoes because of the ethylene gas that is given off by the fruits as they ripen in storage. Even very low concentrations of ethylene may produce adverse effects on other crops.

Chapter ✿ 18   MARKETING

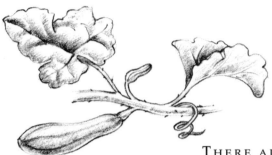

THERE ARE MANY MARKETING POSSIBILITIES FOR the quality-conscious small grower. The standard options are restaurants, farm stands, and farmers' markets. They are tried-and-true outlets, and there are excellent real-life models available to study. At one time or another I have used all of them.

Plan To Succeed

To do successful business with restaurants, the grower needs hustle and dependability—hustle in order to find potential restaurant customers and convince them to buy from you and to offer new crops, extended-season production, and gourmet items in order to increase the business once it is developed, and dependability to keep that business once you have it by never defaulting on a promised order.

The secrets to success at farm stands and farmer's markets are attractive surroundings, ease of access, cleanliness, orderliness, cheerful service, and early produce. Access to the parking lot must be open and inviting. The general level of cleanliness, neatness, and organization will be the first thing a customer notices. Make sure it speaks well of you. The employee or family member on duty at the stand must be friendly and informative. Make sure it is a pleasure for customers to shop there. Say "yes" to special requests whenever possible. Always make amends for any customer complaint.

Our guarantee was ironclad. We gladly offered money back, replacement of the vegetables, even double money back without argument. It is important that customers know you stand behind the quality of what you sell. That policy never cost us more than $10 a year, and it gained us priceless customer good will. Nothing is more expensive for a retail business than unhappy customers.

We planted perishable crops such as lettuce in the fields closest to the stand so customers could choose their lettuces and have them cut fresh on the spot. Free copies of the vegetable recipe of the day were posted to whet our customers' appetites. Customers were encouraged to wander along the harvest paths and view all the crops. Their presence encouraged us to keep up on our cultivation so the place looked orderly and presentable. A prominent herb garden inspired gourmet cooks. We also had our own "green stamps"—a cut-flower garden free for the picking to anyone who purchased vegetables.

We wanted our operation to stand out from all the others. We established a reputation for having everything all the time. We pursued that policy by raising the broadest range of crops and by using succession plantings. The broadest range of crops meant some forty different vegetables. Succession plantings meant planting as often as necessary to assure a continuous supply of each crop from the time it first matured till the end of the growing season. It was an ambitious goal, but a remunerative one.

Another marketing approach might have been to specialize in salad crops. That is especially effective if it is planned for year-round production. More than any others, salad vegetables bespeak freshness, crispness, and purity. What a successful drawing card that is for any small-farm operation.

Whatever the style of marketing, presentation is crucial. Potential customers will quickly become aware of the quality of produce you offer if your high production standards are matched by the inviting way you present your produce. The following paragraph from a 1909 book, *French Market Gardening*, by John Weathers, shows the timelessness of this good agricultural advice:

> Perhaps one of the most difficult problems connected with commercial gardening is the disposal of the produce at such a price as to yield reasonable profits. In this connection much depends not only upon the way the "stuff" is grown, but also upon the way it is prepared for sale. It is well-known that the very finest produce in the world

stands a very poor chance of selling at all, unless it is packed in a neat, clean, and attractive way. . . . Originality, combined with neatness and good produce, very often means remarkably quick sales.

The Food Guild   I was not dissatisfied with my market stand, but I think there is an innovative approach that will be more economically successful for the small farm, more satisfying to the customer's needs, and use less farm labor. I call it a "Food Guild." I choose the word "guild" because it is defined as a voluntary association for mutual benefit and the promotion of common interests. That is an accurate description of this idea. What I envision as the ideal marketing system for the small farm is a farmer-consumer symbiosis, a relationship that benefits both parties.

I first heard of this concept in 1980 from a member of the USDA Organic Farming Study Team who had recently returned from an information-gathering tour of organic farms in Japan. It seems that many Japanese organic producers, who farm on the scale that we are talking about here, found that the best market was a limited group of loyal customers. The farm unit becomes the complete food supplier to whatever number of families the farm production can accommodate—not just for a few products but to supply all the vegetables and any other farm foods over the course of the year. The customer families, who were signed up in advance, were encouraged to become involved with the farm. Everything from choosing varieties of lettuce to determining the number of roasting chickens per year was done in consultation with the customers. Thus they became aware of the source of their daily food to the degree that many would voluntarily show up in their spare time to help out on "their" farm.

I have since learned of many other examples of this style of marketing in European countries where the idea has a long history. In all cases the basic concept is that the farm has contracted with a group of customers to provide them with a broad-based diet of as many farm foods (vegetables, eggs, milk, poultry) over the course of the year as the farm wishes to produce. Obviously, the more complete the offering and the longer the season of availability the more attractive the program is to potential customers.

Under this system, the consumers of the produce become loyal and devoted customers because they realize the connection between their support for the farm and the farm's ability to supply them with top-quality, farm-fresh produce. The farmer benefits because marketing is no longer a time-consuming process. The customers have a dependable supply of first-class food almost as if they had their own private gardener.

Obviously, if one requires this sort of devotion from consumers, they have to receive an equal value in return. What they will receive is safe food in an increasingly chemicalized world. The advantage of our biologically based production techniques is that they are non-chemical. The guild customers will sign up because they can be sure that the farm's food is pure, free from chemicals, and grown with meticulous attention to detail. They need no longer concern themselves with problems of chemical residues in and on their food.

Starting a Food Guild

A "Food Guild" program can be set up for any degree of participation by the customers, depending on the desires of a particular group.

- The customers could help with harvesting and distribution as in a food co-op, or the farm could hire interested customers or outsiders for picking and packing.

- The customers could come to the farm (say, twice a week) to pick up their food supplies, or the farm could deliver to a centralized pick-up spot (in a town or city) or to individual customers on whatever schedule was selected.

- The farm could provide just the raw materials, and the customers would be responsible for any processing. Or the farm could freeze or can the storage items for the customers and provide them with the finished products.

- The customers could store out-of-season foods in their own freezers and cellars, or the farm could provide bulk facilities for freezing and storage that the customers could then draw upon as needed.

- There could be a specified list of products supplied each week throughout the year, and customers could have the flexibility to request greater quantities of one or the other item either by paying more or by trading off against something else: more Chinese cabbage, less lettuce, more chicken, or less pork.

The variations, refinements, and possibilities of a guild marketing program are unlimited. There are some approaches that may initially seem more workable than others, but the real determinant will be the desires of the guild participants. Some areas of the country and some groups will require entirely different arrangements than others. What we have here is a system of marketing in harmony with the biological diversity of farming itself. There are as many marketing choices as there are agricultural choices to accommodate different soils, climates, and locations. It is refreshing to think that this program could potentially be as individual to the farm as are the production practices themselves.

From my marketing experience I would suggest that the more services the guild provides, the more attractive the program will be in a world ever more attuned to supermarket convenience. Although as a producer I know that quality is my first consideration, I realize that for many potential customers — those who are not yet aware of differences in quality — service and convenience rank higher. If I want their business, I must take account of that reality.

Pricing The choice of the either-ors we talked about above would determine the price of the food and the level of service. Logically, the more services the farm provides, the more the food will cost. With the exception of the most personalized service, the cost should be similar to standard store prices for comparable items. But where items are more expensive to produce, their sale price must cover the increased costs. Since this is a mutually beneficial relationship, the customers will be cognizant of the vital importance of a local farmer to their own happiness and well being. A price must be agreed upon that will allow the farmer and farm workers a realistic income for providing such an important ingredient in the lives of their customers.

The biological production technologies I recommend are designed to keep small producers in business by lowering their costs. The resultant higher quality of the crops should further aid small producers by increasing their income. Food prices should reflect quality just as prices do in other consumables. There has to be a premium paid for quality and the skill and caring that creates it or it won't exist. If the small farmer is turning out a premium product, then he must demand a fair return.

Stay Small

These days, when a business succeeds there is always the tendency to multiply the success by getting bigger. Don't. That admonition may sound heretical given the dictates of modern economics, but my experience confirms it. I have seen too many successful producers make the expansion mistake. Without exception, they have each become just another company trading on the reputation they established before expanding. If demand exceeds supply, bring the two back into line by raising prices. Income will increase just as it would by expansion, but quality will not be compromised.

Chapter 19 SEASON EXTENSION

WE LIVE IN AN AGE OF SUPERMARKET THINKING where customers have come to expect out-of-season produce. The supermarket sells tomatoes in April and peas in October. In order to compete, local growers should attempt to come close to those goals for the period of the year when their marketing operation is open. For almost all vegetable crops a longer growing season is desirable if it can be attained economically. Vegetable growers can capture and hold new markets and receive higher prices by having produce available as early or as late as possible compared to unprotected outdoor crops. The grower meeting a local demand or running a market stand will find that a policy of "everything all the time" pays off handsomely.

The secret to success in lengthening the season without problems or failures is to find the point at which the extent of climate modification is in balance with the extra amount of time, money, and management skill involved in attaining it. When planning for a longer season, remember the farmer's need for a vacation period during the year. The dark days of December and January, being the most difficult months in which to produce crops, are probably worth designating for rest, reorganization, and planning for the new season to come. In any season extension, the aim is always to keep the systems as simple and economical as they can be without relinquishing the dependable control necessary to ensure the success of the protected cultivation. A broad range of options are available. This review will run through most of them and then recommend those that fit best into a small-scale vegetable operation.

Climate Modification

When considering the possibilities for extending the growing season, we should be aware of options other than building a greenhouse or moving south. There exist many low-cost or no-cost practices that can make a significant contribution to modifying climate conditions in the grower's favor. Any human modification of climate involves altering the existing natural parameters in order to achieve more than those parameters would otherwise allow. As a rule of thumb, the more we wish to modify the climate, the more energy we must expend in doing so. For example, growing tomatoes in January in New England obviously requires a far more expensive and extensive effort than merely speeding up the ripening of summer tomatoes by setting out the plants in a particularly warm and sheltered spot.

The simplest way to improve the growing conditions for early crops is to find, create, or improve such *warm and sheltered spots*. We can temper the climate with minimum energy expenditure if we work with natural tendencies and try to augment their effects. Three common natural parameters that are logical candidates for modification are the degree and direction of slope of the land; the amount of wind exposure or protection; and the heat-absorbing potential of the soil (soil color). Earlier I discussed land aspect and wind exposure among the criteria for choosing farm land.

Soil color is a third factor that adds to the effects of the first two. The beneficial out-of-season growing conditions created by the combination of a southern slope and wind shelter can be augmented even more by darkening the soil. Certain soils warm more rapidly than others, and this natural power of absorption can be increased. Dark colors absorb more heat than light colors, and soils are no exception. Charcoal, carbon black, and coal dust have all been used successfully to darken and increase the heat absorption of soils.

In an experiment conducted to test the way in which soil color affects the rate of heat absorption, 3 plots were prepared on a natural sandy loam. The first was covered with soot to make it black, the second was left with its normal soil color, and the third was dusted with lime to whiten it. Thermometers were placed at a 4-inch depth in each plot. By midafternoon, on a sunny day in early May, the blackened surface had raised the temperature at the 4-inch level 7°F above the normal soil and 12°F above the whitened surface. The darker soil also retained the heat gained by a few degrees at night. The emissive power of radiation of the longer wavelengths radiated by the earth is not affected by color, so the black soil did not lose heat more rapidly than the others.

Depending on the speed of growth and type of crop, the heat-absorbing effect of a darkened soil will diminish over a 4- to 10-week period as the plants grow and their leaves shade the soil. This is a harmless development, since it is only in the spring that soil temperatures need to be raised.

Plastic Mulch

The next logical step beyond charcoal dust is a simple sheet of material laid on the ground as a mulch to aid in warming the soil. Polyethylene plastic is the standard material. Plastic strips 4- to 6-feet wide and as long as convenient are laid on the soil with the edges buried to anchor them against the wind. Four things contribute to the popularity of plastics as a commercial mulch. Plastic mulch retains moisture, warms the soil, can prevent weed growth, and is readily adaptable to mechanization for application and removal. Both tractor-mounted and hand-cart-mounted implements are available.

Although clear plastic will warm the soil more effectively than black (the clear acts like a low greenhouse), black plastic is more commonly used since it also shades out weeds. Studies have shown, however, that the weeds under clear plastic are not a great problem. The increased soil warming under clear plastic and its benefit to the crop also counterbalance any slight disadvantage of the weeds. Growers should experiment with clear plastic, at least for the earliest crops. Ground-covering plastics are available in smooth-surfaced, textured, biodegradable, and perforated styles. The perforated style allows moisture to pass through to the soil.

Low Covers

The next step beyond mulches is some sort of low covering or structure over the plants. The advantage of these simple, low structures is their flexibility. They can be moved or erected to cover specific crops as necessary. Whereas plastic

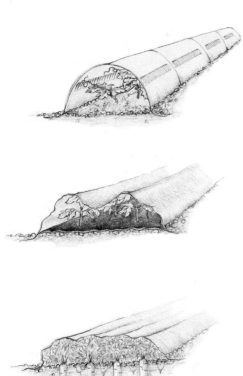

mulch used alone will justify its cost in earlier maturity of warm-season crops, in practice it is usually combined with a low plastic cover for even more improved results.

Lightweight, translucent, low plant covers have been used in horticulture for as long as the materials have been available. The problem that arises with any plant covering during the changeable weather of a typical spring is the need to ventilate the structures when the weather is too warm and close them up again as temperatures cool off. The extra labor and attention needed for such ventilation control can be a strain on the grower's resources. Recent modifications and new products have been aimed at combining cover and ventilation in one unit through slits or holes that allow the passage of air. These designs do not give as much frost protection as unperforated covers, but the difference is small and the trade-off benefit in the form of self-ventilation makes this idea very practical.

There are two common types of self-ventilating covering materials. The first is a clear polyethylene plastic 5 feet wide and 1½ to 2 mils thick, with slits or holes for ventilation. These are popularly known as slitted row covers. The second idea is a spun-bonded, translucent plastic cloth that permits the passage of air and water without the need for additional slits. These are referred to as floating covers. This is a rapidly developing field, and new products appear every day. I expect that future developments will supersede the design but not the intent of these covers.

The slitted row cover is laid over hoops made of No. 8 or No. 9 wire with the ends inserted in the ground on either side of the black plastic mulch. The structure stands about 16 inches high in the form of a low tunnel. The floating covers are laid directly on the plants, which raise the cover as they grow. In both cases, the edges of the covering material are buried in the soil as an anchor against wind. Since these structures are low and don't easily allow for cultivation inside the cover, a black plastic mulch is usually considered indispensable for weed control. For crops where a black plastic mulch is inappropriate (such as early direct seedings of carrots, radish, and spinach) the cover must be removed periodically for cultivation once the crop seeds have germinated.

Benefits Low covers offer much more than just frost protection. In my opinion, frost protection is probably their least valuable contribution, since it amounts to only a few degrees at best. What low covers do well is create a protected micro-climate beneficial to crop growth that does not otherwise exist outdoors early in the season. Low covers shelter the plant like a horizontal windbreak. They inhibit the excessive evaporation of soil moisture, allow both soil and air to warm to a more favorable temperature during the day, and maintain that improvement, albeit smaller, at night. They also provide protection against insects and birds.

Slitted row covers are labor intensive. I prefer the floating covers, which don't require hoops, are more resistant to wind, and maintain a more moderate temperature range. With reasonable care they can be used a second year. They are also available in widths of up to 50 feet, which allows large areas to be covered quickly, with fewer edges to bury to hold them in place.

Spring Use   Low covers can be used as early as the grower dares, depending on the crop. Since the covers provide only a few degrees of frost protection, tender crops like tomato transplants are more of a risk than hardy seed crops like carrot and radish. Many growers successfully sow extra early carrots under floating covers, which are removed periodically for cultivation.

Removal   Covers are usually left on for 4 to 6 weeks, or until outdoor temperatures rise. Removal of the covers must be done as carefully as any hardening off procedure. Partial removal and replacement for a few days prior to total removal is recommended so that all the advantages gained are not lost. If possible, final removal of the covers should be done on a cloudy day, ideally just before rain. Definitely avoid bright sunny periods accompanied by a drying wind, as those conditions will worsen the transition shock for the plants.

The floating covers are worth reusing over fall crops. This sometimes involves modifying the technology. When floating covers are used for spring crops, the covers will be removed before the crops mature, while with fall crops, the covers remain on the mature plants. In windy conditions this sometimes results in abrasion of the plant leaves, which can mar the appearance of a leafy crop. In that case, the film could be supported on wire hoops like the slitted row covers, or bowed fiberglass rods, so it no longer rubs against the vegetable crop.

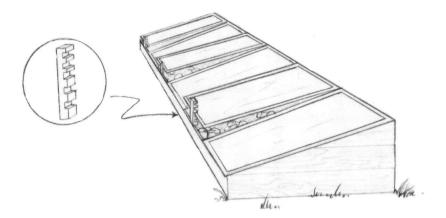

Cold Frames   Traditional low structures such as glass cold frames and their improved variants (Dutch lights, continuous cloches), with which I have had experience over the years, are not recommended in this system. Much as I like glass for frames because it lasts longer and (to me at least) is prettier than plastic, its disadvantages in extra work and initial high cost outweigh its benefits in better frost protection and ventilation. While I will probably continue to use a range of glass frames as well as plastic covers, I recognize that it is more for nostalgia rather than efficiency or economics.

If you want to extend the season further than is possible with low covers, consider stepping up the size of the structure to a walk-in tunnel.

Walk-in Tunnels   By walk-in tunnels, I mean most unheated structures consisting of a single layer of plastic supported by spaced arches or hoops tall enough to walk and work under. In design they vary from very lightweight units on the one hand to structures indistinguishable (except for the lack of supplementary heat) from a greenhouse. I have seen them 200 feet long, although 100 feet is a more common length, and 50 feet may be more manageable in climates requiring close attention to ventilation. Six feet is the usual minimum width and 17 feet the maximum, although most are 12 to 14 feet wide. In practice, the width is a function of the materials used, the planting layout, and the range in styles from simple to complex.

Walk-in tunnels are similar to a Quonset-shaped, bowed pipe-frame greenhouse. The materials, however, are usually lighter and less permanent, since tunnels are designed to be moved. Fiberglass rods, plastic pipe, metal rod, reinforcing bar, electrical conduit, and even bowed strips of wood can be used for the structure. In the lightweight models (up to 15 feet wide) the arches are made like large versions of the wire hoops used to support the slitted row covers. Their ends are inserted into the ground. Larger walk-in tunnels are anchored by pipes driven into the ground to provide support for the arch frame. The arches are usually spaced 4 to 6 feet apart.

The plastic covering is secured in a number of ways. For the 6- to 8-foot-wide units, the plastic can be pulled tight at each end and attached to a stake driven into the ground. The plastic just touches the soil on each side of the tunnel and is not buried. The arches hold the plastic up, and stretch cords run over the top of the plastic from one side to the other to hold the plastic down. Ventilation is provided by raising the plastic sheet up along the bottom edge.

The friction between the arch and the cord keeps the plastic at the desired height above the ground. Ventilation, up during the day and down at night, can be accomplished quickly with a little practice. Since a larger growing area is being ventilated per unit of labor, the extra management involved is more justifiable than for the low structures. Access to the tunnel is gained by raising the plastic along one edge and ducking under.

As walk-in tunnels become wider the design changes. The ends are usually framed up separately and include a wide door. In some cases the plastic covering is secured by boards attached 3 feet above the ground, along either side of the

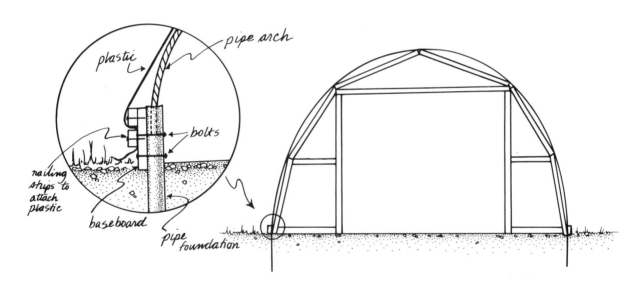

arches, and extends down to a long board lying on the ground. In this system, the plastic can be rolled up for ventilation on either side by means of the long boards. At night the cover is rolled down and the board is held in place on the ground by rocks or concrete blocks.

At the upper end of walk-in tunnel design, the plastic is attached to base boards as in a conventional pipe-frame greenhouse. The base boards are bolted to foundation pipes spaced 4 feet apart and driven 18 inches or so into the ground.

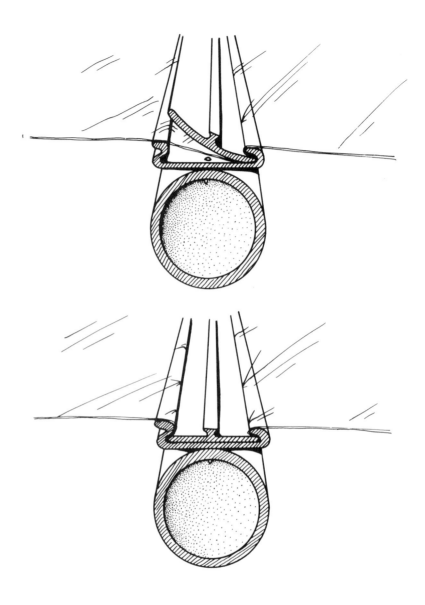

The interior diameter of the foundation pipe is slightly larger than the outside diameter of the pipe arch. The pipe arch is erected by inserting the ends of it into the foundation pipes. The arch rests on the upper of the two bolts that secure the base board.

In models without roll-up sides, ventilation is provided by large doors or roof vents. The doors are framed up as large as the tunnel width permits. The roof vents can be opened and closed by hand or by automatic temperature-activated

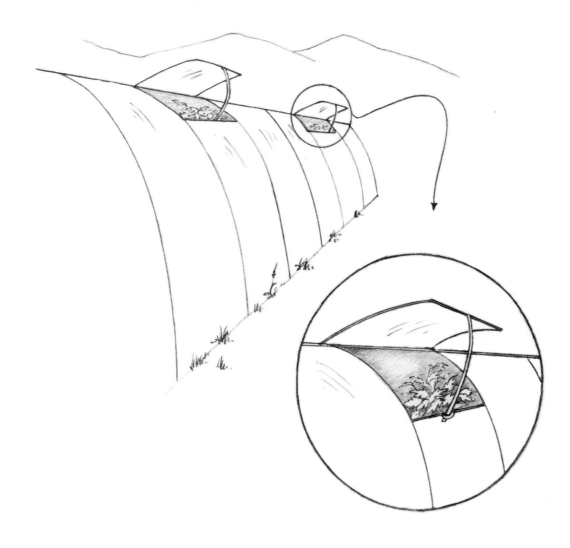

spring openers. The roof vents are an interesting construction in themselves. The desired vent sections are framed out in the roof of the tunnel, either with the same material used in the structure or with wood. The most common spacing is one vent for every four hoop sections. The plastic covering is secured around the edges of the roof opening, most easily with a two-part fastener (a hard plastic channel and an insert strip) attached to the edges of the vent opening to hold the plastic. The two parts snap together and provide a strong, reliable grip on the edge of the plastic. A lightweight frame for the roof vent hatch is covered with plastic, hinged at one end, and attached to the temperature-activated opening arm.

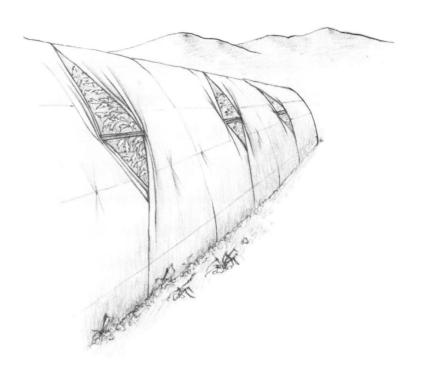

In protected areas, where wind is not excessive, a far simpler roof-venting system can be tried. Instead of putting the plastic on the tunnel the conventional way (lengthwise), the cover is put on side to side. For example, if you are using 25-foot-wide plastic, there would be a cross seam every 25 feet (actually, every 24 feet, since a 12-inch overlap to cover the edge from the prevailing wind is recommended). Venting hot air through the roof or sides is made possible by spreading the two seam edges apart and holding them open with a prop. Fancier systems use pull cords and pulleys to open and close a number of these seam vents along the length of the tunnel.

With any plastic structure, even when conventionally covered, wind whipping and abrasion can be a serious problem. No matter how carefully the cover is tightened when it is first put on, it always seems to loosen. There are two ways to deal with this. The simplest is to run stretch cord over the top of the plastic from one side to the other as with the 6- to 8-foot-wide tunnels. One cord between every fourth rib is usually sufficient. The tension of the stretch cord will compensate for the expansion and contraction of the plastic due to temperature change and will keep the cover taut at all times. The second solution is to cover the tunnel with two layers of

plastic and inflate the space between them with a small squirrel cage fan. This creates a taut outer surface that resists wind and helps shed snow.

The final step beyond these advanced walk-in tunnels is to add a source of heat other than the sun. At this point you have a greenhouse, so it might be better to deliberately build one from the start.

Greenhouses

The simplest greenhouse is only a stronger and slightly more complicated walk-in tunnel. The major differences are that the greenhouse has greater structural stability and provides supplementary heat. A greenhouse can be built of 2 by 4s and will look very similar to a house frame. Or it can be constructed in the same bowed-pipe Quonset design as the walk-in tunnels using a heavier gauge tubing. I prefer the latter style. Bowed-pipe arch greenhouses can be home-built or purchased in modular units that are simple to erect, lengthen, or move as desired. Pipe, being less massive and less numerous than wooden structural members, casts almost no shadows and allows a maximum amount of light to enter.

The two layers of air-inflated plastic mentioned above are commonly used for greenhouses. This air-inflation idea adds strength and utility and makes the greenhouse more rigid. The outer plastic skin remains tight in all temperatures and is not subject to flapping, abrasion, and tearing that single layers experience during windy weather. Furthermore, the stressed curve of the surface sheds snow better, and except in the heaviest storms, it will not need to be swept or shoveled off. When inflated, the two layers are separated by about 4 inches of air, providing an insulation layer that results in a 25- to 35-percent savings in heating costs compared to an identical greenhouse covered with a single layer.

Supplementary heat for the greenhouse can be provided by burning any number of fuels, but the most popular small greenhouse heaters, and the ones I recommend, burn natural gas or propane. They come equipped with a fan blower and are vented to the outside. Installation is relatively simple, and the units can be moved along with the greenhouse.

Energy is an important issue. Some growers may want to explore the greenhouse heating potential of wood, decomposing organic matter, passive solar storage, or some other fuel. I heartily concur with this concern. All I suggest is that you postpone solving the energy problem for a few years. My goal is to present a farming system that works, and you must decide at the outset where you priorities lie. Is this a horticultural unit or a forum for experimenting with new energy technologies? For beginners it is always a wise practice to use a dependable conventional technology because most of the problems have already been worked out by others.

Along with the provision of heat comes the need to mechanize the ventilation system. Thermostatically controlled fans and automatic shutters do the best job and are conventionally used in greenhouse temperature-management systems. Two-stage thermostats allow for different quantities of air to be moved, depending upon temperature demands, and will prove the most effective in precisely regulating the ventilation system.

Another piece of advice is appropriate here. Although the idea of two-stage thermostats, automatic shutters, and ventilation fans may seem overly technological and complicated, they emphatically are not. A greenhouse structure can quickly overheat to temperatures that are deadly to plants. A dependable ventilation system is crucial. Occasionally, such mechanisms may malfunction, and yes, they are more expensive than hand-operated vents or roll-up sides. But they are parts of a successful system, and that system works reasonably well. Any questions should wait until you have gained some experience with greenhouses. Once you are involved with greenhouse growing, you'll see the system makes sense. The rest of the vegetable farm will be demanding enough so that you will appreciate having some automatic assistants to look after a few details.

Cover, Tunnel, or Greenhouse?

I've presented a wide spectrum of technologies, from the use of southern slopes to automatic greenhouses, to help define all the options available for lengthening the season. What follows are selections from that spectrum that best meet the needs of the small-scale grower.

The growing area used for early and late production should have as ideal a microclimate for plant growth as you can create. If it can be located on a south slope with an effective windbreak to the north and unimpeded cold-air drainage downslope, those qualities will add to the effectiveness of the structures. Most important is a windbreak. The temporary shelter from a snow fence or windbreak netting can be used until it is certain where and what ought to be planted for more permanent shelter.

Low Covers

In my opinion, the floating covers are the best of the low-cover options. When used in conjunction with a black plastic mulch they offer dependable season extension for transplanted crops such as tomatoes, peppers, melons, and cucumbers. When used without mulch they can provide significantly earlier harvest for the following direct-seeded crops: carrots, beets, parsley, radish, scallions, spinach, turnips, beans, and potatoes. Floating covers used in spring and fall over early and late crops of transplanted lettuce can justify their cost on this crop alone.

Large floating covers (20 to 50 feet wide) are more efficient to use than the narrower single-row models. There are fewer edges to bury in order to secure them. Burying the edges can also be dispensed with by laying 20-foot lengths of ½-inch re-bar on top of the edges. The weight and the rough surface of the bar effectively hold the cover against wind lifting. The re-bar can be removed as needed, and the cover edges do not become as soiled or torn as they do when they are buried. This helps extend the life of the cover for future use.

In extended-season production, each crop requires a decision by the grower as to whether an earlier maturity justifies the cost. When growing for a local *multiple-crop market* (as opposed to a wholesale single-crop market) it makes most sense to use covers to advance the harvest just enough for each crop to supply the demand until the earliest unprotected crops mature. Once the outdoor crops are available, the economic benefit of protected cultivation disappears. When approached within that framework the amount of land to be covered is not excessive, even when many crops are involved.

Walk-in Tunnels

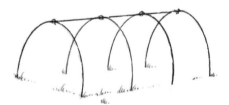

The recommended walk-in design is as follows. The width should be 12 feet and the length no longer than 48 feet for better control of ventilation. A farm-fabricated structure can be made of bowed 20-foot lengths of ½-inch fiberglass rod, ¾-inch Schedule 20 PVC pipe, or 1-inch-thick heavy-wall electrical conduit bent on a jig. The fiberglass rod is the simplest to set up and remove. One 20-foot length can be formed into a half circle with a diameter of 12 feet. Each bow makes one supporting arch. The ends of the rods are pushed into the soil to the depth of about a foot. The arches are set 4 to 5 feet apart and are connected by a ridge purlin.

I make a ridge purlin from other fiberglass rods by tying them to the apex of the arches with strips of rubber inner tube. The ridge purlin can be neatly finished off at the ends of the tunnel with a plastic T connectors used to join plastic plumbing pipe. The cross of the T is slid over the end hoop and the end of the purlin is inserted into the stem of the T. The minimum-protection version of this fiberglass rod tunnel can be covered with 20-foot-wide floating material. For a heavier covering use regular polyethylene. The edges are held down by burying them with soil. The ends can be closed by pulling the covering material together and securing it to a stake with strips of inner tube as in the smaller hoop tunnels in the illustration. For a more permanent tunnel, the ends can be framed up with wide doors for easy access and maximum ventilation. These doors are covered with a single layer of poly attached to the door frame at the top and to a board at the bottom so it can be rolled up for ventilation. A section of the two-part hard-plastic channel and insert-strip fastener mentioned earlier can be used on the side of the door frame to close the plastic tight in windy conditions.

If you decide to upgrade this tunnel, there are three logical steps. First, a small portable heater and fan can be included for frost protection at night and extra ventilation during the day. The fan is also useful, when the greenhouse is not being vented, to move inside air around the plants and prevent stagnation. Second, a conventional greenhouse heater can be installed and run with the thermostat set low (40° to 55°F). Fuel costs will be minimal, and this sort of arrangement is useful for cool-temperature crops in spring and for extending the fall season on tomatoes through October and lettuce to late November.

Third, if the heater is to be run for warm-temperature crops (55° to 70°F), then it pays to add a second layer of poly with an air-inflation blower to save on fuel costs. Unless the tunnel is to be run warm, however, a single layer is preferable. The second layer will cut out an additional 10 percent of the light and will not help retain the sun heat radiating back out from the soil at night. There are new infra-red reflecting plastics on the market that claim to hold in the radiated heat. I have not yet found them to be worth the extra cost.

Greenhouses

Of course, by the time you add air inflation and a heater, you almost have a greenhouse. For commercial vegetable production, a 17- to 33-foot-wide, 50- to 100-foot-long bowed-pipe arch model covered with double-air-inflated polyethylene plastic best meets the needs of the small-scale producer.

The smaller houses are an efficient size to grow in and are manageable enough to move when desired. Wider houses are even more convenient, as long as they fit a grower's production system. Three points will need to be considered. First, in a multi-crop production system there is greater flexibility with two or more smaller houses than with one large one. Since there will be different crops grown, each requiring

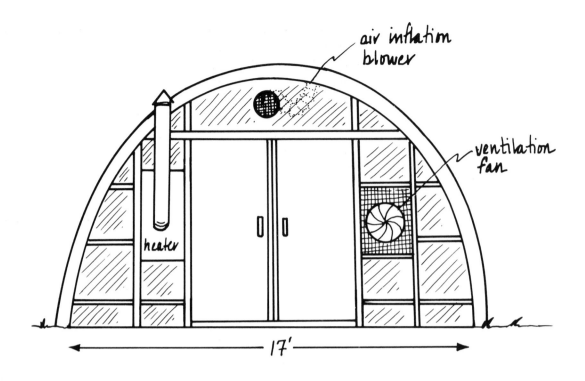

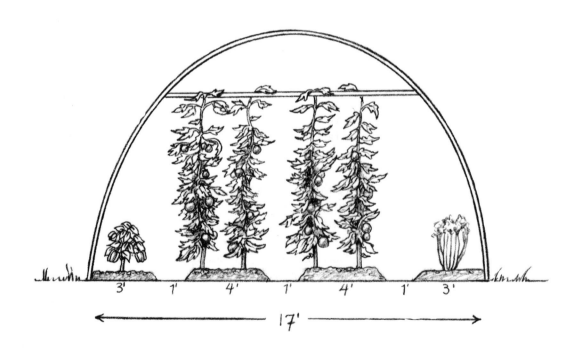

a different temperature regime, a whole house can be given over to one crop or a group of crops with similar cultural needs. Second, if something does go wrong, it will threaten only a part of the production rather than all of it. And third, a wider house is constructed of two bow pieces rather than one. This involves more time and complication when moving the house around. Some growers recommend moving a greenhouse to new ground every few years to renew the soil. Based on the equipment available and the grower's cultural practices, the necessity for moving houses should be decided on an individual basis. I have not yet found it necessary to move a house, provided I can rotate crops in the stationary house.

Growing in a Greenhouse

The aim of a greenhouse is to create *climatic conditions* that are optimum for plant growth. The same should apply to *soil conditions*. Plant growth is intensified in the greenhouse, so extra care must be taken with soil preparation. All the factors that were stressed in the chapter on soil fertility are triple stressed here. Compost applications of 100 tons to the acre are common for successful greenhouse culture. Greenhouse tomatoes and cucumbers are two of the most demanding crops and need adequate compost not only for soil preparation but also for a 2- to 3-inch top dressing every 6 weeks. Lettuce, the other major greenhouse crop, will do well in a rotation with either tomatoes or cucumbers without further soil amendment.

Out-of-season greenhouse production of high-demand crops is a valuable leader to attract customers to the rest of the farm's produce. It can also be a highly lucrative area of specialization in its own right. But it should not be jumped into without considerable thought. Growing high-quality greenhouse vegetables demands a real commitment to management and an attention to detail. Serious commercial-greenhouse production should be postponed until the farm is well established and more capital can be acquired. Then I would recommend it. Books with detailed information about greenhouse vegetable production are listed in the bibliography.

Tomorrow's Answers

The progressive grower always keeps one eye on doing a job and the other on how it could be done better. You should always be alert to improve both the practical and economical aspects of your present production technologies not in order to follow the future, but rather to lead it. The future can often be predicted based on today's patterns of development. The trend in season extension is quite clear. The pattern runs in the direction of making the structures lighter, simpler to manage, and more mobile.

The old-style cold frames had heavy glass covers and permanent concrete bases. Lighter-weight glass covers and wooden frames followed. The development of the continuous cloche added mobility by making the structure out of glass panes held rigid by a wire frame. In the next development, plastic was substituted for glass, and widely spaced wire hoops became the framework. All of the above had to be ventilated by hand. The slitted row covers simplified the ventilation problem through the use of slits in the plastic. The floating covers go two steps further. They eliminate the structure and incorporate the ventilation into the construction of the material itself. In view of these trends, it is safe to assume that the future will see even more refinements in floating covers. These might include better anchoring, more positive ventilation, and improved performance in light transmission and frost protection.

The trend in greenhouses has followed a similar path. The early heavy-framed glass houses needed a strong structure to support the glass covering. When houses began to be designed for plastic, the rafters could be spaced much farther apart because the covering was so much lighter. The metal pipe arch frames are lighter yet, both visually and substantially. This minimal framework blocks very little of the incoming sunlight and is easy to put up and take down, something that cannot be said for an old-time greenhouse. The logical continuation of this trend is toward an even lighter, simpler, and more mobile superstructure coupled with an even more stable (and easier to put on) air-inflation cover.

One fact that cannot be ignored in all of this is the temporary nature of plastics as opposed to the greater permanence of glass. Greenhouse plastics last three years, at best, before they need to be replaced. They must also be disposed of. If the use of plastics in horticulture continues to expand, concerned growers should make three demands of the manufacturers: recycling programs should be initiated so these materials do not end up in a landfill; biodegradable forms of plastic should be developed that decompose *safely* into the environment when their practical life is over; and resource-efficient forms should be developed that are made from corn starch or other renewable plant products rather than petroleum. If extending the vegetable season has to result in perennially expanding the plastic-waste problem, then the old-time permanence of glass for cloches, cold frames, and greenhouses becomes a more responsible, though expensive, solution.

Today's ideas were yesterday's improvements. Tomorrow's ideas will rise from today's problems. The best new concepts come from experienced practitioners and were devised to answer their needs. Once you gain experience, always keep your mind working on finding a better way. The next improvement for you as a small grower, and for countless other food producers, is waiting to be conceived.

CROPS FOR SEASON EXTENSION STRUCTURES

Floating cover plus black plastic mulch:
Tomato
Pepper
Cucumber
Melon
Summer squash

Floating cover:
Bean
Beet
Broccoli
Cabbage
Carrot
Corn
Lettuce
Parsley
Potato
Radish
Scallion
Spinach

Walk-in tunnel (early crops):
Beet, carrot, celery, cucumber, eggplant, lettuce, parsley,
pepper, radish, scallion, tomato

Walk-in tunnel (late crops):
Celery, cucumber, lettuce, mache, parsley, radish, scallion,
tomato

Walk-in tunnel (overwinter crops):
Carrots, mache, lettuce, parsley, scallion

Greenhouse (principal crops):
Tomato
Lettuce
Cucumber

Greenhouse (subsidiary crops):
Celery
Parsley
Pepper
Radish
Scallion
Summer squash

EXPECTED HARVEST DATES FOR SELECTED CROPS GROWING UNDER SEASON EXTENSION STRUCTURES: A SAMPLE LIST COMPILED FOR MID-VERMONT.

Date	Greenhouse	Tunnel	Cold Frames or Low Covers	Outdoor
2/28	Lettuce	Mache* Carrot*		
3/5	Parsley			
3/10	Radish			
3/15	Scallion			
3/20				
3/25				
3/30		Parsley* Scallion*		
4/5				
4/10				
4/15				
4/20		Lettuce*		
4/25		Radish	Scallion* Mache*	
4/30	Tomato Cucumber		Spinach*	
5/5	Zucchini			
5/10		Lettuce	Parsley*	
5/15		Spinach		
5/20			Lettuce Radish	
5/25			Spinach	
5/30				Lettuce
6/5	Celery			Radish Spinach
6/10				
6/15		Tomato Cucumber		
6/20		Zucchini Carrot		
6/25			Tomato	
6/30			Cucumber Zucchini	
7/5			Carrot	
7/10		Celery		Tomato Cucumber
7/15				Zucchini Carrot

*wintered over

SPECIFICATIONS FOR SEASON-EXTENSION STRUCTURES

	Floating Covers	Slitted Row Covers	Walk-in Tunnel	Greenhouse
SHAPE	Flat	Quonset	Quonset	Quonset
SUPPORT	none	#8 or #9 wire	electrical conduit, PVC pipe, fiberglass rod.	1½", 17-gauge galvanized steel pipe bows.
SOURCE	–	homemade	homemade or purchased	purchased
WIDTH	4'	4'	12' to 14'	17'–33'
LENGTH	100'	100'	48' or 96'	48' or 96'
COVERING	porous spun-bonded cloth	2-mil poly	6-mil UV resistant poly	6-mil UV resistant poly
LAYERS	1	1	1	2
INSULATION	none	none	none	air inflation
HEAT	sun	sun	sun plus portable heater for frost protection	propane or natural gas greenhouse heater
VENTILATION	open weave	slits	large doors, vents, small fan	exhaust fan, automatic shutters
ALIGNMENT	conforms with garden rows	conforms with garden rows	E–W	E–W
END CONSTRUCTION	cover buried in soil	cover buried in soil	framed for large door and covered with poly.	framed for door and vents, double poly covered.
DOOR	none	none	roll-up 6-mil plastic	wide opening double doors
SEASON	spring & fall	spring & fall	Mar. 1 to Nov. 15	year-round

Chapter *20* LIVESTOCK

ONE WAY TO DIVERSIFY THE FARM'S POTENTIAL marketing options and simultaneously improve soil fertility for vegetable crops is to include livestock in your system. Because adding livestock to the farm can increase the management load considerably, you should not acquire livestock until the basic vegetable-growing operation is firmly established. Even then, a lot of thought must be given to the added hours of work and the possible need for extra workers.

If you feel comfortable taking on these new responsibilities, the addition of livestock is the next logical step in enhancing your farm's stability and economic independence. Livestock can be considered as a separate operation altogether or as a part of the crop-rotation plan.

Free Manure Many vegetable growers keep livestock separate from the rotation, using mainly purchased feed for their farm animals. The stock are not usually kept for profit, but rather as a source of free manure. For example, if the farm has barn space, you might decide to raise dairy bull calves to beef market weight on purchased hay and grain. As a supplementary farm activity this is not likely to yield a profit per se. The costs will likely equal the income from selling the animals.

But the profitability must be calculated from the savings gained by not purchasing manure and the further benefit of having the quantity and quality of manure you need, produced right on the farm.

Horses

From my experience with different manures as fertilizers for vegetable growing, I would recommend horses over cattle. If the facilities were available I would choose to board horses for the winter. In many ways this may be a simpler option. First of all, winter is the slackest time in the vegetable grower's year, and the livestock responsibility would not be continued through the busier half of the year. Second, I could charge enough to feed the horses well and bed them on straw to produce a quality manure-straw mixture. Last, even if my return from the operation were only enough to cover expenses (I could thereby underbid other horse boarders to get the number of animals I desired), I would have produced, at no cost, a year's supply of what I consider to be the ideal soil amendment for general vegetable crops—horse manure and straw bedding. This fibrous horse manure-straw combination has been the preferred fertilizer throughout the history of market gardening.

The size of the livestock operation can be calculated according to the farm's manure requirements. In order to manure half the acreage every year at the rate of 20 tons per acre (as recommended in this system), a 5-acre operation would need 50 tons of manure. Since a horse will produce 15 tons of manure (with bedding) per year, that would equal .066 horse per ton. For a six-month boarding operation, that factor must be doubled to .133; .133 horse per ton of manure $\times$ 50 tons = 6.65, call it 7 horses. Boarding 7 horses bedded on straw for 6 months would give you 50 tons of first-class vegetable fertilizer.

Managing the Manure

There would be one problem to contend with. On the scale of production we are considering, I would be faced with a great deal of work managing that manure properly (by composting it) and spreading it on the field. However, if the stalls were cleaned every day and the manure added to a steadily growing compost windrow, the composting part would be manageable. Spreading that quantity of manure is a more formidable task. I have spread 50 tons of manure by hand in a year, and I've done it for many years of vegetable growing. Yes, it is hard work, but certainly not beyond the ability of most people. It is usually accomplished over a period of time, and in retrospect it is not all that difficult.

I will agree that spreading 50 tons of manure would be a lot easier with some machinery. Since I don't believe you can economically justify the expense of a tractor and front loader on a 5-acre farm, the best solution is to hire a custom operator. The difficulty, of course, is to find someone who can do the job when you need it done. If that can be arranged, hired machinery would be a viable solution.

Rotating Livestock and Crops

As I said, *were I* to operate such a program, I would choose horses. But there are other considerations which convince me that the first option, including livestock in the rotation, may be a better solution:

• Small livestock products such as fresh eggs or range fed poultry can be valuable as a means of attracting and keeping customers for the vegetable operation. The livestock-soil fertility combination will then contribute directly to farm income.

• The winter months are the grower's only opportunity for vacation. I guarantee that most people will be more effective the rest of the year if they take some time off.

• The ideal soil structure and organic matter benefits conferred by adding manure to the soil can also be achieved by growing a mixed legume-grass sod for two or three years.

• There is a livestock choice that will make optimum use of a legume-grass sod, provide a readily saleable item, not require winter care, and effectively produce manure and spread it for you in the process.

Poultry

The best livestock to complement vegetable production are poultry ranged on sod in the rotation. Chickens or turkeys thrive when run on short grass pasture, known as "range." According to varying experience, pasture can provide up to 40 percent of their food needs. In this option poultry are grazed on a green manure crop that is included in the crop rotation. In that way the legume or grass crop grown for soil improvement also feeds the livestock and they, in turn, manure the field.

Studies show that grazing a green manure results in a higher crop yield than an identical green manure that was mowed with the clippings left in place. There is a significant soil-fertility benefit from the biological activity of animal manure, even though its ingredients came from the field itself and some nutrients were actually removed by the livestock. If grazing is supplemented by feeds purchased off the farm, the fertility gain will be even greater. On average, 75 percent of the fertilizer value of the feed consumed is returned to the soil in manure.

Poultry on range thrive best when the grass is kept short and succulent, a stage at which it is also highest in protein. Grass can be kept short by mowing, at the cost of time and fuel, or by grazing sheep at little expense. Determining the ideal ratio of sheep to poultry to pasture acreage requires some observation and experience on the grower's part. It usually falls somewhere around 4 sheep and 200 chickens (or 50 turkeys) per acre, depending on the size and breed of stock and the productive capacity of the soil. Overstocking causes crowding and bare spots and should be avoided. You can always mow a little, if necessary. The first requirement in this range system is for some sort of movable poultry house.

The Solar Hen House

There are many ways to house poultry on range. Range-rearing systems were used extensively prior to the 1950s, and many styles of shelter were devised. When we began with range poultry, we modified those early designs to make the houses smaller and lighter so they could be moved without a tractor. We also built them with larger wheels for easier rolling. They were very successful, though they had a limit of about 50 chickens to a house. But they were strong and were secure at night against predators. We tried lighter construction materials, but they weren't predator proof.

It was the new woven electric mesh sheep fences that allowed us to make the next design innovation. The right models provide secure predator protection. Since this meant that the predator protection was now separate from the house, we could build the house from very light materials.

Our present field houses are larger and lighter than anything before and house 300 birds. They are also much less expensive. Because an electric fence provides predator protection from skunks, coons, foxes, and dogs, all the house has to provide is shelter. So what we did was to convert one of our plant-growing tunnels into a poultry shelter. The present design is basically a movable greenhouse for poultry.

The Hoop Coop

The hoop coop, as our solar hen house has come to be called, consists of a sliding base frame and a hoop superstructure covered with plastic. It is anchored to the ground with a short length of rebar driven in at each corner.

The base for the 12- by 20-foot coop consists of a pair of parallel 20-foot-long 2 by 6s set on their edges. The ends are beveled so they slide along the ground.

The superstructure is made of 20-foot lengths of fiberglass rod (it could be metal or plastic pipe) bowed into hoops the same as for the field tunnels described in the preceding chapter. The hoops are erected every 4 feet into holes drilled in the upper edge of the 2-by-6 runners. The hoops are covered with a single layer of plastic.

The doors are framed at both ends. The door frames hold the sides of the coops apart. The door shape is triangular, rather than rectangular, for greater strength. These triangular door frames are best made of metal pipe welded together in the shape of an A.

After the hoops are erected, the plastic covering is put on

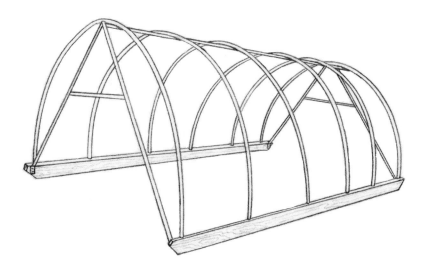

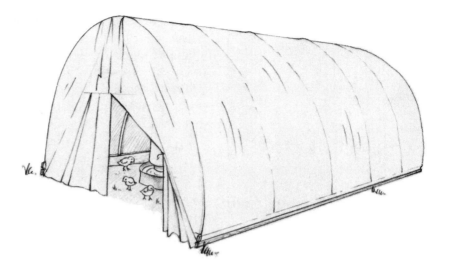

and attached tightly to the 2-by-6 base boards. The plastic is held on with narrow lath strips as described for covering greenhouses.

The ends of the plastic are attached to the door frame. You can use either the plastic inserts used around the edges of the greenhouse vents or sections of rubber pipe or hose slit lengthwise so they can be opened up enough to slide over the A-frame pipes and hold the plastic to them tightly. The door material (composed of the same plastic covering) extends from one side of the A-frame and closes diagonally.

In the mid-summer heat, two options will keep the house cooler. An opaque white plastic can be used instead of the clear plastic, but at the expense of losing some of the early-season heat gain. Or greenhouse shade cloth can be stretched over a clear plastic to block the sun. The shade cloth mesh also serves to protect the plastic from other livestock when they graze with the poultry. The hoop coop offers the following management benefits in conjunction with a range-poultry system.

Low Initial Cost   The two 20-foot-long 2 by 6s for the base frame and the welded metal door frames are the only special components. The fiberglass rods for the hoops are the same as those used for a 12-foot-wide field tunnel. The only continuing expense is the yearly replacement of the plastic cover.

Mobility   This house can be used on a wide variety of terrain. The house should be moved to a clean site every day. The A-frame door design allows moving even with poultry inside because there are no cross bars at ground level. The house is moved by means of a rope or chain attached to the runners. If the fiberglass hoops are reinforced with a ridge purlin like the field tunnels, then feeders can be hung from the hoop frame and thus will move with the house. Waterers and any outside range feeders will have to be moved separately, but that can be done every other day.

Cleanliness   The house itself is easy to clean because there is so little structure involved. The 6-mil plastic covering should be replaced after each season. The ground underneath and around the house is changed daily. All crops and livestock benefit from a rotation where they are moved to new ground periodically. A movable chicken house prevents the build-up of disease and parasites in the environs of the shelter because it never spends too long in one place.

Flexibility   We have used this design for range poultry from start to finish. The house is intended to be the only shelter necessary from the day the chicks arrive. When used for starting baby chicks, the grass upon which the house sits should be mowed very short. Ventilation is managed by adjusting the door coverings. With the doors rolled down and a brooder hung inside, the atmosphere is warm enough for starting baby chicks from about mid-May.

Simpler Feed   Studies have shown that poultry on good range will grow well on just whole grains and mineral supplements without the need for the complicated feed mixtures fed to birds raised in confinement. The grass, worms, and insects provide extra protein plus all the known and unknown ancillary feed factors. This can result in a savings of up to 40 percent in feed costs. If desired, the poultry diet can be supplemented from the garden with trimmings or unsold crops.

Less Work   This is one poultry house that doesn't need to be shoveled out, whether day or night droppings fall onto the pasture. Since the house is moved to a new location every day, the manure ends up being spread lightly and evenly across the range. When poultry are grazed with other livestock, bird-scratching helps to incorporate all the manures into the soil. Scratching also benefits the pasture by aerating the surface of the soil and encouraging the growth of the finer grasses.

Better Health Grass, insects, and outdoor living contribute greatly to the health of the poultry. Pasture has long been recognized as one of the most important guarantees of poultry health. Poultry raised on range do not need to be protected with drugs and medications like those raised in confinement.

Better Flavor And do they ever taste better! I have yet to meet anyone who doesn't notice the difference. There is no meat or dairy product that the consumer associates more with poor flavor and overmedicated treatment than poultry. When they are raised on clean grass range, the improvement is so considerable it almost seems like the meat of a superior species. Anyone who can provide the market with range-fed birds will find customers beating a path to their door.

Hoop-Coop Chicks

Poultry are purchased as day-old chicks, or poults, and are housed right from the start in the hoop coop. A brooder lamp or a floor brooder is placed in the house for warmth (specific details about temperature and feeding needs for baby poultry can be found in many books, extension pamphlets, or from the poultry supplier itself). In colder weather chicks can be started indoors then moved to the hoop coop when the weather warms up. Or you could provide supplementary heat in the hoop coop.

There are advantages to starting in the range house. First, the chicks identify with the house and will return to it at night after they are let out on pasture. Second, the hoop coop allows them to have that important early access to grass. The very earliest grass area for chicks should be clean ground that has not been grazed by poultry for the past few years. That is one of the advantages of incorporating poultry in a crop-rotation system where clean, new ground can be assured.

When poultry are on pasture, a simple but specific management schedule should be followed: in the morning sprinkle scratch feed, pull the re-bar anchors, move the house a short distance, and drive in the anchors again; in the evening refill the feeders and waterers. Feed can be provided inside from hanging feeders or outside from range feeders. Each has advantages. The inside hanging feeder is moved automatically when the house is moved. The large covered out-

side range feeder holds more feed and needs refilling less often. The waterers are usually set outside the hoop coop and moved periodically.

Poultry Plus Sheep   As mentioned earlier, poultry on range do best when the grass is kept short. Closely clipped pasturage is higher in protein and easier to digest. To keep the grass short, either mow it from time to time or graze it with animals. Sheep will do it best. To avoid year-round livestock care, sheep should be purchased as lambs in the spring, grazed during the poultry season, and sold at the end of the year. There is not much profit here; money saved in mowing time and expense is the principal return.

When poultry are on pasture with other stock, the feed should be available from inside the range house where the other stock cannot get at it. A few bars across the A-frame door will keep the sheep out of the house. A range feeder is no proof against hungry sheep, who will often knock over and spill it even if it is redesigned to make access more difficult for larger animals.

Fencing

The same predator-proof woven electro-plastic netting serves for both poultry and sheep. The simplest electric source is one of the battery-powered chargers. Since these fencing systems are extremely portable, the fence can follow the hoop coop to all parts of the farm. This allows any small or odd-shaped piece of the property, even lawns or brushy areas, to be grazed periodically.

Breeds

With sheep, you can use whatever breed is locally available. However, downland breeds, which are more pure grazers than part-browsing upland breeds, may be the best bet. With turkeys, the smaller varieties are usually better rangers than the larger ones. Of the large turkeys, the bronze are better foragers than the white, in my experience. With chickens, breed is a difficult but important choice. Certain commercially popular broiler crosses, such as the Rock Cornish, may not be the best. Their nutritional requirements are so specific due to their rapid growth that they must be fed high-protein commercial feeds. Although they do well on range as long as those feeds are used, there are few savings in feed costs because they don't take advantage of the pasture.

The most desirable chicken breeds for this system are active foragers. Their only disadvantage is that, although they are a perfectly nice bird, they don't provide the unbelievably plump carcasses of the hybrid broiler crosses. If those carcasses are what the market wants, then a grower will have to try out the different hybrid strains to see which one is most adaptable. For those interested in the older breeds, I recommend White Rocks, Dark Cornish, and Mottled Houdans. All of these breeds thrive on range plus a simple diet and reach market size at 12 to 16 weeks. The last two breeds are especially adapted to ranging and provide an ideal product for a market that appreciates the best in gourmet chicken.

Chapter 21 A FINAL QUESTION

ALTHOUGH I INTEND THIS BOOK TO BE COMPRE-
hensive, there is one question I cannot answer that readers
must answer for themselves. Until the answer to this question is resolved, all the best instruction in the world won't
help. Let me address you directly. The final question is,
"Why do you want to be a farmer?"

Why Do You Want To Farm?

I suggest sitting down with pen and paper and coming up
with some answers to that question. I've found that the best
way to sort out fuzzy thinking is to compose ideas in a
readable form. Is it only the idealized lifestyle that you crave?
A touch of "over the river and through the woods to grand-
mother's house we go?" Think carefully about whether a
desire to farm is a positive action toward farming or a negative reaction against what you do now.

Dissatisfaction with your present career, an intolerance for
city living, a sudden concern with a lack of excitement in
your life may generate that negative reaction. Future hopes
are often naively focused on rural life because it fulfills the
bucolic fantasies that we all share in the back of our minds. I
encourage thinking long and hard about what you really
want to change, where you really want to go, and why.

In a negative reaction, the would-be farmer has suddenly had enough of the city, the dead-end job, or simple boredom and jumps impulsively for the fantasy of fresh air and farm living. In contrast, a positive action stems from a long-term desire to farm, which may have been set aside for practical or economic reasons. Such an action is based on knowledge of the hard work and discipline that a career in agriculture demands. In a positive action, the move has been planned carefully and the farmer is only waiting for the parts to fall into place and the time to be right.

Whether the motivation is understood or not, there is one option that clearly makes sense — go and work on a farm. Try out the idea by laboring (and learning) with someone else. Experience the good times and the bad, the realities and the rewards. If possible, work on more than one farm. The more background and experience you can get, the better off you'll be.

The requirements for success in farming are like those for any small business — organizational aptitude, diligence, financial planning, the ability to work long hours, and the desire to succeed. Added to these are the need for the ability to work with your hands, a sensitivity towards living creatures, a high level of health and fitness, and a love of what you are doing. Farming offers a satisfying challenge found in no other profession to those who can meet its demands, overcome its difficulties, and reap its rewards.

Groups, Schools, and Institutions

My production system is well suited to the needs of organized groups that may wish to produce some or all of their own food. I highly recommend such a course of action, but the decision should not be entered into lightly by groups any more than by individuals. Before beginning, the organizers should ask themselves some hard questions. Is this a serious commitment or just a passing fancy? Is everyone willing to share in the work or is it going to fall on an enthusiastic few? Do we have the time and interest to carry this idea through and do a first-class job of preparing the land, planting the crops, maintaining the garden, and distributing or storing the food? For the organized group wishing to start a food production program, this book is a reliable guide. One of the long-time exponents of institutional food production is the Mountain School in Vershire Center, Vermont. Since its founding in 1963, the Mountain School has produced the bulk of the school's food as part of its traditional academic program. Those years present a clear picture of the benefits and practical soundness of participatory food production.

Food can be produced (1) with simple, dependable, low-cost equipment; (2) by interested amateurs without expensive professional supervision; and (3) by practicing an environmentally sound cultural system that stresses selected varieties, crop rotation, green manuring, and compost. The food produced can be harvested and stored inexpensively for periods when it is not being produced by using the facilities of the average institutional kitchen and using amateur labor under in-house supervision. Money can be saved; fresher, better tasting, and more nutritious food can be served; and the consumers can enjoy participation in the resource-efficient system by which their food is supplied.

Furthermore, organized groups, schools, and other institutions actually have many advantages over commercial operations. These advantages exist on the one hand because of the unique situation of schools and institutions and on the other through the mutual benefits that accrue from group efforts. First is land. Land for growing crops is not likely to be a limiting factor. On most institutional premises, a surprising amount of land can be found that is suitable for growing food. These underutilized acres vary from abandoned land overgrown with brush to extensive lawn areas presently requiring mowing and upkeep. If you visualize an acre as a square approximately 210 feet (70 average paces) on each side, it is easy to picture where and how gardens can fit into an existing landscape. The production from 1 acre can easily feed 40 people all their vegetables for a year. Or feed a far greater number of people if, for example, only salad or fresh produce is grown. Moreover, the entire area used for food production does not have to be contiguous. Production on a number of smaller pieces is no problem and may actually be an advantage where different soil types are involved. In short, land, the first requirement, is often readily available at little or no cost other than mowing or clearing. And in the case of schools, institutions, and charitable organizations, the land they use is tax exempt.

Next is labor. Most vegetable operations are dependent upon a supply of seasonal labor at specific times of the year. Arranging for and managing that labor is a major concern of the farmer. In a group food-production program, labor is provided by the participants as a recreational, educational, or therapeutic activity. No salaries need be paid since the benefits received by the participants (acquisition of a skill, exercise, satisfaction, better and fresher food) are the main rewards. Any labor problems of a participatory group will lie more in using it effectively and fairly than in locating it.

Third is marketing. On average, as I have stated earlier, I think that 50 percent of the success in an agricultural operation depends on marketing skill. That includes all the operations involved in the sale and distribution of the produce. In the case of participatory food production, the difficulties of marketing are avoided entirely since the participants provide their own market. This can result in a further advantage. Frost, hail, drought, sun scald, and minor pest problems can cause superficial damage to crops, resulting in a low price or no sale at all on the commercial market even though in all other aspects the crop quality is high. A participatory food production program would suffer no loss since cosmetic appearance would not affect its "market."

Despite all these benefits, food production by groups, schools, and institutions, once a widespread practice, has mostly been abandoned with the exception of a few unique operations like the Mountain School. The practice was abandoned because within the limitations of previous agricultural concepts, it was considered necessary to hire professional horticulturists and laborers to run the professional side of the program. Their salaries made the economic side uneconomic. That need no longer be the case. The simplified equipment and production methods detailed in this manual make the doers into the professionals whether participant, teacher, or supervisor. Food production can now be incorporated into any standard activity program at minimal cost and with maximum educational benefit. But it is more than just another activity. It is an economically productive activity, the end product of which supplies the otherwise increasingly expensive ingredients for a nutritionally sound diet.

L'ENVOI

Chapter
✤ 22

The miraculous succession of modern inventions has so profoundly affected our thinking as well as our everyday life that it is difficult for us to conceive that the ingenuity of men will not be able to solve the final riddle—that of gaining a subsistence from the earth. The grand and ultimate illusion would be that man could provide a substitute for the elemental workings of nature.

—FAIRFIELD OSBORN
Our Plundered Planet

THERE ARE NO SIMPLE SOLUTIONS OR SHORT-CUTS in this work. No panaceas exist. There are, however, logical answers. Viable production technologies exist that address environmental and economic realities. Some of these production technologies may require new ways of thinking, while others may appear to revive old fashioned or outmoded ideas. On closer examination, it will be found that the "outmoded" practices were never discredited but rather discarded during a period of agricultural illusion when science *did* seem to promise simple solutions and substitutes.

The production technologies of this biological agriculture nurture and enhance "the elemental workings of nature." They synthesize a broad range of old and new agronomic practices into an economically viable production system. These technologies are the result of a reasonable and scientifically grounded progressive development, not a return to the "old ways." This agricultural system consists of a series of interrelated plant and soil cultural practices which, when done correctly, are no more difficult, albeit possibly more thought-provoking, than chemical food-production technologies.

The information presented herein is as up-to-date as it can be. But it will change. I will modify my approach as I learn new techniques, and I will revise one practice or another. However, I have used these methods long enough to assure readers that they will not go wrong in following my recommendations. Still, all of you will want to change parts of this system. Not only will you want to adapt it to fit your own particular conditions but also to keep from getting into a rut. It is crucial to experiment, adapt, and improve. We owe a great debt to all those farmers and researchers who have gone before us whose work has either solved problems or has left clues that will help us solve them. All the information for further improvement is out there waiting for us to discover it.

The skill that most benefits you as a farmer is learning how to incorporate new knowledge as a productive addition to your present system. Do not hesitate to discard present practices when experience or evidence prove them faulty. But how do you decide? By what criteria can small steps or sweeping changes be judged? In the final analysis, the only truly dependable production technologies are those that are sustainable over the long term. By that very definition, they must avoid erosion, pollution, environmental degradation, and resource waste. Any rational food production system will emphasize the well-being of the soil-air-water biosphere, the creatures which inhabit it, and the human beings who depend upon it.

CHAPTER NOTES

Land   Some interesting books on microclimate are: *Climates in Miniature* by T. Bedford Franklin (London: Faber, 1945); *Shelterbelts and Windbreaks* by J. M. Caborn (London: Faber, 1955); and *Climate and Agriculture* by Jen-Hu Chang (Chicago: Aldine, 1968).

Recent investigations have shown that many soil-test labs do not perform very accurate tests. The lab I use, which is generally agreed to be one of the best, is Woods End Laboratory, RD 2, Box 1850, Mount Vernon, Maine 04352. If you want a second test for comparison, I recommend using your local state university soil testing service. If there is a considerable difference between the two tests, then ask hard questions of both labs.

Marketing Strategy   Some books that deal with the ideas of food quality as it is related to the use of fertilizers and pesticides are: *Silent Spring* by Rachael Carson (Boston: Houghton Miffin, 1962); *Nutritional Values in Crops and Plants* by Werner Schuphan (London: Faber, 1961); *Mineral Nutrition and the Balance of Life* by Frank Gilbert (Norman: University of Oklahoma Press, 1957); *Nutrition and the Soil* by Dr. Lionel Picton (New York: Devin Adair, 1949); and *The Living Soil* by E. B. Balfour (London: Faber, 1943).

Planning and Observation   Many of Helen and Scott Nearing's ideas and experiences as small farmers are described in their book, *Living the Good Life* (Harborside, Maine: Social Science Institute, 1954).

Further information on succession planting of greenhouse lettuce can be found in *Lettuce Under Glass*, Grower Guide No. 21, Grower Books, 50 Doughty Street, London WC1N 2LP.

Crop Rotation The most complete bibliography of studies on all aspects of crop rotations up through 1975 is collected in "Bibliografia Sull Avvicendamento delle Colture" by G. Toderi in *Rivista di Agronomia*, 9, 434–468, 1975.

The bulk of the University of Rhode Island crop-rotation experiments is reported in the following two studies: "A Half-Century of Crop-Rotation Experiments" by R. S. Bell, T. E. Odland, and A. L. Owens in *Bulletin* No. 303 (Kingston: Rhode Island Agricultural Experiment Station) and "The Influence of Crop Plants on Those Which Follow V" by T. E. Odland, R. S. Bell, and J. B. Smith in *Bulletin* No. 309 (Kingston: Rhode Island Agricultural Experiment Station).

Photocopies of almost any articles, studies, book chapters, or other printed agricultural data can be obtained by writing or calling the National Agricultural Library, 10301 Baltimore Boulevard, Beltsville, Maryland 20705 (301-344-3755). The copying fee is quite reasonable.

Green Manures The most comprehensive treatise on green manuring is still the classic *Green Manuring* by Adrian J. Pieters (New York: John Wiley, 1927). Obviously, good basic information is never out of date.

For a complete discussion of the decomposition of green manures in the soil, see *Soil Microbiology* by Selman A. Waksman (New York: John Wiley, 1952). *Soil Micro-Organisms and Higher Plants* by N. A. Krasilnikov, 1958, which is available from the U.S. Department of Commerce, 5285 Port Royal Road, Springfield, Virginia 22161, provides an amazing wealth of information about the effects of different crops on soil properties.

Tillage An excellent bibliography is the "Annotated Bibliography on Soil Compaction" available from the American Society of Agricultural Engineers, 2950 Niles Road, Saint Joseph, Michigan 49085-9659.

The book that first inspired me to think in terms of surface cultivation was *Intensive Gardening* by Dalziel O'Brien (London: Faber, 1956). It is also a first-class work on the subjects of small-scale growing, compost, soil fertility, and labor management.

Soil Fertility

There are a large number of books, pamphlets, and theories on composting. For the extra-fine compost used in blocking mixes, I follow the procedures suggested by Dalziel O'Brien in *Intensive Gardening*, cited above. For farm-scale composting, I make windrows by winging the materials out of the back of a manure spreader. There is an excellent presentation of all the imaginable material on the benefits of organic soil amendments in Krasilnikov's *Soil Micro-Organisms and Higher Plants*, cited above.

Powdered or pelleted soil amendments need to be spread evenly. At one time or another, I have used the following methods: (1) Mix them together with compost or manure, and (2) spread with a metered spreader, such as the Gandy, which can be adjusted for accurate coverage. I recommend the latter. A four-foot-wide Gandy spreader is easy to pull or tow with the walking tractor and allows for accurate spreading at almost any rate of application.

For very light applications of trace elements, use a hand-cranked, chest-mounted seeder filled with the soil amendment rather than seed.

Composts and manures can be successfully applied over the green manures in late fall. The green manures will take up any nutrients leached, but this should be minimal during the winter where the ground is frozen. In warmer areas, the growth of hardy-winter green manures will benefit from the manure or compost application.

Pests?

This chapter stresses my belief that the emphasis in farming must be redirected toward practices that enhance the vitality of the crops rather than chemicals to destroy the pests. I am aware that this approach will be taken only as an "ideal" of pest control by many people. I expect some readers would rather I concentrated on providing "magic organic solutions" for instant relief. Those in need of such help will find many books specializing in that approach. One of them is *The Encyclopedia of Natural Insect and Disease Control*, edited by Roger Yepsen (Emmaus: Rodale Press, 1984).

For my part I suggest below a few temporary palliatives I have used reluctantly. But I make these suggestions knowing that on the occasions I've used such palliatives, they were a temporary stop-gap rather than a long-term answer. I make no apology for treating "natural" pest-control agents so cavalierly. They don't solve the basic problem. Like chemical pesticides, they treat the symptom rather than correcting the cause.

If you read the toxicity data on many natural pesticides, you will learn that it is hard to defend them as safer for humans to use. Both rotenone and nicotine products are toxic to most animals. Diatomaceous earth contains high levels of free silica, which damages the lungs and can cause silicosis. Precautions should be taken when using any of them. The safety factor in using "natural products" is that they do occur in nature, do not persist, and do not leave man-made chemical residues in the environment. I recommend considering the residue issue for any products you intend to apply.

I have used rotenone to control potato beetles and it works reasonably well. The new bacillus thuringiensis strains also appear to be effective in early trials. I have used finely ground rock powders like basalt dust as an innert pesticide by dusting them over the plants. (Basalt is safer for you than diatomaceous earth because it contains almost no free silica.) These finely ground powders are very effective in dry weather. In contact with the insect, they either adsorb or wear off the exterior wax layer that protects the insect skeleton and the insect dries out. There are no residue problems since Basalt dust is also used as a slow-release soil amendment.

Vacuum collection of insects is an effective measure, especially against Japanese beetles. A standard shop vacuum can be used on a small scale. Commercial-scale bug vacuums have recently been developed for tractor use.

Strongly flavored or astringent substances such as garlic and horseradish extracts or tannic acid can also be effective as repellents that prevent the insects from eating the plants. The floating row covers described in the season-extension chapter work quite well as physical barriers providing they are placed over the crop before the insects arrive. Unfortunately, none of these are selective and will inhibit the beneficial as well as the harmful insects. They can be effective only as a *temporary* measure. The long-term solution is to learn how to grow the plants correctly so you don't need palliatives the next time around.

Harvest A good (although dated) book on farm work efficiency is *Farm Work Simplification* by L. M. Vaughan and L. S. Hardin (New York: John Wiley, 1949).

Season Extension A good book for those getting started in greenhouse vegetable production is *Greenhouse Tomatoes, Lettuce and Cucumbers* by S. H. Wittwer and S. Honma (East Lansing: Michigan State University Press, 1979).

For a manual of general information on all aspects of greenhouses, see *Greenhouse Engineering* by Robert A. Aldrich and John W. Bartok, Jr. (Storrs: University of Connecticut, undated). Other books are listed in the bibliography.

ANNOTATED BIBLIOGRAPHY

Contemporary Sources of Information

A common characteristic of many successful organic growers is that they learned what they know without outside help. They managed to decipher the whys and wherefores of biological systems on their own plucky initiative. This prevalence of self-education is not surprising, since so little *specific* instructional material and consultation has been available. In such a situation the best teachers, after experience, are good, basic, *general* reference sources on soils, plants, and techniques. The information can be interpreted to meet the grower's specific needs. These books are not light reading, but they do offer a wealth of useful ideas and can provide the "hard data" that serve as the springboards to improved performance.

Balls, R., *Horticultural Engineering Technology*. London and New York: MacMillan, 1985. This book, along with M.F.J. Hawker and J.F. Keenlyside's *Horticultural Machinery* and John Robertson's *Mechanising Vegetable Production* (see below), are valuable both as background on how things work and as sources of ideas for home-fabricated solutions to the same tasks on a smaller scale. As a handy old Maine neighbor used to tell me, "Wal, if you can give me an idea what you want, I 'spect I can gump something up for ya." Good inspirational books for "gumpers."

Bleasdale, J. K. A., *Plant Physiology in Relation to Horticulture*. London: MacMillan, 1984. It is always nice to know what is going on behind the scenes. This book has all the "inside" information. A lot heavier going than the Bleasdale books below, but well worth the trouble for the hard facts and excellent bibliographic references.

Bleasdale, J. K. A., P. J. Salter, and others, *Know and Grow Vegetables, I and II*. London and New York: Oxford University Press, 1979 and 1982. Wonderful little books for the amateur as well as the budding professional. The authors, from the National Vegetable Research Station in England, obviously like their subject and delight in providing the reader with first-class information both from their experience and their experiments.

Bunt, A. C., *Modern Potting Composts*. University Park: Pennsylvania State University Press, 1976. To an Englishman like Bunt, potting composts is the term for potting soils. This is my favorite of all the books I consulted on the subject. Everything you ever wanted to know.

Flegmann, A. W., and Raymond A. T. George. *Soils and Other Growth Media*. London and New York: MacMillan, 1979. The heaviest of the bunch, but still worth having as a reference work.

Fordham, R., and A. G. Biggs, *Principles of Vegetable Crop Production*. London: William Collins Sons (distributed in USA by Sheridan House, Inc.), 1985. Very complete and not overly dry. Lots of little tidbits of useful information tucked here and there.

Grower Guides: No. 3, *Peppers and Aubergines*; No. 7, *Plastic Mulches for Vegetable Production*; No. 10, *Blocks for Transplants*; No. 21, *Lettuce Under Glass*; No. 26, *Vegetables Under Glass*. Parts of a continuing series published by Grower Books, 50 Doughty Street, London, WC1N 2LP (Telephone 01-405-7135). These are consistently informative booklets, usually under 100 pages, which do a thorough job of treating each individual subject. New titles appear frequently.

Hawker, M. F. J., and J. F. Keenlyside, *Horticultural Machinery*. New York: Longman, 1985. See my comments under R. Balls (above).

Mastalertz, John W., *The Greenhouse Environment*. New York: John Wiley, 1977. A complete factual presentation of all aspects of greenhouse growing.

Ministry of Agriculture, Fisheries and Food, *Plant Physiological Disorders*, Reference Book 223. London: Her Majesty's Stationary Office, 1985. Problems do occasionally arise, even for the best of us. When they do, books like this—and J.B.D. Robinson's and Roorda van Eysinga and Smilde's (below), are nice "consultants" to have on hand. Clear color photos, detailed diagnoses, solid advice, and excellent references make these books a worthwhile investment for the serious grower.

Nelson, Paul V., *Greenhouse Operation and Management*. Reston, VA: Reston Publishing, 1978. A complete presentation of all aspects of greenhouse growing.

Robertson, John, *Mechanising Vegetable Production*. Ipswich, Suffolk, England: Farming Press, 1978. See my comments under R. Balls (above).

Robinson, D. W., and J. G. D. Lamb, editors, *Peat in Horticulture*.

New York: Academic Press, 1975. Everything you ever wanted to know about peat, all its uses and horticultural qualities.

Robinson, J. B. D., general editor, *Diagnosis of Mineral Disorder in Plants, Volume I–Principles, Volume II–Vegetables, Volume III–Glasshouse Crops*. London: Her Majesty's Stationary Office, 1983, 1983, 1987.

Roorda van Eysinga, J. P. N. L., and K. W. Smilde, *Nutritional Disorders in Glasshouse Tomatoes, Cucumbers and Lettuce*. Wageningen, The Netherlands: Centre for Agricultural Publishing and Documentation, 1981.

Tite, R. L., *Growing Tomatoes: A Greenhouse Guide*. London: Her Majesty's Stationary Office, 1983. This is a British ADAS (extension) publication. A very well-done, small (32 pages) introductory booklet that will help any greenhouse tomato grower get off on the right foot.

Wittwer, S.H., and S. Honma, *Greenhouse Tomatoes, Lettuce and Cucumbers*. East Lansing: Michigan State University Press, 1979. A shade dated but still good basic information. This is the book I started with.

Classic Sources For The Organic Grower

Here is a listing of those "classic" sources that I believe most merit the attention of serious growers. Many of these are out of print, especially the classic English sources. I've noted which titles have been recently reprinted. Most of the rest can be found in a good library.

As you might expect, the authors of these books do not always agree with each other. Some have written on the periphery of biological agriculture, while others were deeply involved and knowledgeable practitioners. It is important to read critically, check references, compare, and see what the other side has to say in order not to become, like so many proselytizers of a new idea, "a man of vast and varied misinformation."

Albrecht, William A., *Soil Fertility and Animal Health*. Webster City, IA: Fred Hahne, 1958. An outstanding survey of the subject by the most respected American exponent of intelligent farming. Albrecht begins with an old quote, "All flesh is grass," and proceeds to demonstrate the importance of the quality of that grass to animal health.

Aubert, Claude, *L'Agriculture Biologique*. Paris: LeCourrier du Livre, 1970. An able presentation of the case by a leading European expert. In French.

Baker, C. Alma, *The Labouring Earth*. London: Heath Cranton, 1940. A survey of agriculture from the bio-dynamic point of view.

Balfour, Lady Eve, *The Living Soil*. London: Faber, 1943. The important early work by a founder of the Soil Association. Lady Eve documents the evidence for biological agriculture. A fine book that should be in everyone's library. Reprinted 1975.

> *It would save much confusion if we all adopted the name "biological farming" rather than "organic farming." We should then keep the emphasis where it belongs, on the fostering of life and on biological balance, and not on just one of the techniques for achieving this, which, if narrowly interpreted, may be effective only in a certain set of circumstances.*
> Lady Eve Balfour, *The Journal of the Soil Association,*
> January 1954

Billington, F. H., *Compost for Garden Plot or Thousand Acre Farm.* London: Faber, 1943. An early work giving thorough treatment to all aspects of composting. Five specific methods are described in detail. There is also a more recent edition revised and co-authored by Ben Easey.

Blake, Michael, *Concentrated Incomplete Fertilizers.* London: Crosby Lockwood, 1966. A discussion of the faults and consequent abuses of chemical fertilizers.

Bromfield, Louis, *Pleasant Valley.* New York: Harper, 1946. This is the first of Bromfield's farming books. In it, he relates how he returned to Ohio and became a farmer, and discusses the details of the early farm plans, soil conservation, and the Friends of the Land.

———, *Malabar Farm.* New York: Harper, 1947. Continues the story begun by *Pleasant Valley* and covers the year-round rhythm of activities at Malabar. Also focuses on Bromfield's other interests with such chapters as "Grass the Great Healer," "Malthus Was Right," and "The Organic-Chemical Fertilizer Feud."

———, *Out of the Earth.* New York: Harper, 1948. Stresses the need for knowledge of the many intricate, interrelated sciences involved in agriculture as a complement to the knowledge of the farm itself. Bromfield condemns the idea that "anybody can farm." Practical intelligence and dedication are necessary for success.

———, *From My Experience.* New York: Harper, 1955. The last of the farm books and the best of the lot. Outstanding accounts of a roadside market, farming in Brazil, building topsoils, living with the weather, and a chapter titled "A Hymn to Hawgs" make enjoyable and informative reading.

Bruce, Maye, *From Vegetable Waste to Fertile Soil.* London: Faber, 1940.

———, *Common-Sense Compost Making.* London: Faber, 1967. Both of Bruce's books describe composting with the aid of herbal extracts. The extracts supposedly activate the heap and produce a superior finished product. The standard work. Recently reprinted.

> *Feeding quality is the most important matter of all. If a plant is healthy, and growing up to its own perfection, it must have great vitality, and it is the vitality, the living force of the plant, that heightens its food value. A vegetable cannot give what it has not got; what it has, it gets from the soil. It cannot reach its 'own perfection' in starved ground, still less in ground doped with chemicals.*
>
> Maye Bruce, *Common Sense Compost Making*

Cocannouer, Joseph A., *Weeds, Guardians of the Soil*. New York: Devin-Adair, 1952. Cocannouer is an enthusiastic advocate of the virtues of weeds.

———, *Farming With Nature*. Norman: University of Oklahoma Press, 1954. A general work with some good information. Recently reprinted under the title *Organic Gardening and Farming*.

———, *Water and the Cycle of Life*. New York: Devin-Adair, 1958. A searing indictment of the mistaken farming practices that led to the dust bowl and their effect on the ecology of water.

Corley, Hugh, *Organic Farming*. London: Faber, 1957. "But the reason for farming well is that it is right." Corley fills this book with useful interpretations of what "farming well" is all about.

Donaldson, Frances, *Approach to Farming*. London: Faber, 1941. This book states that the "health" of the soil, of the livestock, and of the produce is the paramount consideration on any farm.

Easey, Ben, *Practical Organic Gardening*. London: Faber, 1955. An outstanding work, almost a textbook. Very thorough and documented. Contains a lot of material found nowhere else.

Elliot, Robert H., *The Clifton Park System of Farming*. London: Faber, 1907. In its introduction, Sir George Stapledon calls this book an "agricultural classic." First published in 1898 under the title *Agricultural Changes*, it was later the work that inspired Sykes and Turner. Elliot writes of grass, pasture, and especially of his extensive seed mixture, "calculated to fill the land with vegetable matter."

Faulkner, Edward H., *Plowman's Folly*. Norman: University of Oklahoma Press, 1943. Louis Bromfield wrote that everyone including Hollywood actresses asked him about this book. It ultimately sold millions of copies. An effective condemnation of the moldboard plow.

———, *A Second Look*. Norman: University of Oklahoma Press, 1947. In this book Faulkner attempts to restate his case more clearly in view of the controversy stirred up by *Plowman's Folly*.

———, *Soil Restoration*. London: Michael Joseph, 1953. Faulkner applied his techniques to bring a worn-out farm back into production as a market garden. This is the story of that experiment.

> *As always in my experience, the destructive activity of insects came only when plants were in an abnormally weak condition.*
>
> *Formerly I believed that solely by virtue of the best possible soil conditions one could banish both insects and disease. I have learned better. Most diseases do seem to disappear completely as the soil improves, but insects are not so easily disposed of.*
>
> Edward H. Faulkner, *Soil Restoration*

Graham, Michael, *Soil and Sense*. London: Faber, 1941. An unpretentious but informative book about grasses, pastures, livestock, and their relationships to one another.

Hainsworth, P. H., *Agriculture: A New Approach*. London: Faber, 1954. A fairly reasoned and well-documented study of biological agriculture by a successful market grower. Contains a lot of new and stimulating material.

Henderson, George, *The Farming Ladder*. London: Faber, 1944.

———, *Farmer's Progress*. London: Faber, 1950.

———, *The Farming Manual*. London: Faber, 1960. If you only read one author on farming, read Henderson. The first two books cover his entry into farming with his brother and their experience over the years. The third is a detailed guide to farmwork. Henderson infuses all these books with his own love of farming and an invaluable sense of craftsmanship and pride in a job done well.

> *It is the same with almost everything; we studied, compared, and observed before attempting it. Somewhere there is always someone who is doing a job a little better and there are many who are doing it a great deal worse; from either a lot can be learned.*
>
> George Henderson, *The Farming Ladder*

Hills, Lawrence, *Russian Comfrey*. London: Faber, 1953. Comfrey is a perennial crop used for feed, mulching, and compost. This book details many useful ways of employing comfrey in the farm economy.

———, *Down to Earth Fruit and Vegetable Growing*. London: Faber, 1960. With typical thoroughness Lawrence Hills, Director of the Henry Doubleday Research Association, covers every aspect of the garden with straightforward, practical, and detailed instructions.

Hopkins, Cyril G., *Soil Fertility and Permanent Agriculture*. Boston: Ginn and Company, 1910. This is Hopkins' best-known work and his most thorough exposition of the concept of a "permanent agriculture."

Howard, Sir Albert, *An Agricultural Testament*. London: Oxford University Press, 1940. The most important seminal work of biological agriculture, it inspired countless readers to try his ideas. The book presents ways and means by which the fertility of the soil can be restored, maintained, and improved by natural methods.

————, *The Soil and Health*. New York: Devin-Adair, 1947. A continuation of the ideas of the *Agricultural Testament*, presented in a more popular form. "I have not hesitated to question the soundness of present-day agricultural teaching and research ... due to failure to realize that the problems of the farm and garden are biological rather than chemical."

> *By 1919 I had learnt how to grow healthy crops, practically free from diseases, without the slightest help from mycologists, entomologists, bacteriologists, agricultural chemists, statisticians, clearing-houses of information, artificial manures, spraying machines, insecticides, fungicides, germicides, and all the other expensive paraphernalia of the modern experiment station.*
> *This preliminary exploration of the ground suggested that the birthright of every crop is health.*
>
> Sir Albert Howard, *The Soil and Health*

Howard, Louise, *The Earth's Green Carpet*. London: Faber, 1947. A popular recounting of the ideas of Sir Albert Howard through the eyes of his wife. Well done.

————, *Sir Albert Howard in India*. London: Faber, 1953. Traces the development of Howard's thought during his years as a researcher in India. A valuable record of his scientific work.

Hunter, Beatrice T., *Gardening Without Poisons*. Boston: Houghton-Mifflin, 1964. Undoubtedly the best documented and most thoroughly researched work on the subject. Well organized with an excellent index and bibliography.

Jenks, Jorian, *The Stuff Man's Made Of*. London: Faber, 1959. The origin, the philosophy, and the scientific evidence behind biological agriculture. Jenks, for many years editor of the *Journal of the Soil Association*, has an encyclopedic grasp of the subject.

King, F. C., *The Compost Gardener*. Highgate: Titus Wilson, 1943. This small book lays down the general principles of cultivation for all the popular vegetables. Contains some unique information.

————, *Gardening With Compost*. London: Faber, 1944. Compost preparation and use, comments on chemical fertilizers, and sections on weeds and earthworms.

————, *The Weed Problem*. London: Faber, 1951. King is doubly unorthodox. He defends the control rather than elimination of weeds and he condemns turning over the soil.

King, F. H., *Farmers of Forty Centuries*. London: Jonathan Cape, 1927. A granddaddy of them all, this classic was first published in 1911. King's trip through China, Korea, and Japan showed him how soil fertility had been preserved by returning all organic wastes to the land. Hundreds of photos and fascinating information. Recently reprinted.

Konnonova, M. M., *Soil Organic Matter*. New York: Pergamon, 1961. A technical work well worth reading for a better understanding of the processes involved in biological agriculture.

Maunsell, J. E. B., *Natural Gardening*. London: Faber, 1958. A book of unconventional gardening techniques. Maunsell is the most thorough of the no-diggers and his use of the spading fork for "disturbing" the soil is worth noting.

Northbourne, Lord, *Look to the Land*. London: Dent, 1940. One of the early inspirational works. "Mixed farming is economical farming, for only by its practice can the earth be made to yield a genuine increase."

O'Brien, Dalziel, *Intensive Gardening*. London: Faber, 1956. This book of original ideas describes a meticulously efficient market garden. From the layout, to the philosophy, the composting and fertilizing procedures—even to a motion study of transplanting—everything is covered. Veganic (without animal manure) compost is used.

> *We are not out to convince anyone of the truth of the discoveries we have made of the way the soil transforms itself in three years using our methods, for we are confident ourselves that time will do that for us. We put forward this method as an alternative to the orthodox gardening techniques, which to-day involve growers in heavy labour costs and outlay on stable and artificial manures, things which bite so deeply into the profits of intensive cultivation of vegetables and plants. When we describe how something should be done, we have done it that way and made a profit out of it.*
> Dalziel O'Brien, *Intensive Gardening*

Oyler, Philip, *The Generous Earth*. London: Hodder and Stoughton, 1950. A classic. Tells the story of the timeless farm life in the Dordogne Valley of France, "the land of all good things." It shows how the operation of sound farming practices will sustain fertility indefinitely.

———, *Sons of the Generous Earth*. London: Hodder and Stoughton, 1963. More on Oyler's experience in France. A valuable story from a man who values hard work, rural skills, wholesome food and drink, and a simpler way of life.

Pfeiffer, Ehrenfried, *Bio-Dynamic Farming and Gardening*. New York: Anthroposophic Press, 1938. Presents the case for non-chemical farming in general, and bio-dynamic farming in particular.

———, *The Earth's Face and Human Destiny*. Emmaus, PA: Rodale, 1947. A discussion of landscape characteristics and their value to the natural system.

Picton, Dr. Lionel, *Nutrition and the Soil*. New York: Devin-Adair, 1949. Mostly on nutrition but partly about the soil. One of the earliest works on the subject and therefore of some historical interest.

Rayner, M. C., *Problems in Tree Nutrition*. London: Faber, 1944. A report of the work done by Dr. Rayner at Wareham Heath. The use of composts in forestry to encourage the growth of seedlings in a sterile soil by stimulating the development of mycorrhizal associations.

Rodale, J. I., *Stone Mulching in the Garden*. Emmaus, PA: Rodale, 1949. An almost forgotten work and one of Rodale's best. Mulching with stones, an old and effective practice, is clearly explained in photos and text.

————, *Encyclopedia of Organic Gardening*. Emmaus, PA: Rodale, 1959.

————, *How To Grow Vegetables and Fruits by the Organic Method*. Emmaus, PA: Rodale, 1960. This and the encyclopedia above are large (1,000-page) books covering all phases of the art.

Rowe-Dutton, Patricia, *The Mulching of Vegetables*. Farnham Royal, Bucks, England: Commonwealth Agricultural Bureau, 1957. A valuable compilation of all the research on mulching up to the date of publication.

Russell, E. J., *The World of the Soil*. London: Collins, 1957. A thorough study of the soil by a director of the Rothamsted Experimental Station in England. Reliable background information for anyone.

Seifert, Alwin, *Compost*. London: Faber, 1952. An outstanding book on the hows and whys of producing and using first-class compost.

Shewell-Cooper, W. E., *The Complete Fruit Grower*. London: Faber, 1960.

————, *The Complete Vegetable Grower*. London: Faber, 1968. Encyclopedic coverage of both subjects in a readable format. Excellent.

Smith, Gerard, *Organic Surface Cultivation*. London: Faber, 1961. Another of the no-digging books. Deals with composts, garden planning, plus an assortment of hints and ideas.

Soil Association, The, *Journal of the Soil Association*, 1947–1972. Walnut Tree Manor, Haughley, Stowmarket, Suffolk IP14 3RS, England. A quarterly journal of invaluable reference information.

> *I remember the time when the stable would yield,*
> *Whatsoever was needed to fatten a field,*
> *But chemistry now into tillage we lugs*
> *And we drenches the earth with a parcel of drugs.*
> *All we poisons, I hope, is the slugs.*
> *Punch, 1846, as quoted in*
> *The Journal of the Soil Association,*
> *April 1956*

Stephenson, W. A., *Seaweed in Agriculture and Horticulture*. London: Faber, 1968. Documents the use of seaweed—especially in liquefied form—in farming, by examples of research from various parts of the world. Those interested in the subject will find some additional information in *Seaweed Utilization* by Lily Newton (London: Sampson-Low, 1951) and *Seaweeds and Their Uses* by V. J. Chapman (London: Methuen, 1970).

Sykes, Friend, *Humus and the Farmer*. London: Faber, 1946. The transformation of unpromising land into one of the showplace farms of England by methods described as humus farming. Covers renovating old pastures, making new ones, subsoiling, harvesting, and related topics.

———, *Food, Farming and the Future*. London: Faber, 1951. The further development of humus farming plus many peripheral subjects.

———, *Modern Humus Farming*. London: Faber, 1959. Discusses the danger to the soil caused by worship of "technical efficiency" and "getting more for less." Sykes puts forth his case that humus farming is as effective and productive as any other system.

Turner, Newman, *Fertility Farming*. London: Faber, 1951. Turner is a practical farmer who learned conventional agriculture in college but when he applied the teachings the results were disastrous. He then "unlearned" all his formal training and formulated his own system. Fascinating reading.

———, *Herdsmanship*. London: Faber, 1952. Dedicated "to the Jersey Cow which combines beauty with efficiency." Comprehensive treatment of dairy cow selection and management from Turner's point of view. Excellent descriptions of all major dairy breeds plus sections on herbal veterinary practices.

———, *Fertility Pastures*. London: Faber, 1955. The value of the herbal ley (temporary pasture) is the central theme of this book. The detailed information on the character and properties of herbs and grasses for grazing is extremely interesting. Turner determined the composition of his pasture seed mixtures by "consulting the cow."

Voisin, Andre, *Grass Productivity*. London: Crosby Lockwood, 1958.

———, *Soil, Grass and Cancer*. London: Crosby Lockwood, 1959.

———, *Better Grassland Sward*. London: Crosby Lockwood, 1960. Voisin, a leading French authority of grassland management was deeply concerned with the biological quality of produce.

Waksman, Selman A., *Soil Microbiology*. New York: John Wiley, 1952. A valuable book, Waksman details the needs of soil microorganisms and their importance in the soil. His information is consistent with the best practices of biological agriculture.

The addition of large amounts of organic matter, especially fresh plant and animal residues, to the soil completely modifies the nature of its microbiological population. The same is true of changes in soil reaction which are brought about by liming or by the use of acid fertilizers, by the growth of specific crops, notably legumes, and by aeration of soil resulting from cultivation.

Selman Waksman, *Soil Microbiology*

Whyte, R. O., *Crop Production and Environment*. London: Faber, 1960. A book of plant ecology. It treats the effects on the plant of what Whyte considers to be the primary factors of aerial environment: temperature, light, and darkness.

Wickenden, Leonard, *Make Friends with Your Land*. New York: Devin-Adair, 1949. Wickenden was a professional chemist who became interested in organic growing. In this book he attempts to cut through some of the myths and to investigate the claims from a scientific perspective. An interesting book for the skeptical beginner.

———, *Gardening with Nature*. New York: Devin-Adair, 1954. One of the best for beginner and experienced gardener alike. A practical, comprehensive and intelligent treatment of all aspects of gardening.

Wrench, G. T., *Reconstruction by Way of the Soil*. London: Faber, 1946. A historical survey of soil mistreatment and its influence on civilization from earliest times. Wrench views farming as a creative art.

Wright, D. Macer, *Fruit Trees and the Soil*. London: Faber, 1960. Soil management in the orchard as the key to better quality fruit.

Note: Wherever possible the publisher and date are given for the earliest edition of each book listed in this bibliography.

Appendix 1 Recommended Tools & Supplies

Tools have their own integrity;
The sneath of the scythe curves rightly to the hand,
The hammer knows its balance, knife its edge,
All tools inevitably planned,
Stout friends, with pledge
Of service; with their crochets too
That masters understand, . . .

—V. Sackville West

Soil Preparation

Colloidal Phosphate and Greensand Your local organic fertilizer dealer should be able to supply colloidal phosphate and greensand at retail or order them for you in commercial quantities.

Powdered or pelleted soil amendments need to be spread evenly. At one time or another, I have used the following methods: (1) mix them together with compost or manure; or (2) spread with a metered spreader, such as the *Gandy*, which can be adjusted for accurate coverage. I recommend the latter. A four-foot-wide *Gandy* spreader is easy to pull by hand or tow with the walking tractor and allows for accurate spreading at almost any rate of application.

For very light applications of trace elements, use a hand-cranked, chest-mounted seeder filled with the soil amendment rather than seed. A wide assortment of these models are available from A. M. LEONARD, P.O. Box 816, Pique, Ohio 45356. *Gandy* spreaders can be ordered from GANDY COMPANY, 528 Gandrud Road, Owatonna, Minnesota 55060.

Broadfork The original and still the best of the many models of this hand-powered sub-soil loosener is the *Grelinette*. It is available from SMITH & HAWKEN, 25 Corte Madera, Mill Valley, California 94941.

Chisel Plow There are a number of manufacturers of small (5-shank) chisel plows that can be pulled by a 35-HP tractor. Ask your local farm-equipment dealer.

Two-Wheel Walking Tractor-Tiller This is the basic power source on the small farm. They are manufactured in a wide range of sizes and working capabilities. The best models imported into this country are from Italy. My favorite is a *Goldini* 12-HP gas-powered model. I recommend it. The *Goldini* is available from MAINLINE, Box 526, London, Ohio 43140.

Seeding and Transplanting

Seeds My favorite seed catalogs are JOHNNY'S SELECTED SEEDS, Foss Hill Road, Albion, Maine 04910; VESEY'S SEEDS, York, Prince Edward Island, Canada COA 1PO; STOKES SEEDS, Box 548, Buffalo, New York 14240; and SHEPHERDS SEEDS, 30 Irene Street, Torrington, Connecticut 06790.

Seeders Models of the seeders described in Chapter 11 are available from: FLUID DRILLING, LTD., Queensway Industrial Estate, Leamington Spa, England (fluid drill); MAHIER, Z. I. de Belitourne, 53200 Chateau-Gontier, France (vacuum model); STANHAY WEBB, LTD., Exning, Newmarket, Suffolk CB8 7HD, England (belt model); NIBEX, Nibe-Verken AB, S-285 Markaryd, Sweden (cup model).

The seeder that I prefer, a plate seeder — *Earthway Precision Garden Seeder*, Model 1001B — is lightweight, inexpensive, and very adaptable to modification for even greater flexibility with different seed sizes or sowing distances. The manufacturer will make special seed plates on request at a reasonable charge. It is available from EARTHWAY PRODUCTS, INC., P.O. Box 547, Bristol, Indiana 46507.

I prefer the *Earthway* to a similar seeder made by LAMBERT CORP., P.O. Box 66, 519 Hunter Avenue, Dayton, Ohio 45404. However, since the Lambert seed plates also fit the Earthway and offer a slightly different range of sizes, I recommend purchasing a set of plates from Lambert.

My five-row seeder was constructed by bolting five Earthway seeders side by side with a common front axle and a common push bar joining them at the back.

Soil Blockers The best equipment for hand-powered soil-block production is made by Michael Ladbrooke in England and sold in the U.S. by SMITH & HAWKEN, 25 Corte Madera, Mill Valley, California 94941. Ladbrooke's models include the mini-blocker, which makes 20 cubes ¾ inch on a side; 1½- and 2-inch hand models, which make 5 blocks and 4 blocks, respectively; 1½-, 2-, and 3-inch floor models making 20, 12, and 6 blocks each, respectively; and 4-inch models, which make one maxi-block.

Most of the motorized block makers are produced in Europe. In my opinion, the best designs are those from VISSER TUINBOUWMASCHINEN, P.O. Box 5103, 3295 ZG's Gravendeel, The Netherlands.

Blocking Mix Ingredients I buy *peat* sold by FAFARD, INC., P.O. Box 3033, Springfield, Massachusetts 01101. They have dealers throughout the country. They sell both the dark humus peat (*terre noire*) and a premium-grade brown peat.

The *calcined clay* product, *Terra Green*® (coarse), that can be used in place of sand and is available from OIL-DRY CORPORATION OF AMERICA, Chicago, Illinois 60611.

Weed Control   *Cultivators* The *Old-style Planet Jr. wheel hoes* are still available from DALTON, COOPER AND GATES CORP., 215 N. Main Street, Freeport, New York 11520. My preference is for the newer, lighter-weight models equipped with stirrup hoes. They are made by WERNER GLASER, Gschwind & Cie, Werkzeugfabrik A. G., Stefan Gschwind-Strasse 17, CH-4104, Oberwil/BL, Switzerland.

There are a number of different models of the lightweight, in-line *cultivating hoe* (also called the *collineal hoe*). The best is carried by SMITH & HAWKEN, 25 Corte Madera, Mill Valley, California 94941. They also sell a long-handled *stirrup hoe*, which is useful if you allow the weeds to get larger than cultivating-hoe size.

Harvest   *Knives* *California-style knives* are sold by JOHNNY'S SELECTED SEEDS, Foss Hill Road, Albion, Maine 04910.

Carts Heavy-duty *wheels* for building your own *harvest cart* can be purchased from GARDEN WAY MANUFACTURING CO., 102nd Street and 9th Avenue, Troy, New York 12180.

Season Extension   *Low Covers* The following are good sources for *low covers*: KEN-BAR, 24 Gould Street, Reading, Massachusetts 01867, and KIMBERLY FARMS, 1400 Holcomb Bridge Road, Roswell, Georgia 30076.

Field Tunnels and Greenhouses Manufacturers of *fiberglass rods* that can be used for field tunnels are MORRISON MOULDED FIBERGLASS, Box 580, Bristol, Virginia 24203, and MOBAY CHEMICAL CORP., Mobay Road, Pittsburgh, Pennsylvania 15205.

Automatic temperature-activated ventilator-arms are made by DALEN PRODUCTS, 201 Sherlake Drive, Knoxville, Tennessee 37922.

The *hard plastic channel and insert strip*, known as *Poly-Fastener*, is available from NORTHERN GREENHOUSE SALES, Box 42, Neche, North Dakota, 58265.

For inexpensive 12- to 17-foot-wide *hoop greenhouses*, I have been pleased with the models from X. S. SMITH, Drawer X, Red Bank, New Jersey 07701.

Another source for *hoop tunnels*, and especially for larger greenhouses that are well adapted to greenhouse tomato culture, is HARNOIS INDUSTRIES, INC., 1044 Main Street, Saint Thomas of Joliette, P.O. Box 150, Quebec, Canada J0K 3L0.

Livestock

Electric Fence   In my experience, the best *electric fence* equipment is sold by PREMIER SHEEP SUPPLIES, Box 89, Washington, Iowa 52353. Greenhouse shade cloth for livestock shelters is also available from Premier.

Poultry   I've found the following suppliers of *poultry chicks* to be dependable: WELP, INC., Box 66, Bancroft, Iowa 50517 (Cornish Rock Cross); REICH POULTRY FARMS, RFD 1, Marietta, Pennsylvania 17547 (Barred Rock Cross); MURRAY McMURRAY HATCHERY, P.O. Box 458, Webster City, Iowa 50595 (Dark Cornish and Mottled Houdan); and MAPLEVALE FARM & HATCHERY, P.O. Box 58, East Kingston, New Hampshire 03827 (turkey poults, especially Maplevale medium which are very successful on free range).

Caring for Tools

Keep Them Clean   Clean all tools after using them and before putting them away. Use a wooden or metal scraper to remove dirt, a wire brush for the finer material, and wipe dry with a rough rag.

Keep Them Sharp   A number of benefits accrue from keeping garden tools well sharpened. The work can be done better; the tools require less effort to use; more can be accomplished in a given time; and the worker will be much less tired at the end of the job. It is best to touch up the edge of a tool frequently to keep it sharp rather than waiting until it has become dull. For most horticultural tools, a flat metal file is the implement of choice for sharpening. A whetstone should be used for sickles and scythes. Knives and pruners are most effectively sharpened on an oilstone.

Keep Them Lively   Most good tools will have strong, straight-grained ash handles. These handles need to be coated occasionally with pure linseed oil to prevent the wood from drying out. Dry wood loses the valuable resilience of a properly maintained handle and is more likely to break.

Keep Them Around   One of the neatest, best-kept, and most efficient tool rooms I have ever seen was on a small farm in Germany. There was a prominent sign over the workbench that translated to:

"EVERYTHING IN ITS PLACE SAVES ANGER,
TIME, AND WORDS"

Hang small tools on cup hooks or a pegboard. If the location is marked by a painted outline, the tool can be easily returned to its place after use and noticed when it is missing. Another worthwhile practice is to paint a conspicuous color (red, light blue, or orange) on a non-wearing area of the metal part of the tool so it can be seen easily if it is left lying about the fields.

A well-planned tool shed should be constructed either as part of the farmer's house or in close proximity to the fields. It should be equipped with electricity, water, a concrete floor, woodstove for heat, a work bench with vises, and adequate safe-storage facilities for gas, oil, parts, and all tools.

Appendix *From Asparagus To Zucchini:*
2 *The Major Vegetable Crops*

Over the years I have picked up lots of little tidbits of useful information and preferred techniques. For the most part these tidbits are not the standard ABCs (which are well covered by the books in the Annotated Bibliography or by other standard reference works) but rather those little refinements that are the fruits of a good deal of experience and are so often left untold. The preferences described below for each crop are the best that I have arrived at. Names of specific varieties are given where I think they offer a real advantage to the organic grower.

Asparagus   This is a perennial crop and therefore is not part of the rotation. A well-cared-for planting can be productive for more than 20 years. I start asparagus from seeds rather than buying roots. Plant early, January 1 to February 1, in order to gain an extra year of growth. Cover the seeds and germinate at 72°F in mini-blocks. Pot on immediately to 3-inch blocks. Grow on at 60°F and transplant to the field after the last frost.

Prepare the soil with rock powders and manure. Make sure the pH is up to 7. An extra 50 tons to the acre of manure, if available, is well spent in preparing for this crop. Set asparagus out in rows 5 feet apart with plants 2 feet apart in the row. Make a hole 8 inches deep with a post hole digger. Place one soil block plant in each hole, and fill halfway so the greens are still above the soil. Fill the planting hole to the surface later on once the greens have grown above ground level.

Seed a leguminous green manure—one pass with the five-row seeder—between each row of asparagus. I use a green manure rotation, starting with white clover the first year, then sweet clover, red, alsike, and back to white. As early in the spring as possible, till the surface of the bed shallowly to turn under the previous year's green manure and the asparagus fern debris.

If the seeds were started early you can begin a light pick the year after planting. Otherwise, wait a season. Cut asparagus spears with a sharp knife just below the soil surface to include a bit of white stem. It keeps longer that way. Cool it immediately after harvest. Store at 32° to 36°F with 95 percent humidity. When picking is over each year, sow the inter-row strip down to green manure again. My favorite variety — *Viking* or one of the new all-male types.

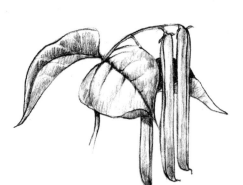

Bean The difficulty with beans is getting them picked economically. The mechanical bean pickers used on large-scale operations are tough price competition for the small grower who picks by hand. Given that reality, the grower can either treat beans as a loss leader (a crop that needs to be grown to keep customers happy even though it is not economical) or only grow the specialty varieties such as the extra-thin French types that sell for a sufficiently higher price to justify the picking costs. I recommend the latter, even though these gourmet varieties need to be picked every day for highest quality.

Either bush or pole varieties can be grown. The pole varieties may seem easier to pick because they are upright, but a good picker can pick faster with the bush types. Although beans are a legume, they respond well to a fertile soil. Rotted horse manure will grow better beans than any other fertilizer. I grow beans in 30-inch rows, and I aim for a plant every 4 to 6 inches in the row. Beans germinate poorly under cool, wet conditions and should not be seeded outside until the soil warms up. For the earliest crop, beans can be transplanted successfully using soil blocks. Use a 1½-inch block for single plants and a 2-inch block for multi-plants (nice for pole beans). Transplant when two weeks old.

Beans don't need to be iced after harvest. Wilting can be prevented by high humidity. Store them at 45°F and 90- to 95-percent humidity. The containers should be stacked to allow for good air circulation in storage. My favorite variety — any of the "filet" French types.

Beet This is a multi-season vegetable. Sales begin with beet greens then move to baby beets and on to storage roots in the fall. Different varieties are best suited to different stages. Read the variety descriptions carefully.

I plant beets in 18-inch rows and aim for a plant every 3 inches in the row. Beet seeds are actually fruits containing 1 to 4 seeds and they need to be thinned. Mono-germ varieties, with only 1 seed, are available but are not my favorites. The earliest crop can be transplanted in soil blocks. Plant 4 seeds per block. Thinning isn't necessary, since the dominant seedling in each fruit will usually prevail. Transplant at 4 to 5 weeks. Set out 4 to 8 inches apart in 18-inch rows. Set them closer for greens, farther away for baby beets.

Beets grow best with a neutral pH and an adequate supply of boron. I have found the best answer to supplementing soil boron to be a pelleted borax with a 10-percent elemental boron content. Carefully calculate the amount to be spread. Three pounds of elemental boron to the acre is usually a safe rate for beets in soil with adequate organic matter. Pelleted borax can be spread accurately with a hand-cranked, chest-mounted seeder. Beets with greens must be cooled quickly after harvest. Store at 36°F with the humidity at 95 percent. Store in well-ventilated containers. My favorite variety — *Vermillion*.

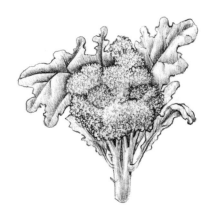

Brassicas   This heading includes broccoli, Brussels sprouts, cabbage, and cauliflower because they have similar growing needs. I find that all four of these crops grow vigorously and are free of root maggot damage if they are grown after a leguminous green manure. In lieu of a green manure, exceptional crops of brassicas can be grown where autumn leaves were tilled into the soil the fall before. When the leaves decompose in the spring, they provide a shot of nitrogen for the crop just like the legumes do.

I grow all these brassicas from transplants. These seeds should be covered when seeded in the soil block. They are set out in 30-inch rows at 24-inch spacing. Closer in-row spacings can be used where the grower does not plan to undersow the crop. Succession plantings will spread the harvest from early summer through late fall.

Broccoli varieties with smaller central heads and better side-shoot production are ideal for the salad bar market. For a late fall harvest, choose Brussels sprout varieties with good leaf cover to protect the sprouts. Brussels sprout plants should be topped in early fall to encourage even sprout maturity for a once-over harvest. Self-blanching cauliflowers make life easier for the grower, but even with them, a leaf should be folded over the head to provide more assured blanching conditions. Long-standing cabbage varieties give the grower some leeway in scheduling cabbage harvest.

Harvest broccoli, cabbage, and cauliflower by cutting the stem with a sharp knife. Snap Brussels sprouts off the stem with a quick side motion. To harvest sprouts for storage, remove the leaves from the plant, cut the whole stem, and store with the sprouts attached. Broccoli, Brussels, and cauliflower should be cooled quickly after harvest. All the brassicas keep best stored at 32°F with a humidity of 90 to 95 percent. Excellent aeration in storage is important.

My favorite varieties — Broccoli *Emperor*, Brussels *Jade Cross*, and Cabbage *Bergkabis* (extra early) and *Chieftan Savoy* (flavor).

Carrot   I have noticed over the years that consumers can readily distinguish the superior flavor of organically grown carrots more than any other vegetable. That is not surprising since petroleum distillates are used as herbicides on conventional carrot crops, and they taste like it. Furthermore, studies have shown that carrots take up pesticide residues from the soil and concentrate them in their tissues. The quality grower can truly excel with this crop by growing succession plantings and selling fresh over as long a season as possible.

Varieties should be chosen for flavor. The earliest crop can be planted in an unheated tunnel as soon as the ground thaws. A late-planted crop can be covered with an unheated tunnel and baby carrots harvested from under a covering of straw throughout the winter. These will be the sweetest, tenderest carrots anyone has ever eaten.

Carrots are planted in 6- to 12-inch rows at a spacing of 1 to 4 inches in the row. Under tunnels, 6-inch rows with seeds at 4 inches in the row have been shown to give the earliest harvest, although I find 8 by 2 inches more productive and almost as early. I sow field carrots in 12-inch rows and aim for 1-inch spacing. Either pelleted or naked seed can be used depending on the seeder. It is worth running your own germination test on pelleted seed before using. Germination can be disappointing. For dependable germination of carrots, it is vital to keep the soil moist from the time of seeding until they emerge. I always direct-sow carrots because I have never found a dependable system for transplanting this taprooted crop.

Don't plant carrots in a weed-infested soil. The in-row weed problems will be overwhelming. On a reasonably clean soil, one handweeding and careful between-row weeding with the wheel hoe will give excellent control. In the fall it is a good idea to hoe soil up over the shoulders of mature carrots to forestall greening and as extra protection against freezing prior to harvest. Carrots can be loosened in the soil by using the broadfork to make them easier to pull. When bunching carrots, cut off the upper half of the tops after tying to prevent excess moisture loss. Bunched carrots must be kept moist and cool to keep the roots from wilting.

Store carrots at 32°F with a relative humidity of 95 percent. Well-grown, mature carrots will keep in excellent condition for 6 months. Stored carrots can turn bitter when stored with apples, pears, tomatoes, melons, or other fruits and vegetables that give off ethylene gas in storage. My favorite varieties—*Napoli* (early and late tunnels), *Scarlet Nantes*, and *Ingot*.

Celery Celery is not a common crop on the small farm, but I believe it should be. There is a ready market for organically grown celery. The ideal conditions are a highly fertile soil with lots of organic matter and a steady supply of moisture. The grower must make sure that the soil contains adequate supplies of calcium and boron. If you are near a hatchery that has egg wastes, they are a great soil improver for celery. Irrigation is a must for successful celery crops.

Start celery in mini-blocks at 72°F. Mist the blocks frequently until germination occurs. Pot on to 2-inch blocks and grow at 60°F or warmer. Temperatures below 55°F will cause celery seedlings to bolt to seed in the first year. Transplant celery into 12-inch rows at 12-inch spacing in the row. Early outdoor transplantings must be protected with a tunnel or other heat source to keep them from bolting to seed if the weather turns damp and cool. I grow my earliest crop along the edges of the early-tomato greenhouse where the roof is not tall enough for staking tomatoes.

Store celery at 32°F with a relative humidity of 95 percent. Burlap spread on the floor of the storage room and moistened with water

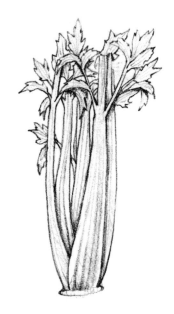

is one way of keeping up storage-room humidity. The same advice applies to celeriac as well as celery. Celeriac, however, is slightly more forgiving about bolting and moisture requirements. My favorite varieties — Celery *Ventura* and *Tendercrisp*, and Celeriac *Jose*.

Chard   Swiss chard is a relative of the beet and responds to similar growing conditions. I start chard in 1½-inch blocks and thin to 1 seedling per block. I transplant into 18-inch rows at 12 inches in the row for a cut-and-come-again harvest, or into 12-inch rows at 6-inch spacing for the cut-the-whole-plant-one-time harvest. I think the eating quality is best from the latter, but a market that demands large leaves with prominent mid-ribs will require the former. Like most leafy greens, chard does not store well. Cool it quickly after harvest, and keep the humidity as high as possible.

Corn   This crop causes a frustrating decision for the small grower. Financial return per acre from sweet corn is low, but the popularity and demand for the crop are high. What to do? If you are marketing in a guild system, you will want to grow just enough to meet your responsibilities. If you are growing a more limited list of crops, corn is not likely to be one of them unless you have extra land. If you market at a stand, sweet corn is one of the most dependable crops you can buy from other growers.

I plant corn in 30-inch rows and aim for 1 plant per foot. Corn can be transplanted for the earliest crop by using soil blocks. Place the blocks in a bread tray. With the mesh bottom, air gets to all sides of the block and prevents the tap root from growing out of the block. Do not plan to hold corn seedlings more than 2 weeks before transplanting. Out door plantings are dependent on the temperature. Corn germinates poorly if the soil temperature is under 55°F. I have begun to experiment with pre-germinating the crop before planting in order to be able to make early seeding more dependable. All you want is to break the seed dormancy, not have a root sticking out. The idea looks promising, and I suggest that other growers may want to try their hand at it.

For a continuous supply of sweet corn, the grower should plant a number of varieties with successive harvest dates. Some experience will be necessary to determine the best varieties, since in practice varieties do not always mature as progressively as the catalog information indicates. The sugar content in corn begins to decrease after harvest, so the fresher the corn, the better the flavor. If you wish to preserve that sweet corn quality, it is most important to cool the crop quickly and keep it cool. The new supersweet corns do not lose their sweetness as quickly after harvest, but I think there is more to eating corn than sweetness. I do not believe these varieties are as nutritious, either.

Cucumber   This is a warm weather crop, one that grows best in the most fertile soil you can provide. Greenhouse cucumber growers have always used more manure and compost for this crop than for any other. Composted sheep and horse manure have always been

the favored soil amendments. Cucumber pest problems are usually a result of imbalanced fertilization—excess nitrogen from chicken manure or a lack of trace elements. Most cucumber-growing problems can be cured by amending the soil with a well-finished compost plus dried seaweed for trace elements. The results are worth the effort. Many home gardeners grow cucumbers. Your market will be determined by excelling their quality. This is best done by growing one of the European-style, thin-skinned varieties. Most of these need to be grown in a greenhouse or tunnel. They must also be pruned to one stem and to one fruit at each leaf node.

Growing cucumbers vertically pays off in yield per square foot. Trellising the crop upwards makes the most efficient use of your highly fertile and best-protected growing areas. The plants can be trained up a mesh netting with 6-inch squares (for ease of picking) or up single strands of a strong garden twine. At the top of the support, the plants are pruned to 2 stems, which then descend back to the ground while continuing to produce cucumbers. Total production of the greenhouse varieties can reach 50 cukes per plant.

I start all cucumbers as transplants. Germinate them in 1½-inch blocks at 85°F. Pot them on to 4-inch blocks and grow at 65°F. Use bottom heat at 70°F to keep them growing well. Transplant them to greenhouse, tunnel, or protected outdoor bed at 4 weeks of age. I plant 2 rows of staking cucumbers in a 60-inch bed at 30-inch spacing each way. Give them plenty of water and plan to top dress with extra compost at monthly intervals. Pick them every day to keep the quality high. Overgrown cucumbers put an extra strain on the plants and lower the yield. Store cukes at 50°F with a relative humidity of 90 to 95 percent. Ethylene from apples, tomatoes, and other produce will cause accelerated ripening and cause the green color to change to yellow. My favorite varieties—*Sweet Success* (an outdoor European type) and *Aurelia* (a greenhouse variety).

Garlic   Fall-planted varieties are a better bet than spring-planted. The fall varieties are planted in October, winter over in the soil, and mature in summer when customer interest is high. There is time for a green manure or succession crop to be established after harvest. My experience with garlic varieties is that they can be very specific to soil types. When you start out growing garlic, you should try as many different cultivars as are available and then choose the one that does the best on your soil. After that save your own seed every year and select for large-sized bulbs. Garlic must be well cured and dried after harvest. It stores best at 32°F and at a humidity of 65 percent.

Kale   Kale is a relative of the cabbage family, and the same soil fertility suggestions apply. I grow all kale as transplants in 1½-inch soil blocks and set them out in 18-inch rows at 12-inch spacing. Smaller plants can be grown in 12-inch rows.

I have sold kale both as bunches of leaves and as whole plants. As with chard, I recommend the latter. The eating quality of the whole

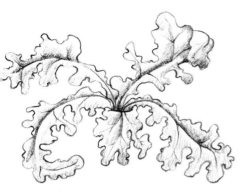

young plants is better. Kale is most flavorful in the fall, after a few light frosts, and so I plant it as a succession crop. Since brassicas grow very well following a member of the onion family, kale could be the ideal crop to follow garlic. Kale can be left in the ground and harvested right up through hard frosts. Any kale still around very late in the fall makes a tasty green treat for laying hens. My favorite variety—*Winterbor*.

Lettuce Lettuce, in contrast to sweet corn, is a very high dollar-return-per-square-foot crop. On some intensive market gardens, lettuce is the major crop. That complicates crop-rotation planning. Extra compost is needed where the same crop is grown at too short an interval.

I grow all lettuce from transplants for a number of reasons. First, I want to be sure of a full crop without gaps in the rows. Since lettuce seed germinates poorly in hot, dry weather, I prefer to sow it under controlled conditions indoors. In very warm weather the seeded blocks can be germinated in 2 days in a cool cellar and then brought up to grow. Second, since most leaf lettuces are a 60-day seed-to-harvest crop, they can spend a third to a half that time as seedlings before transplanting. During the 3 to 4 weeks the lettuce seedlings are in the blocks, an unrelated crop can occupy that same ground. This not only increases production but lessens crop-rotation problems. And third, lettuce is a fast-growing crop, and I want a vigorous seedling grown under ideal conditions to go into a fertile soil and grow quickly. The excellent lettuce transplants from soil blocks give me just that. Information on the timing of succession lettuce plantings is presented in the planning chapter.

I grow greenhouse lettuce at a 10- by 10-inch spacing and outdoor lettuce at 12 by 12 inches. The greenhouse lettuce grows on the residual fertility of the tomato crop. The outdoor lettuce receives an application of well-finished compost lightly mixed into the topsoil just before transplanting. The key to successful lettuce culture is quick growth. You want to make all the growing conditions as ideal as possible. That means not only soil preparation and irrigation, but also the quality of the transplants. Treat the lettuce transplants gently so they go into the ground without torn leaves or soil-filled hearts. When the weather conditions are too warm, you will want to harvest the lettuce at a younger age to keep up the quality and double-bag them (sell two smaller heads for the price of one). My favorite varieties—*Buttercrunch* (bibb), *Green Ice* (leaf), *Nancy* (Boston), *Crispino* (head), *Diamante* (fall greenhouse), and *Salina* (spring greenhouse).

Mache This crop, also known as corn salad in this country, is quickly growing in popularity, and deservedly so. It looks like a very small leaf lettuce, but it is no relation. As a salad ingredient, it complements lettuce or can be used on its own. It is very tasty. But best of all, it is extremely cold-hardy and can be harvested in midwinter.

I sow mache in late summer to early fall with the five-row seeder.

I aim for a plant every 2 inches in the row, but plant about twice that close because mache germination is poor. I cover the plants with a field tunnel and basically pay very little attention to them except to weed and water. By December they are full-grown (about 3 inches high and wide) and usually frozen solid. Any time there is a thaw for a day or two, or if the tunnel temperature is above freezing, mache can be harvested. It almost seems to like having been frozen and shows nearly no damage. To harvest, you cut the plant at ground level. I then wash and store them whole. They are usually served mixed in a tossed salad or with cold cooked beets or used in one of many mache recipes. This is a great mid-winter sale item. My favorite variety — *Vit*.

Melon This is another warm-weather crop, even more so than cucumbers. Any extra heat that can be provided through soil-warming mulches, windbreaks, or a sheltered site will pay off in a better outdoor crop. Fiberglass rod field tunnels protected with a floating cover material make for excellent melon growing. The cover should be removed at pollination time. The same soil conditions apply here as for cucumbers. The more fertile the soil, the better the melon crop. A sandy soil is often preferred for melon growing, since it warms up more quickly. Extra organic matter helps a sandy soil hold water.

Muskmelons should be harvested at full slip (the stem separates easily from the fruit) for best flavor. Many of the European *Charantais* varieties have to be harvested before slip to be at their best. Be sure to read the catalog descriptions. Melons can be stored at 40°F at high humidity for a short time after harvest. My favorite variety — *Gold Star*.

Onion This is the crop that taught me the value of multi-plant blocks. Since I prefer a round globe-shaped onion (as opposed to the flattened globe from sets), I grow onions from transplants. But transplanting and subsequent in-row weed control were not as efficient as I would have liked. Multi-plant blocks changed all that.

With multi-plant blocks, 6 seeds are sown in each 1½-inch block 5 to 6 weeks before the earliest outdoor transplanting date. Onions, like the brassicas, grow better seedlings if the seeds are lightly covered with potting soil. The blocks are set out in rows 12 inches apart at 12 inches in the row with the same equipment used for other block transplants at that spacing. In-row weeds are no problem, since the space between the blocks can be cultivated in both directions. The onions grow together in the clump, pushing each other aside for more room as they get bigger. At harvest, each clump is a circle of 4 to 6 onions the same size as if they had been spaced normally in the row.

Onion-family plants are greatly affected by the preceding crop in the rotation. The most favorable preceding crops are a fine grass (red-top), lettuce, or a member of the squash family. In my rotation, onions follow winter squash. I grow the onions right where the squash rows grew. I have found they do best where no green manure was sown. Carrots or some other root crop is grown in the alternate beds that did grow green manure the previous year.

I use the same multi-plant technique for scallions, but at an even higher density. Ten to 12 seeds are sown per 1½-inch block and set out 6 inches apart in 12-inch rows. At maturity, the clumps are already prebunched for harvest. The same technique works for leeks. Four seeds are planted per 1½-inch block and are planted out in deep holes made with a bulb planter. They don't get quite as large as individual leeks, but the time saving is worth it.

The onion crop is ready for harvest when the leaves begin to die down naturally. If weather conditions are good (warm and dry), pull the onions, cut the tops, and leave them to dry in the field. If conditions don't allow for field curing, remove the crop to a storage room and dry on racks at 80°F with fans blowing the air around. The same bread trays used for holding soil blocks make excellent onion-drying racks. Heat can be provided with a small woodstove. Household fans provide the air movement. The complete drying procedure will take about 2 weeks or so until the necks are completely dry. After drying, store at 32°F with a relative humidity of 65 percent. These practices will give you the highest-quality onions for sale and storage. My favorite varieties—*Norstar* (yellow) and *Redman* (red).

Parsley This is one of my favorite foods, and I snack on it while I work. I think that with some marketing effort it could be a much more important crop for the small grower than it is. The choice of flat- or curled-leaf varieties will be determined by the market.

I grow all parsley from transplants. It is started in mini-blocks at 72°F and then transplanted on to 2-inch blocks. Soil blocks are the only consistently efficient and dependable way to transplant a tap-rooted crop like parsley. I set out succession crops of parsley in any odd corner, both in the field and in the greenhouse. I harvest by cutting the whole plant and then letting it regrow new greens before the next cut. Parsley can be stored with cool temperatures and high humidity for a month or so, but I prefer to harvest and sell it fresh. My favorite variety—*Darki*.

Parsnip Even though I enjoy eating parsnips and grow them for my own table, I do not think that the return from this crop is sufficient to justify including it in any but a guild marketing system. Parsnips need to be planted early, cultivated through the season, and ideally left in the ground to be harvested early the following spring. The freezing winter temperatures turn some of the starch to sugar and make parsnips a real spring treat for those who enjoy them.

A good precision seeder like the Earthway can plant raw parsnip seed adequately, although the rows will need to be thinned. For other seeders, pelleted parsnip seed is available from some suppliers. I plant parsnips in 18-inch rows and aim for a spacing of 3 inches in the row. If a market exists, parsnips do have the advantage that they can be sold at a time of year when there is usually

very little farm income. It is important to dig them just as soon as conditions permit and before they begin to sprout. Fall-harvested parsnips that can be held at a temperature of 32°F for 2 weeks in storage can attain a sweetness close to those left over winter in the field. The humidity level must be kept at 95 percent.

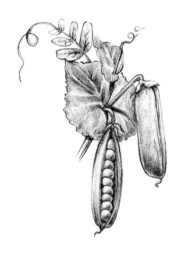

Peas Peas have more variability than almost any other crop. There are low varieties, tall staking varieties, smooth seeded, wrinkle seeded, regular peas, snow peas, and sugar snaps. The problem with peas, as with beans, is getting them picked economically. For that reason, the more exotic types like sugar snaps and snow peas may be the best bet in some markets because their prices better reflect the real costs.

I grow both the early low-growing varieties and the later staking types in order to spread out the harvest season. I plant all peas in double rows 6 inches apart. For low peas, these double rows are 30 inches from the next, and for staking peas the distance is 60 inches. With the low-growers, the 2 rows lean against each other to keep them more upright. With the staking peas, the rows climb either side of a 78-inch-tall, 6-inch mesh netting supported by wooden posts and cross bars.

Peas can be transplanted for an extra-early crop. Plant 4 seeds in each 2-inch block. Place the blocks in bread trays with mesh bottoms to get air to all sides and prevent root emergence. Transplant at 2 weeks of age.

Peas need to be harvested frequently (at least every other day) for highest quality. They should be rapidly cooled to 32°F as soon as possible after picking. I suggest selling them the day they are picked. Old peas are bad business. My favorite varieties—*Maestro* (dependability), *Lincoln* (best flavor), and *Sugar Snap* (hard to beat).

Pepper This is another warm-weather crop that will repay the grower any climate improvement he can provide. Floating covers, plastic mulch, and field tunnels will all aid the production of the pepper crop. I use the spaces between my greenhouses to provide a warm microclimate for a rotation of peppers, melons, and celery.

I start peppers in mini-blocks at 72°F. They are potted on to 2- and then 4-inch blocks in order to grow the finest early transplants. Nighttime temperature minimum is 62°F. I do not let fruit set on the plants before the blocks are transplanted to the soil. I get much greater production later on by reducing that early strain on the plants. It is best to avoid highly nitrogenous soil amendments like chicken manure. The extra nitrogen makes the pepper plants go more to leaf than to fruit.

After harvest, peppers should be stored at 50°F at a humidity of 90 to 95 percent. Temperatures below 45°F predispose these hot-weather fruits to bacterial decay. My favorite variety—*Ace* (for very short seasons).

Potato The best return in potato growing comes not from the maincrop but from extra-early harvest of baby new potatoes. That

is especially true if one of the yellow-fleshed varieties like *German Fingerling*, *Yellow Finnish*, or *Bintje* is chosen. The gourmet market will pay handsomely for the crop, and the field is available for a succession planting of another vegetable or a green manure.

I plant potatoes in 30-inch rows at a spacing of 8 to 12 inches, depending upon the variety and the size desired. I pay a great deal of attention to the rotational position and soil fertility for potatoes. I do not grow them at a low pH, but I try to prevent scab by providing excellent potato-growing conditions and preceding them in the rotation with a scab-suppressing crop. As I mentioned earlier, the potato beetle is the one insect that causes economic loss in my system. I have not yet found the ideal growing conditions to enhance the resistance of the potatoes. Certain practices have helped, however. Chisel plowing the potato field to break up any pan and improve soil aeration for root growth has had a positive effect. So has careful irrigation to prevent moisture stress on the plants. I am continuing to explore all further cultural options.

A one-row potato digger can be purchased as an attachment for walking tractors. It is a worthwhile investment if you grow many potatoes. For best storage, potatoes need a period of 2 weeks at 50°F to heal cuts and bruises. After that, storage temperatures of 40°F to 45°F with 90-percent humidity will keep them in fine shape. Storage temperatures below 38°F tend to make the potatoes undesirably sweet through a change of some of the starch to sugar. Potatoes that have been stored in too cool a place can be reconditioned by holding them at 70°F for about two weeks before use. My favorite variety—*Kennebec* (main crop).

Pumpkin and Squash   I include both pumpkins and squashes together, since their growing requirements are similar. Both crops thrive on a fertile soil with lots of organic matter. Both are vining crops, and both are planted in widely spaced rows. Pumpkins may only be valuable as a Halloween crop. I think the best "pumpkin" pies are actually made with winter squashes.

These are good crops to plant on weed-infested land. Since they are frost tender and thus planted late, the field can be tilled a couple of times before planting to initiate the weed-seed germination and control process. After planting, the wide spaces between the rows and the slow early growth of the plants before they begin to vine provide further opportunities for clean cultivation. Finally, once the vines and large leaves begin to cover the ground, they do a pretty good weed-smothering job of their own.

Both pumpkins and squash can be started in 3-inch blocks and transplanted in 2 to 3 weeks. In some short-season areas, starting the plants ahead may be the only way to assure full maturity of the fruits. I plant in rows 10 feet apart and aim to have a vigorous plant every 18 to 24 inches in the row. It is best to harvest just before frost in fall. Frost damage can inhibit the keeping qualities of the fruits. After harvest, a curing period used to be recommended, but that has been shown to be unnecessary. Store at a temperature of 50° to

55°F with a relative humidity of 50 to 75 percent. Hubbard squashes are less liable to storage rot if the stems are completely removed before storage. My favorite variety—*Buttercup* (winter squash).

Radish   A well-grown radish is a wonderful salad vegetable. In order to fulfil its potential, it must be grown quickly in a very fertile soil. Growing temperatures on the cool side will help. I like to grow radishes as a fall crop in unheated field tunnels.

Radish rows can be spaced as close as 4 inches. The seeds should be sown about 1 inch or so apart. I plant them with the same five-row seeder used for green manures. Succession sowings every few days assure the best quality. If root maggots have been a problem, use the same autumn leaf fertilizer as for brassicas. Till leaves under in fall (up to 25 cords to the acre), and till again before planting. Leaves used this way as a soil amendment release nitrogen in a form that seems to help the radishes grow right past their pests.

Radishes should be cooled quickly after harvest. Don't bunch them with the tops on except for immediate sale. The tops will expire moisture and cause the roots to wilt. The crisper the radish, the better the sale. My favorite variety—*Marabelle*.

Rutabaga   I grow these because I like to eat them. The market is not overwhelming for this under-appreciated root crop, but if served mashed half-and-half with potatoes, they will usually convert doubters to fans.

I grow rutabagas in 18-inch rows, and I aim for a plant every 4 inches in the row. The same soil-improving techniques for brassicas and radishes also apply to this related crop. I sow the rutabagas around the first of July. The best spot is where an overwintered leguminous green manure crop has been tilled under about 3 weeks beforehand. The rutabagas will then grow a marvelous crop with no problems.

Spinach   The trick with spinach is not growing it in season, which should be relatively easy on a fertile soil, but growing it out of season. Spinach is a cool-weather crop, but the demand for it as a salad component and as an ingredient in many gourmet dishes extends year-round. There are a number of ways to meet that demand.

A clay soil has more body and is a better choice for growing hot-weather spinach than a sandy soil. A sandy soil can be improved with plenty of compost, however, and a good irrigation system. Under difficult conditions, spinach responds to the same feeds as celery and so egg wastes or crab shells as fertilizer are also effective. If a spinach crop is planted toward the end of the summer and then protected with a field tunnel and just enough heat to keep it from freezing, the harvest can extend well into the winter months.

Spinach is not often transplanted but it is easy enough to do. Sow 4 to 5 seeds per 1½-inch block. Transplant 3 week-old seedlings every 6 inches in rows spaced at 12 inches. Instead of being transplanted, however, the early crop is usually sown the fall before and wintered over. Young spinach plants are quite hardy and will normally survive the winter with no protection if there is a covering of snow. If snow isn't dependable, a light mulch of pine branches or a floating cover will provide the extra protection. The spring crop can be speeded up by placing a field tunnel over it as soon as the ground thaws.

Spinach is usually harvested plant by plant with a knife. I saw a much more efficient and productive system in Holland. The spinach was planted in close rows using something like our five-row seeder. It grew very thick and upright. Harvesting was done by mowing carefully with a scythe equipped with a net cradle to collect the spinach. Spinach should be cooled quickly after harvest and covered with crushed ice. The relative humidity should be in the 90- to 95-percent range. My favorite variety—*Tyee*.

Tomato   When a selected tomato variety is well grown and fully ripened on the vine, there is no more appealing snack. Vine-ripened greenhouse tomatoes, along with lettuce, are the two most remunerative crops for the intensive salad grower. I most emphatically do not mean "greenhouse tomato" in the sense that consumers have come to regard it. This is not the tasteless, plastic-looking object with no flavor that was picked green, ripened artificially, and sold for its looks alone. I mean *real* tomatoes grown in a greenhouse in order to extend the season and *improve* quality.

I recommend growing greenhouse tomatoes for a number of reasons. The tomato is a popular crop, but the outdoor season is short. Greenhouse production can greatly extend that season and bring customers to your farm. Many of the diseases of outdoor tomatoes, such as blight, are related to weather stress. Under both greenhouse and tunnel production, those stresses are lessened or non-existent, and blight is not a problem. Much of the eating quality of a warm-season crop comes from ideal weather conditions. In the northern tier of this country those conditions do not usually exist. In the southern tier they do not exist long enough to fully extend the tomato season. In most cases, long-season production of vine-ripened tomatoes under controlled conditions is a viable option.

I grow only *beefsteak* varieties. Seeds can be planted from mid-November on. I sow my first crop here in early January. Seeds are started in mini-blocks at 72°F. After 8 to 10 days they are potted on to 2-inch blocks and grown at 62°F night temperature. After another 10 to 14 days they are potted on once more, this time to 4-inch maxi-blocks. I use a high-pressure sodium lamp for supplemental lighting. I transplant to the greenhouse when the plants are 6 to 7 weeks old. Without supplemental light, it will take 7 to 10 days longer.

I grow greenhouse tomatoes in 5-foot-wide beds that are heavily amended with compost. I grow at a night temperature of 62°F, and I ventilate at 75°F. The soil temperature should be no lower than

60°F for best growth. To warm the soil, cover the beds with clear plastic for at least 2 weeks before planting, and leave it on until the first compost top-dressing about 6 weeks later.

The plants are grown in 2 rows 30 inches apart so as to provide 4 square feet per plant. The plants are pruned to a single stem and side shoots are removed every few days. The plants are trellised to overhead supports. Strong twine (untreated) is tied loosely to the base of the plant and attached to the overhead support. As the plant grows, it is twisted around the twine. For optimum production without stressing the plants, the fruit clusters should be pruned to 5 fruits on the first 2 clusters and 4 fruits thereafter. A top-dressing of another inch or so of compost should be added to the soil every month. Cover the soil surface with a mulch of straw to prevent the surface from drying out. Irrigate regularly.

When the plants reach the overhead support (ideally, 8 feet above ground), they either can be stopped for a short production season or the plants can be lowered. In order to lower the plants, a practice known as "layering," you will want to have left an extra length of twine at the top. By this stage of growth, the bottom cluster of fruit will have been harvested, and the lower stem will be bare. Untie the twine at the top and lower the plant so the bare stem approaches the soil. Do this to all the plants in the same direction along the row. At the end of the row, start training the plants around the corner and then back down the other side of the bed. Each time the plant top reaches the support, it should be lowered in this same way. As long as the top 5 feet or so of the plant is vertical it will grow normally. The bare plant stems will eventually contact the soil and send out new roots where they touch. In this way an early planting can be kept productive right through to late fall. For more detailed information consult the books on greenhouse tomato-growing in the bibliography.

My first harvest is around May 1 and continues until the middle of November. I pick these tomatoes only when they are vine ripe and ready to eat. The flavor will bring customers back in a steady stream. My favorite varieties—*Vendor* (an older, open-pollinated variety with the best flavor of all) and *Buffalo* (a new, more productive hybrid variety with exceptional flavor and quality).

Zucchini   I will include yellow summer squash in this category as well. These are crops whose extra virtues are beginning to be appreciated. There is an increasing market for fruits picked small (a lá the French courgette). There is also a market for fruits picked with the blossom attached and for male blossoms. Special varieties have been developed for the blossom market.

As with other fast-growing crops, these squashes will thrive under the best growing conditions you can provide. They can be transplanted to field tunnels for an early crop. For the outdoor crop, I prefer direct seeding. The main key with zucchini and summer squash is to pick them on time. If picking small fruits, pay close attention to the plants. These squashes are only valuable

when young and fresh. They are so productive that a new harvest is ready every day and even twice a day in hot weather. Handle the fruits very carefully when harvesting. Some growers wear soft gloves to avoid scratching the tender and easily bruised skin. Don't plan to hold them for long after harvest. My favorite varieties— *Zucchini Elite* and *Senneca Prolific*.

APPENDIX 3

A SCHEMATIC OUTLINE OF BIOLOGICAL AGRICULTURE

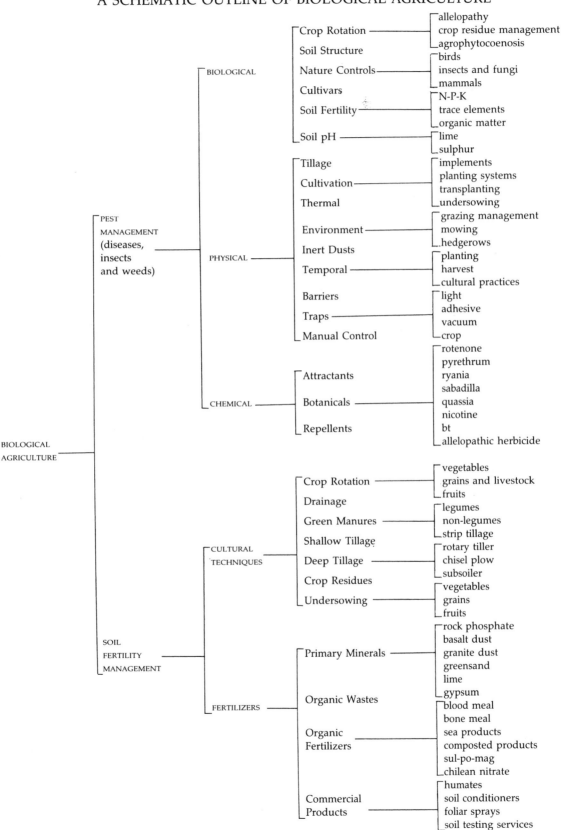

INDEX

NEW ORGANIC GROWER was designed by Dede Cummings.
It was typeset in Palatino by Dartmouth Printing Company.
It was printed on Finch Opaque, an acid-free paper,
by Command Web Offset.